FOUR
VIEWS
ON

THE ROLE OF WORKS
AT THE FINAL JUDGMENT

Books in the Counterpoints Series

Church Life

Bible and Theology

FOUR VIEWS ON

THE ROLE OF WORKS
AT THE FINAL JUDGMENT

Robert N. Wilkin

Thomas R. Schreiner

James D. G. Dunn

Michael P. Barber

Alan P. Stanley, general editor
Stanley N. Gundry, series editor

COUNTERPOINTS
BIBLE & THEOLOGY

ZONDERVAN®

ZONDERVAN.com/
AUTHORTRACKER
follow your favorite authors

ZONDERVAN

Four Views on the Role of Works at the Final Judgment
Copyright © 2013 by Alan P. Stanley, Robert N. Wilkin, Thomas R. Schreiner, James D. G. Dunn, Michael P. Barber

This title is also available as a Zondervan ebook. Visit www.zondervan.com/ebooks.

Requests for information should be addressed to:

Zondervan, *Grand Rapids, Michigan* 49530

Library of Congress Cataloging-in-Publication Data

Stanley, Alan P.
     Four views on the role of works at the final judgment / general editor, Alan Stanley ; contributors, Robert N. Wilkin ... [et al.].
        pages cm. — (Counterpoints)
       Includes indexes.
       ISBN 978-0-310-49033-3 (softcover)
       1. Judgment Day 2. Good works (Theology) 3. Reward (Theology) 4. Merit (Christianity) I. Stanley, Alan P. II. Wilkin, Robert N., 1952-
BT883.F68 2013
236'.9 — dc23
2012039881

Cover design: *Tammy Johnson*
Cover photography: *M. Trischler*
Interior design: *Matthew Van Zomeren*

Printed in the United States of America

HB 03.22.2024

CONTENTS

ABBREVIATIONS

AB	Anchor Bible
ABD	*Anchor Bible Dictionary*, ed. David Noel Freedman, 1992.
AYBRL	Anchor Yale Bible Reference Library
BBR	*Bulletin of Biblical Research*
BDB	Francis Brown, S. R. Driver, and C. A. Briggs, *Hebrew and English Lexicon of the Old Testament*, 1907.
BECNT	Baker Exegetical Commentary on the New Testament
BSac	*Bibliotheca sacra*
BZNW	Beihefte zur Zeitschrift für die neutestamentliche Wissenschaft
CBQ	*Catholic Biblical Quarterly*
EBC	*Expositor's Bible Commentary*
ESV	English Standard Version
ETSMS	Evangelical Theological Society Monograph Series
EvQ	*Evangelical Quarterly*
ExpTim	*Expository Times*
GNTC	*Grace New Testament Commentary*
HCSB	Holman Christian Standard Bible
HNTC	Harper's New Testament Commentary
ICC	International Critical Commentary
IVPNTC	InterVarsity Press New Testament Commentary
JBL	*Journal of Biblical Literature*
JETS	*Journal of the Evangelical Theological Society*
JGES	*Journal of the Grace Evangelical Society*
JSPL	*Journal for the Study of Paul and His Letters*
JTS	*Journal of Theological Studies*
NCBC	New Century Bible Commentary
NICNT	New International Commentary on the New Testament
NIGTC	New International Greek Testament Commentary
NIV	New International Version
NIVAC	NIV Application Commentary

NovTSup	Novum Testamentum Supplements
NPNF1	Nicene and Post Nicene Fathers, series 1
NRSV	New Revised Standard Version
NTS	*New Testament Studies*
PL	Patrologia latina
PNTC	Pillar New Testament Commentary
RSV	Revised Standard Version
SBLDS	Society of Biblical Literature Dissertation Series
SNTSMS	Society for New Testament Studies Monograph Series
SP	Sacra pagina
TNTC	Tyndale New Testament Commentary
TrinJ	*Trinity Journal*
WBC	Word Biblical Commentary
WEC	Wycliffe Exegetical Commentary
WUNT	Wissenschaftliche Untersuchungen zum Neuen Testament
ZECNT	Zondervan Exegetical Commentary on the New Testament
ZNW	*Zeitschrift für die neutestamentliche Wissenschaft und die Kunde der älteren Kirche*

INTRODUCTION

ALAN P. STANLEY

It's the end of time, the place is heaven; the scene resembles a courtroom. Front and center is a great white throne, unapproachable, encircled by a multifaceted display of shining and sparkling jewel-like colors. An exceedingly powerful electrical storm emerges from the throne; flashes of lightning and peals of thunder produce an audio-visual display out of this world. Ineffable heavenly beings surround the throne spellbound, enthralled, fascinated, awestruck, captivated, mesmerized by the holy one seated on the throne. Others too, worship without hesitation, adoring the incomparable worth of God, the King of the universe.

The Judge appears in glorious splendor. He is powerful, majestic, beyond description, awesome, and dressed in a long robe with a golden belt circling his chest; his head and hair are white as snow, his eyes blazing like fire, and his feet shining like fine bronze in a furnace. He speaks. His voice is like the sound of a great waterfall. In his right hand he holds seven stars. A sharp, two-edged sword protrudes from his mouth, and his face blazes like the sun.

Heaven and earth flee from his presence. But the dead, great and small, stand before the throne, where very thick books lie open. Another book, the book of life is opened. And the dead are judged according to the information in the books.

This is the final judgment, commonly known as the Great White Throne Judgment (Rev. 20:11–15). It is the last and final act of history before God dwells with his people forever. We may disagree on other things, but all agree that this is the *final* judgment.

Judgment in Scripture

Judgment in the Old Testament

That God is the rightful "Judge of all the earth"[1] (Gen. 18:25) has been

---

1. The Bible translation used in this introduction is the NIV 2011. Any italics in the NIV text have been added for emphasis.

a stalwart of the biblical story from the beginning (e.g., 16:5; 31:53). "God will bring into judgment both the righteous and the wicked, for there will be a time for every activity, a time to judge every deed" (Eccl. 3:17). No one will be exempt; "the LORD will judge the ends of the earth" (1 Sam. 2:10; cf. Gen. 18:25; 1 Chron. 16:33) according to people's works (e.g., Job 34:10–11; Ps. 62:11–12; Prov. 24:12; Isa. 59:18; Jer. 17:10; 32:18–19; Ezek. 24:14; Hos. 12:2), bringing "every deed into judgment, including every hidden thing, whether it is good or evil" (Eccl. 12:14).

"Will not the Judge of all the earth do right?" (Gen. 18:25). Yes, he will. He will judge with justice and equity (Pss. 9:8; 72:2; 75:2; 96:10), which means "the wicked will not stand in the judgment" (Ps. 1:5) and the righteous will "sing before the LORD" (98:9). As for when this will happen, God has chosen "the appointed time" (75:2); "that day belongs to the Lord" (Jer. 46:10). But God will save his people. "For the LORD is our judge, the LORD is our lawgiver, the LORD is our king; it is he who will save us" (Isa. 33:22). Since Israel will sing on "that day," they could sing in "their day" (Ps. 75).

Judgment in the New Testament

The New Testament similarly declares that God has "set a day," or so variously called (Acts 17:31; cf. Matt. 8:29; Rom. 2:16; 1 Cor. 4:5; 2 Tim. 4:8). It is "the last day" (John 12:48), "the day of judgment" (Matt. 10:15; 11:22; 12:36; 2 Pet. 3:7; 1 John 4:17; cf. 2 Pet. 3:12), when God "will judge the world" (Acts 17:31; Rom. 3:6). But there is an advance on the Old Testament. This day has come closer. "The ax is already at the root of the trees" (Matt. 3:10). "The hour has already come" (Rom. 13:11). "The end of all things is near" (1 Pet. 4:7). Hence, the Lord "is ready to judge the living and the dead" (1 Pet. 4:5).

But there's more. God has selected *a man* to carry out his judgment, "the man he has appointed." What's more, "he has given proof of this to everyone by raising him from the dead" (Acts 17:31). The man is, of course, Jesus Christ. Thus, "the Father judges no one, but has entrusted all judgment to the Son.... And he has given him authority to judge because he is the Son of Man" (John 5:22, 27). "Christ Jesus," therefore, "will judge the living and the dead" (2 Tim. 4:1), though not independently of the Father (John 5:30). Judgment, therefore, will not be left up to "any human court" (1 Cor. 4:3). We must "wait until the Lord comes"

(4:5). But we must be clear on this: "There is only one Lawgiver and Judge, the one who is able to save and destroy" (Jas. 4:12).

The appointed day and appointed man are therefore key, nonnegotiable tenets of the gospel. Paul declares, "This will take place on the day when God judges people's secrets through Jesus Christ, as my gospel declares" (Rom. 2:16). Similarly, Peter recalls how Jesus "commanded us to preach to the people and to testify that he is the one whom God appointed as judge of the living and the dead" (Acts 10:42). This is basic to Christianity (see 24:25; Heb. 6:1–2).

Since judgment is part of the gospel and since the gospel is truth (Gal. 2:5, 14; Eph. 1:13), God's judgment will also be "based on truth" (Rom. 2:2). Human beings tend to judge by outward appearances (John 7:24; 8:15; 1 Pet. 4:6), but this is not always fair because we lack the full and "true" picture required to make accurate judgments. But God is the "Sovereign Lord" (Rev. 6:10), which means he is able and will judge "people's secrets through Jesus Christ" (Rom. 2:16) and "will bring to light what is hidden in darkness and will expose the motives of the heart" (1 Cor. 4:5). Therefore his judgment will be "true" (John 8:16), "just" (5:30; Rev. 19:11), and "righteous" (Rom. 2:5), for he is "the righteous Judge" (2 Tim. 4:8). He will judge "each person's work impartially" (1 Pet. 1:17; cf. Acts 17:31; Rom. 2:11; 1 Pet. 2:23). Indeed, the Judge of all the earth will still do what is right (Gen. 18:25).

Who, then, will be judged? "God will judge those outside" the church (1 Cor. 5:13), namely, "the enemies of God" (Heb. 10:27), "the unrighteous" (2 Pet. 2:9) and "the ungodly" (2 Pet. 3:7; Jude 14–15), "the inhabitants of the earth" (Rev. 6:10), who judged Jesus to be unworthy of their worship. Jesus said, "There is a judge for the one who rejects me and does not accept my words; the very words I have spoken will condemn them at the last day" (John 12:48). Clearly then, God will judge those who have refused to receive Jesus Christ.

Who Will Be Judged?

Faith and Grace

So far so good! What about Christians; will they be judged? Christians are defined by their relationship to Jesus Christ, a relationship that they are in by faith on account of God's grace and Christ's finished work on the cross. The devil therefore doesn't try to prevent works; he tries to prevent *belief*: "the devil comes and takes away the word from their hearts, so that they may not *believe* and be saved" (Luke 8:12). Those who believe "become children of God" (John 1:12) and are "not condemned" (John 3:18). They "*will not be judged*" for they have "crossed over from death to life" (5:24). One translation captures John 5:24 this way: "They will never be condemned for their sins" (NLT). Hence, "there is now no condemnation for those who are in Christ Jesus" (Rom. 8:1). Faith in Jesus Christ, no condemnation; what Christian doesn't know these fundamental truths? And then, of course, there is John 3:16, evidently the most popular verse in the Bible.[2]

It is a remarkable fact that out of the 155 times the Greek word *charis* (grace) occurs in the New Testament, Paul is responsible for one hundred of them.[3] He, himself "once a blasphemer and a persecutor and a violent man ... [who] acted in ignorance and unbelief" (1 Tim. 1:13), is portrayed in the pages of the New Testament as deeply thankful for God's grace and mercy (1:12; cf. Rom. 7:25; 1 Cor. 15:57; 2 Cor. 9:15). Notice how he lumps himself in with his readers: "At one time *we too* were foolish, disobedient, deceived and enslaved by all kinds of passions and pleasures" (Titus 3:3). "*All of us also* lived among them at one time, gratifying the cravings of *our* flesh and following its desires and thoughts" (Eph. 2:3).

It was on this man — "the worst of sinners" no less — that "the grace of our Lord was poured out ... abundantly" (1 Tim. 1:14, 16). How can this be so? "How can God pour out his grace so abundantly on a vile man like Paul?" The answer in short is Jesus! "Here is a trustworthy saying that deserves full acceptance: Christ Jesus came into the world to save sinners — of whom I am the worst" (1:15). But notice again what Paul says: "Here is a trustworthy saying that deserves full acceptance." In other words, it "is true, and you should fully accept it" (NCV), it's "a word you can take to heart and depend on" (Message), "This statement is completely reliable and should be universally accepted" (J. B. Phillips). "You can take it to the bank!"

But what relevance does this trustworthy statement have for us? Paul shows us: "I was shown mercy *so that* in me, the worst of sinners,

---

2. www.christianpost.com/news/most-popular-bible-verses-revealed–29900/.
3. This assumes that all thirteen epistles attributed to Paul are indeed written by Paul.

Christ Jesus might display his immense patience *as an example for those who would believe* in him and receive eternal life" (1 Tim. 1:16). Paul is an example for anyone who feels as though they're beyond God's grace. Little wonder, then, that he begins and ends all of his letters with the term "grace." His last recorded words are, "*Grace* be with you all" (2 Tim. 4:22).

Case settled then. It is through Jesus Christ *alone* that we "have gained access by faith into this grace" (Rom. 5:2). To "set aside the grace of God" would mean that "Christ died for nothing" (Gal. 2:21). Faith and grace are basic tenets of Christianity (e.g., Heb. 4:16; 6:1; 10:22; Jas. 4:6–10; 1 Pet. 1:3, 5, 9–10, 13; 1 John 5:1, 13). How fitting is it that the New Testament ends with, "The grace of the Lord Jesus be with God's people. Amen" (Rev. 22:21).

Christians and Judgment

So back to the question: What about Christians, will they be judged? Yes. God is "the Judge of all" (Heb. 12:23). Thus, "the Lord will judge his people" (10:30); "it is time for judgment to begin with God's household" (1 Pet. 4:17a). Those who teach the Bible "will be judged" (Jas. 3:1). "The one who plants and the one who waters ... will each be rewarded according to their own labor" (1 Cor. 3:8). In short:

- "Everyone will have to give account on the day of judgment." (Matt. 12:36)
- "We will all stand before God's judgment seat ... each of us will give an account of ourselves to God." (Rom. 14:10, 12)
- "We must all appear before the judgment seat of Christ, so that each of us may receive what is due us for the things done while in the body, whether good or bad." (2 Cor. 5:10)
- "Nothing in all creation is hidden from God's sight. Everything is uncovered and laid bare before the eyes of him to whom we must give account." (Heb. 4:13)

Therefore, "speak and act as those who are going to be judged" (Jas. 2:12). "Since you call on a Father who judges each person's work impartially, live out your time as foreigners here in reverent fear" (1 Pet. 1:17).

The Nature of Judgment

This much is clear then: "The coming Lord is also the judge of the Christian."[4] But what will this judgment entail? We are told that God will judge those who have hypocritically judged others (Matt. 7:1–2), "the adulterer and all the sexually immoral" (Heb. 13:4), "anyone who has not been merciful" (Jas. 2:13), and those who "grumble" (Jas. 5:9). So are these people saved or not? Could it be that they are saved and will lose their rewards? This leads us to some of the more detailed passages concerning judgment. Matthew depicts the Son of Man coming to judge the sheep from the goats. To the sheep he will say,

> Come, you who are blessed by my Father; take your inheritance, the kingdom prepared for you since the creation of the world. For I was hungry and you gave me something to eat, I was thirsty and you gave me something to drink, I was a stranger and you invited me in, I needed clothes and you clothed me, I was sick and you looked after me, I was in prison and you came to visit me. (Matt. 25:34–36)

To the goats he will say:

> Depart from me, you who are cursed, into the eternal fire prepared for the devil and his angels. For I was hungry and you gave me nothing to eat.... (Matt. 25:41–42a)

Many problems surround this passage,[5] but perhaps the most pressing is that "there is no trace of a doctrine of the forgiveness of sins, or of the grace of God.... There is no trace of a saving *faith*.... There is no mercy shown to the accursed."[6] In other words, doesn't this look "dangerously like justification by works"?[7] Craig Keener writes, this "passage explicitly declares that this judgment determines people's *eter-*

---

4. Peter H. Davids, *The Epistle of James: A Commentary on the Greek Text* (NIGTC; Grand Rapids: Eerdmans, 1982), 185.

5. See Sherman W. Gray, *The Least of My Brothers, Matthew 25:31–46: A History of Interpretation* (SBLDS; Atlanta: Scholars, 1989).

6. Francis Wright Beare, *The Gospel according to Matthew* (San Francisco: Harper & Row, 1981), 496–97 (*italics* original).

7. Michael Green, *Matthew for Today: Expository Study of Matthew* (Dallas: Word, 1988), 242.

nal destinies." [8] Okay, but what exactly is the role of works here? "Does acceptance of Jesus Christ by faith count for nothing at the end?" [9] Matthew 25 is not alone. Jesus says, in John, "a time is coming when all who are in their graves will hear his voice and come out—those who have done what is good will rise to live, and those who have done what is evil will rise to be condemned" (John 5:28–29).

Paul wanted believers at Rome to know that "God 'will repay each person according to what they have done.' To those who by persistence in doing good seek glory, honor and immortality, he will give eternal life" (Rom. 2:5–7). James warns his readers, "Don't grumble against one another, brothers and sisters, or you will be judged. The Judge is standing at the door!" (Jas. 5:9). James addresses them as "brothers and sisters," that is, Christians. There are obviously two alternatives: grumble and be judged, stop grumbling and escape judgment. But what would it mean to escape judgment? One thing James *cannot* mean is that pending their behavior, they can expect to forfeit the judgment process altogether. Obviously James is thinking of the outcome of judgment.

But what are the possible outcomes for Christians? To put it simply, if these readers did not heed the warning, what exactly would judgment entail? Donald Bloesch alludes to the issue, maintaining that believers will be at the final judgment but can rest assured God will be merciful (Jas. 2:12). Thus, "all Christians *who are faithful* to the end can be assured that they are in the hands of a God who is ... infinite mercy." [10] But what does this mean then for Christians who are unfaithful?

Justified by Faith, Judged According to Works

Whatever it means, the New Testament ends on a note of expectancy: "Look, I am coming soon! My reward is with me, and I will give to each person according to what they have done" (Rev. 22:12). Hence the Apostle's Creed articulates what four centuries of early Christians had come to believe as orthodox: "I believe in Jesus Christ ... he ascended into heaven ... from there he will come to judge the living and the dead."

---

8. Craig S. Keener, *The Gospel of Matthew: A Socio-Rhetorical Commentary* (Grand Rapids: Eerdmans, 2009), 604 (*italics* original).

9. David Hill, *The Gospel of Matthew* (NCBC; Grand Rapids: Eerdmans, 1981), 330.

10. Donald Bloesch, *The Last Things: Resurrection, Judgment, Glory* (Christian Foundations; Downers Grove, IL: InterVarsity Press, 2005), 70.

It is true that some find the notion of judgment an affront to a loving God. In the late 1960s one scholar wrote, "God is primarily a God who loves, a God who saves. Hence any eschatological statement set in the context of future judgment must take into account the inadequacy of this context and must allow for this inadequacy if conclusions unworthy of God are to be avoided."[11] This attitude still exists half a century on,[12] but an honest reading of the New Testament won't allow it.

So here is the basic tension we have uncovered: the Bible teaches that people are justified by grace through faith in Jesus Christ and yet will be judged according to their works. Are we to conclude, then, that the Bible has created for itself an intolerable impasse? Or should we resort to prioritizing doctrines? In particular, for the believer, what role do works play at judgment?

Martin Luther, the New Perspective, John Piper, and N. T. Wright

Martin Luther

Space precludes even the briefest of sketches of church history on this topic, but we should at least consider Martin Luther (sixteenth century).[13] Luther rejected the Catholic notion of works being meritorious for salvation/eternal life, even if they were preceded by grace, insisting that justification was entirely by faith alone (*sola fides*) apart from works. This is "the true and chief article of Christian doctrine"[14] and is irreversible, continuing until the final judgment.[15] However, Rome was not Luther's only opponent. If Catholicism was steeped in works, antinomians downplayed them altogether. Thus Luther insisted that while works do not justify, they are important for faith—to demonstrate that faith is real.[16] Thus, "if good works do not follow, it is certain that this

---

11. William J. Dalton, *Aspects of New Testament Eschatology* (Perth: University of Western Australia Press, 1968), 7, cited in Richard H. Hiers, "Day of Judgment," *ABD*, 2:81.

12. Cf., e.g., Rob Bell, *Love Wins: A Book About Heaven, Hell, and the Fate of Every Person Who Ever Lived* (New York: Harper One, 2011); Peter W. Marty, "Betting on a Generous God," *Christian Century* 128, no. 10 (May 17, 2011): 22–23, 25.

13. For a fuller synopsis of Luther's thinking on the relationship between faith and works, see Alan P. Stanley, *Did Jesus Teach Salvation by Works? The Role of Works in Salvation in the Synoptic Gospels* (ETSMS 4; Eugene, OR: Pickwick, 2006), 39–46. For the same throughout church history, see pp. 19–70.

14. Luther, *Works*, 35:363.

15. Paul Althaus, *The Theology of Martin Luther* (Philadelphia: Fortress, 1966), 446.

16. Luther, *Works*, 34:124.

faith in Christ does not dwell in our heart." [17] Luther wrestles with the tension between faith and works but is careful to give priority to faith. Works are necessary *but* they do not make a person a Christian. [18] For instance, to be without works at the final judgment would be cause for fear (1 John 4:16-18). [19] However, works by themselves will not alleviate fear since salvation is a free gift grounded in "God's forgiving grace." [20] So yes, works are important, but if one were to appear at the final judgment without them, "we cannot tell anyone in such a situation to do anything else than to believe. If you have no works, then do not be without faith." [21]

The New Perspective and The End of the Twentieth Century

Fast-forwarding to the latter half of the twentieth century, many have sought to reconcile the juxtaposing themes of justification by faith and judgment according to works. Invariably these studies have tended to focus on Paul for it is there that we see the contrast most starkly. Furthermore, E. P. Sanders' 1977 watershed book, *Paul and Palestinian Judaism*, [22] marked a new era in Pauline studies. Arguing that Judaism was not in fact characterized by works-righteousness (i.e., salvation by works), as Martin Luther and most of us had thought from our readings of Romans and Galatians, Sanders' work inevitably spawned a flurry of literature on Paul in what came to be known as the New Perspective. [23] Since the New Perspective impinges on the role of works at the final judgment, [24] much of what has been written has also addressed this issue

---

17. Ibid., 34:111.

18. Ibid., 31:361; 34:165.

19. Althaus, *The Theology of Martin Luther*, 453.

20. Ibid.

21. Ibid., 454–55.

22. E. P. Sanders, *Paul and Palestinian Judaism: A Comparison of Patterns of Religion* (London: SCM, 1977).

23. For responses to Sanders' work and the New Perspective in general, see the two volumes by D. A. Carson, Peter T. O'Brien, and Mark A. Seifrid (eds.), *Justification and Variegated Nomism: The Complexities of Second Temple Judaism* (WUNT 2/140; Tübingen: Mohr Siebeck, 2001); *Justification and Variegated Nomism: The Paradoxes of Paul* (WUNT 2/181; Grand Rapids: Baker, 2004). For an easy to read introduction to the New Perspective, see Simon J. Gathercole, "What Did Paul Really Mean?" *Christianity Today* 51 (Aug. 2007): 22–28, or online: www.christianitytoday.com/ct/2007/august/13.22.html.

24. See, for instance, Sanders' section on "Judgment by Works and Salvation by Grace [in Paul]," *Paul and Palestinian Judaism*, 515–18.

in relation to Paul's doctrine of justification by faith. [25] Nevertheless the last century still brought with it no coherent thought on the subject. [26]

The IVP Bible Dictionaries that came out in the last decade of the twentieth century—and have as their subtitle, "A Compendium of Contemporary Biblical Scholarship"—confirm this point. In the 1992 and 1993 volumes Stephen Travis argued that at the *final judgment* works provide *evidence* as to whether "the basic direction of one's life" has been toward God or away from him. [27] But according to Mark Seifrid, in the 1997 volume, works cannot be reduced to mere evidence. Rather *just recompense* best describes a judgment that is in accordance with each person's works. This does not deny justification by grace since believers must not presume upon grace, for "where saving realities are

25. This is merely a select list of what has been written (given in chronological order): Leon Morris, *The Biblical Doctrine of Judgment* (Grand Rapids: Eerdmans, 1960); Karl P. Donfried, "Justification and Last Judgment in Paul," *ZNW* 67 (1976): 90–110; T. Francis Glasson, "Last Judgment in Rev 20 and Related Writings," *NTS* 28 (1982): 528–39; Nigel M. Watson, "Justified by Faith, Judged by Works: An Antinomy?" *NTS* 29 (1983): 209–21; Klyne R. Snodgrass, "Justification by Grace—to the Doers: An Analysis of the Place of Romans 2 in the Theology of Paul," *NTS* 32 (1986): 72–93; Stephen H. Travis, *Christ and the Judgment of God* (Basingstoke, UK: Pickering, 1986); Don Garlington, *Faith, Obedience, and Perseverance Aspects of Paul's Letter to the Romans* (Tübingen: Mohr Siebeck, 1991); Thomas R. Schreiner, "Did Paul Believe in Justification by Works? Another Look at Romans 2," *BBR* 3 (1993): 131–58; Kent L. Yinger, *Paul, Judaism, and Judgment according to Deeds* (SNTSMS 105; Cambridge: Cambridge University Press, 1999); Thomas R. Schreiner and Ardel B. Caneday, *The Race Set before Us: A Biblical Theology of Perseverance and Assurance* (Downers Grove, IL: InterVarsity Press, 2001); Simon Gathercole, *Where Is the Boasting: Early Jewish Soteriology and Paul's Response in Romans 1–5* (Grand Rapids: Eerdmans, 2002); Christian Stettler, "Paul, the Law and Judgment by Works," *EvQ* 76 (2004): 195–215; Paul A. Rainbow, *The Way of Salvation: The Role of Christian Obedience in Justification* (Milton Keynes, UK: Paternoster, 2005); Chris VanLandingham, *Judgment and Justification in Early Judaism and the Apostle Paul* (Peabody, MA: Hendrickson, 2006); Alan P. Stanley, *Did Jesus Teach Salvation by Works?* (2006); Richard H. Bulzacchelli, *Judged by the Law of Freedom: A History of the Faith-Works Controversy, and a Resolution in the Thought of St. Thomas Aquinas* (Lanham, MD: University Press of America, 2006); Kyoung-Shik Kim, *God Will Judge Each One according to Works: Judgment according to Works and Psalm 62 in Early Judaism and the New Testament* (BZNW 178; Berlin: de Gruyter, 2011); A. B. Caneday, "Judgment, Behavior, and Justification according to Paul's Gospel in Romans 2," *JSPL* 1/2 (2011): 153–92.

26. Rainbow, *The Way of Salvation*, 17, notes that at the beginning of the twenty-first century the issue of how to reconcile justification by faith and judgment according to works was an "unresolved problem." Similarly VanLandingham, *Judgment and Justification in Early Judaism*, 11: "Nothing close to a consensus exists among scholars about how to reconcile judgment and justification in Paul," and Michael F. Bird, "Judgment and Justification in Paul: A Review Article," *BBR* 18/2 (2008): 299: "no solution has won a consensus … and the tension between justification by faith and judgment according to deeds has continued to perplex commentators and preachers."

27. S. H. Travis, "Judgment," in *Dictionary of Jesus and the Gospels* (Downers Grove, IL: InterVarsity Press, 1992), 408–11; idem, "Judgment," in *Dictionary of Paul and His Letters* (Downers Grove, IL: InterVarsity Press, 1993), 516–17; idem, *Christ and the Judgment of God: Divine Retribution in the New Testament* (Hants, UK: Marshall Pickering, 1986), 169.

present they manifest themselves in persevering faith and obedience, which secure the believer in the final judgment."[28]

Admittedly, this is a simplified portrayal of things. The reality is that while there are a limited number of ways of explaining the role of works at the judgment, there are many nuances.[29] Others view the final judgment as the place where divine commendation will be given or withheld. Either way, the believer is saved (e.g., 1 Cor. 3:10–15),[30] and a passage like Romans 2:5–16 is theoretical/hypothetical rather than actual.[31] For others, while rewards and not eternal life is the issue, believers will not be at the final judgment.[32]

John Piper and N. T. Wright

However, many of these debates have occurred in scholarly journals and monographs. This doesn't mean they are not accessible, of course, but generally speaking they have remained in scholarly circles. Yet as one of my former students, now a pastor, said when hearing about this book, "This is not just a scholarly debate ... to get this wrong is serious." Indeed. True, blogs are undoubtedly making a difference, yet most Christians I know are completely unaware of the issues. However, two prominent figures in evangelicalism have brought these issues out into the open in recent years. I am referring to British New Testament scholar N. T. Wright and American pastor John Piper. While the role of works at the final judgment was not the main point of disagreement between the two, it was indeed a major one.[33] The problem was that

28. M. A. Seifrid, "Judgment," in *Dictionary of the Later New Testament and Its Development* (Downers Grove, IL: InterVarsity Press, 1997), 623–24.

29. Dane C. Ortlund, "Justified by Faith, Judged according to Works: Another Look at a Pauline Paradox," *JETS* 52 (2009): 324–31, lists fourteen "nuanced" views grouped under four general headings. For recent surveys on approaches to reconcile justification by faith and judgment according to works (mostly limited to Paul), see Rainbow, *The Way of Salvation*, 16–19; VanLandingham, *Judgment and Justification in Early Judaism*, 11–15; Kim, *God Will Judge Each One according to Works*, 5–13.

30. E.g., Paul Barnett, *The Second Epistle to the Corinthians* (NICNT; Grand Rapids: Eerdmans, 1997), 276–77.

31. E.g., George Eldon Ladd, *A Theology of the New Testament* (rev. ed.; Grand Rapids: Eerdmans, 1993), 611.

32. E.g., Samuel L. Hoyt, *The Judgment Seat of Christ: A Biblical and Theological Study* (Milwaukee, WI: Grace Gospel, 2011), who sees as many as *five* eschatological judgments.

33. See Michael F. Bird, "What Is There between Minneapolis and St. Andrews? A Third Way in the Wright-Piper Debate," *JETS* 54 (2011): 299–309.

Wright, one of the leading proponents of the New Perspective,[34] kept on saying—or at least we all thought he did—that at the final judgment the believer's final justification will be *on the basis of the whole life lived*[35] or something to that effect (e.g., "Justification, at the last, will be on the basis of performance").[36]

Piper tackled Wright head-on in *The Future of Justification: A Response to N. T. Wright.* One of Piper's central concerns was that "Wright makes startling statements to the effect that our future justification will be on the basis of works."[37] Piper believed that

> our deeds will be the public evidence brought forth in Christ's courtroom to demonstrate *that our faith is real....* Our deeds are not the basis of our salvation, they are the evidence of our salvation. They are not foundation, they are demonstration. All our salvation will be by grace through faith.... So when Paul says (in 2 Corinthians 5:10) that each "[will] be recompensed ... according to what he has done," he not only means that our *rewards* will accord with our deeds, but also our *salvation* will accord with our deeds.[38]

So what was Piper's beef with Wright? Actually, it was more that Wright was simply ambiguous on the issue of "faith alone," (pp. 130–31), leaving the door open for a "Catholic" interpretation of justification[39] (p. 183). According to Piper, "it may be that Wright means nothing more here than what I mean when I say that our good works are the necessary evidence of faith in Christ at the last day. Perhaps. But it is not so simple." Thus, "I would be happy," wrote Piper, "for Wright to clarify for his reading public that this, in fact, is *not* what he believes." Piper, as we have seen, does not have a problem with

---

34. See, e.g., N. T. Wright, *Paul: In Fresh Perspective* (Minneapolis: Fortress, 2005). It is actually more accurate to speak of New Perspectives (plural).

35. Ibid., 57, 121, 148.

36. N. T. Wright, "Romans," in *The New Interpreter's Bible* (Nashville: Abingdon, 2002), 10:440.

37. John Piper, *The Future of Justification: A Response to N. T. Wright* (Wheaton, IL: Crossway, 2007), 22.

38. John Piper, *The Purifying Power of Living by Faith in Future Grace* (Sisters, OR: Multnomah, 1995), 364–65 (*italics* original). Watch Piper discuss the role of works at judgment at: www.youtube.com/watch?v=7ZQjP–5ce6Q.

39. Piper, *The Future of Justification*, 130–31.

judgment and even with works being necessary for one's final salvation. His central concern was that for Wright the ultimate *basis* or *ground* of final salvation appeared to be works rather than faith alone in Jesus Christ and his finished work on the cross. [40] For Piper, "Christians are free from law-keeping as the *ground* of our justification" (italics mine). [41]

Wright responded with *Justification: God's Plan and Paul's Vision*, and he qualified that he didn't mean salvation is earned or that a perfect life was required. What he did mean was that because of our union with Christ (Rom. 6:1–11), the presence of the Spirit (2:25–29) and God's work in us, we are now able to live a new life (6:6–11), obey the law (8:4), put to death the misdeeds of the flesh (8:13), and live eternally (8:13). [42] Hence, "humans become genuinely human, genuinely free, when the spirit is at work within them so that they choose to act ... in ways which reflect God's image, which give him pleasure, which bring glory to his name, which do what the law had in mind all along. That is the life that leads to the final verdict, 'Well done, good and faithful servant!'" [43] This is not to do away with faith for "if God justifies people in the present, ahead of the final judgment, faith must be the characteristic of those thus justified." [44]

Wright's response, however, was not enough to stave off his critics. [45] Still ambiguous was the *ground* of final salvation. Wright and Piper were then scheduled to go head to head as plenary speakers at the 2010 Evangelical Theological Society's annual meeting in Atlanta. Piper couldn't make it and Tom Schreiner, the second contributor in this volume, took his place. Schreiner called for a more thoughtful explanation on this issue:

---

40. For the quotes in this paragraph, see Piper, ibid., 22, 43, 88–90, 103, 113, 116, 128–31, 143, 146, 171, 182, 184, 217, 221, 224–25. "The crucial question for the final meaning of justification is: *What will be the final ground of our acceptance in the presence of God?*" (p. 101, *italics* original).

41. Ibid., 221.

42. N. T. Wright, *Justification: God's Plan and Paul's Vision* (London: SPCK, 2009), 167, 205–9.

43. Ibid., 168, cf. 198.

44. Ibid., 183.

45. As is clear, for example, from the subsequent panel discussion to Wright's response between Tom Schreiner, Mark Seifrid, Brian Vickers, and Denny Burke at Boyce College: www.dennyburk.com/schreiner-seifrid-and-vickers-assess-piper-wright-debate-at-boyce-college/.

I think what Wright says about justification by works or judgment according to works could be explained in a more satisfactory way since he occasionally describes good works as the final basis of justification. On the other hand, Wright reminds us of a critical theme that is often ignored in evangelical circles. Paul does teach that good works are necessary for justification and for salvation, and Wright rightly says that those texts are not just about rewards.[46]

Wright helpfully clarified that "justification is anchored firmly and squarely in Jesus the Messiah, the crucified and risen Lord, who is the same yesterday, today, and forever."[47] More specifically, "When I," says Wright, "have spoken of 'basis' ... I have not at all meant by that to suggest that this is an independent basis from the finished work of Christ and the powerful work of the Spirit, but that within that solid and utterly-of-grace structure the particular evidence offered on the last day will be the tenor and direction of the life that has been lived."[48] And again:

> The future justification, then, will be in accordance with the life lived, but the glorious conclusion of [Rom.] chapter 8 makes it clear that this is no ground for anxiety. "If God be for us, who can be against us?" This is looking to the future, trusting that the Jesus who died, who rose, and who now intercedes for us will remain at the heart of the unbreakable bond of love with which God has loved us.[49]

Thus, "the final, future justification, then, is assured for all who are 'in the Messiah.'" As a result, "this future justification, though it will be in accordance with the life lived, is not for that reason in any way putting in jeopardy the present verdict issued over faith and faith alone.... All that I have said looks back to the finished work of the Messiah."[50]

Tom Schreiner responded:[51] "I am delighted that Tom [Wright] now speaks of the final judgment as one that will be in accordance with

---

46. Thomas R. Schreiner, "Justification: The Saving Righteousness of God in Christ," *JETS* 54 (2011): 20–21.

47. N. T. Wright, "Justification: Yesterday, Today, And Forever," *JETS* 54 (2011): 49.

48. Ibid., 60.

49. Ibid., 61–62.

50. Ibid., 62.

51. I am grateful to Tom Schreiner's thoughts on what I have written here. They have proved helpful in what follows.

our works instead of on the basis of our works. I think this adjustment and clarification is exactly right.... I am in full agreement with his formulation: we are judged according to our works, but not on the basis of our works." [52]

However, Wright wrote into one blog cautioning such excitement:

> ... don't get too excited. I haven't retracted anything that I meant in my many, many earlier statements on this subject. How could I, since I was simply stating what Paul states rather than trying to squash him into a dogmatic framework? ... Clearly I did say "basis." But ... I have always made it clear ... that I did not mean or intend the kind of thing that clearly some theologians think that word "must" mean. Since the word "basis" is not itself a biblical word I'm not claiming any great status for it. Obviously people have read it without reading the other things I say and then jumped to conclusions which are not warranted by the fuller exposition I give.... Let me say it again: all I am saying is what Paul says in Romans 2 (and elsewhere). Our own technical terms ("basis," etc.) are fluid and flexible in our discourse and, like all summary terms, need to be teased out in terms of the larger discourse—Paul's, and mine.... The point, again, is that by the Spirit those who are already justified by faith have their lives transformed, and the final verdict will be in accordance with that transformation, imperfect though it remains. [53]

The Four Contributors

This book comes, then, on the heels of these debates, and I hope will serve to make this subject more accessible to the wider church public. The four essays that follow will show that there are indeed things for us to consider that perhaps many of us have not. While there are many scholars that could serve these views well, the four are leading proponents. The first contributor, Bob Wilkin, is the Executive Director

---

52. "Tom Schreiner's Response to N.T. Wright," in the plenary discussion that followed Wright's presentation, can be found at http://schreinerpatrick.wordpress.com/2010/11/23/tom-schreiners-response-to-n-t-wright/.

53. N. T. Wright responding on Denny Burke's blog, 11/20/2010: www.dennyburk.com/n-t-wright-on-justification-at-ets/.

of the Grace Evangelical Society. Bob has devoted his life to this and related subjects, writing and speaking around America.

Second is Tom Schreiner, one of the world's leading New Testament Pauline scholars. Having written often on faith's relationship to works, Paul and the law, not to mention commentaries on Romans and Galatians, it is difficult to think of anyone more qualified to represent the second view.

The third contributor is James Dunn, a leading British New Testament scholar and widely known for his work on Jesus and Paul. As the one who coined the term "New Perspective," he too is particularly suited to represent the third view.

Finally, Michael Barber is Professor of Theology, Scripture, and Catholic Thought at John Paul the Great Catholic University. As the author of several books and host of *Reasons for Faith Live*, a radio show heard weekly across America, Michael presents the Catholic view on the role of works at the final judgment.

Finally, this subject does tend to generate a lot of emotion.[54] There's nothing wrong with passionate debate, of course, but regrettably the Internet has become a place where people can hide behind their computers and serve ad hominem arguments back and forth to people they don't even know. We need to learn how to discuss these issues with the same grace we have received (Rom. 15:7; Eph. 4:1–3; 5:1–2; Phil. 2:5). What's more, at times there is power in remaining silent (Prov. 17:28). Ultimately it's our love for one another that will speak volumes to a lost and watching world (John 13:35; 17:21, 23). Darrell Bock helpfully reminds us:

> Surely our disputes and a multiplicity of approaches to each problem will always be with us. But clarification and better movement toward mutual understanding are realistic goals. Let's be sure to remember the world and pursue our larger mission.... Let's debate fairly, fully and with a dignity that reflects respect for our fellow brothers and sisters in the Lord, until glory comes.[55]

---

54. Cf., e.g., some of the comments to this brief clip by Piper explaining the role of works at the final judgment: //www.youtube.com/watch?v=7ZQjP–5ce6Q.

55. Darrell L. Bock, *Purpose Directed Theology: Getting Our Priorities Right in Evangelical Controversies* (Downers Grove, IL: InterVarsity Press, 2002), 114.

CHAPTER ONE

CHRISTIANS WILL BE JUDGED ACCORDING TO THEIR WORKS AT THE *REWARDS* JUDGMENT, BUT *NOT* AT THE *FINAL* JUDGMENT

ROBERT N. WILKIN

Calls for Christians to persevere occur throughout the New Testament.[1] There is no dispute on this point. The issue is what is at stake. Many people teach that what is at stake is eternal salvation. For example, concerning Matthew 10:22 (also 24:13; Mark 13:13) Tom Schreiner and Ardel Caneday state, "Jesus promises salvation, but he conditions the promised salvation on perseverance 'to the end.'"[2] And concerning 2 Peter 1:5–11, where Peter urges his readers to diligently add godly virtues to their faith so as to "receive a rich welcome into the eternal kingdom of our Lord and Savior Jesus Christ," Schreiner and Caneday add, "Those who practice these virtues will never fall, that is, they will obtain final salvation. The word *fall* refers here, then, to apostasy. Those who practice godly virtues will not turn decisively away from the gospel of Christ." In other words, "final salvation is at stake in [Peter's] call to obedience."[3] Similarly John Piper writes, "The

---

1. See, for example, Matt. 24:13; John 15:1–6; 1 Cor. 9:27; Gal. 6:9; Col. 1:21–23; 2 Tim. 2:3, 12; 4:6–8; Heb. 10:36; 12:1–3; Jas. 1:12; 5:11; 1 Pet. 2:19; 1 John 2:28; 4:17–19; Rev. 2:26.

2. Thomas R. Schreiner and Ardel B. Caneday, *The Race Set before Us: A Biblical Theology of Perseverance and Assurance* (Downers Grove, IL: InterVarsity Press, 2001), 147.

3. Ibid., 290–91 (*italics* original).

condition of final *glorification* is persevering in this same faith and hope ... (Colossians 1:22–23)." [4]

Of course, it is not only Calvinists who believe that perseverance is necessary for "final salvation." Arminians (e.g., Roman Catholic, Orthodox, and many types of Protestants) also see the necessity of endurance to escape eternal condemnation. [5] Though Arminians say that everlasting life can be lost and Calvinists do not, they agree on the necessity of perseverance in faith and good works until death.

However, not all evangelical Christians hold that one must persevere to obtain "final salvation." For example, Jody Dillow writes:

> Contrary to the Arminian, we do not believe [the warnings] are given to raise concerns about forfeiture of one's eternal destiny. Contrary to the Calvinist, they are not the means by which professing believers are to be motivated to examine to see if they are truly regenerate. Nor are they intended to motivate true Christians to persevere by causing them to wonder if they are really saved. God has more sufficient means than fear of hell to motivate His children. Rather, the warnings are real. They are alarms about the possibility of the forfeiture of our eternal rewards and of learning at the judgment seat that our lives have been wasted. [6]

Earl Radmacher agrees:

> As believers, our home with Christ in heaven is secure, but our position of service with Christ in the Millennium depends on whether we endure hardships patiently and faithfully or whether we "deny" Him by failing to undergo difficulties with patience and loyalty to Him. [7]

Let's now consider what the Bible says.

---

4. John Piper, *Future Grace* (Sisters, OR: Multnomah, 1995), 234 (*italics* original).

5. See, e.g., Robert Shank, *Life in the Son* (Minneapolis: Bethany, 1960, 1961, 1989); Robert Sungenis, *Not by Faith Alone: The Biblical Evidence for the Catholic Doctrine of Justification* (Goleta, CA: Queenship, 1996); Grant R. Osborne, "Soteriology in the Gospel of John," in *The Grace of God and the Will of Man* (ed. Clark H. Pinnock; Minneapolis: Bethany, 1989), 258.

6. Joseph C. Dillow, *The Reign of the Servant Kings* (Miami Springs, FL: Schoettle, 1992), 243.

7. Earl D. Radmacher, *Salvation* (Swindoll Leadership Library; Nashville: Word, 2000), 207.

Proof That Perseverance Is the Condition for Eternal Rewards and Not Final Salvation

The Perseverance-Free Promises in John's Gospel

Merrill Tenney famously called the gospel of John "the gospel of belief"[8] since the word *pisteuō* ("I believe") occurs more times in this book than in any other New Testament book. Jesus said it is the one who "believes in Him" (*pisteuōn eis auton*) that "has eternal life." The one who *believes* "will not perish" (John 3:16), "will *never* [*ou mē*] hunger ... will *never* [*ou mē*] thirst" (6:35), and "will *never* [*ou mē*] die" (11:26). The Lord also affirmed, "he who hears My word and believes in the One who sent Me [*pisteuōn tō pempsanti me*] ... shall not come into judgment but has passed from death into life" (5:24).

John 3:16, for example, concerns "whoever believes in Him," not "whoever perseveres in Him." Clearly the one who simply believes in Jesus has eternal life.[9] The New Testament is united on this point.[10]

Not once in John does Jesus ever say that one must persevere in order to obtain or retain eternal life. Rather, He promises eternal security the moment one believes. Once a person drinks the water of life—believes in Jesus—he or she "will never thirst" (John 4:14; 6:35). No perseverance is required. Even the Samaritan woman understood Jesus to mean that a one-time drink would forever quench her thirst (4:15). The one who eats the bread of life—another figure for faith in Christ—"shall never hunger" (6:35). It's a simple point: perseverance in faith or works is excluded by such promises.

We find no statement from Jesus declaring that a believer must persevere to retain eternal life or show evidence of it.[11] Jesus told Martha, "I am the resurrection and the life. He who believes in Me, though he may die, he shall live. And whoever lives and believes in Me shall never die" (11:25–26a). He then asked Martha, "Do you believe this?" She

---

8. Merrill C. Tenney, *John: The Gospel of Belief* (Grand Rapids: Eerdmans, 1948, 1976).

9. See also John 1:12; 3:36; 4:10–14; 5:24; 6:35, 37, 39, 47; 11:25–27.

10. Compare, for example, Gal. 2:15–16; Eph. 2:8–9; Titus 3:5; Jas. 1:17–18; 1 Pet. 1:23; 1 John 2:25; 5:9–13.

11. John 2:23–25 and 8:30–32 are often cited as proof that more than "intellectual belief" is required for salvation. I argue elsewhere that sanctification is in view and not justification/conversion; see *The Grace New Testament Commentary* (Denton, TX: Grace Evangelical Society, 2010), 1:372–73, 408.

replied in the affirmative. Jesus did not rebuke her and say, "But what of your life? How do you know you will persevere? Is it not possible your faith is mere intellectual assent rather than persevering faith?" No, He accepted her profession.

Mind you, while these promises are decisive, they do not prove anything about the relationship between perseverance and rewards. They only say that in John's gospel Jesus did not make perseverance a condition for eternal life. How could He? For John himself wrote *"so that you may believe* that Jesus is the Christ, the Son of God, and *that believing* you may have life in His name" (20:31).

The Parable of the Minas in Luke's Gospel

The parable of the minas starts as follows:

> A certain well-born man planned to travel to a far country to receive for himself a kingdom and then to return. Before leaving, he called ten of his servants and gave them ten minas and told them, "Invest the money until I come back." But his citizens hated him and sent a delegation after him, saying, "We do not want this man to reign over us." When the nobleman returned after having received the kingdom, he commanded to be called to him those servants to whom he had given money so that he might know what each had gained by investing. (Luke 19:12–15)

Jesus then recounts the story of three of these servants, each of whom had received the same sum of money (one mina) and been told, "Do business till I come." The issue in the judgment is productivity, not belief. [12] But only the servant who turned his one mina into ten hears, "Well done, good servant" (19:17). He receives praise and is promised rule over ten cities in the kingdom. Since only those who endure will reign with Christ (cf. 2 Tim. 2:12), we can be sure this first servant endured.

The second servant was halfhearted in his service. Though he could have produced ten minas, he only managed five. His halfhearted com-

---

12. *Pistos* in Luke 19:17 refers to *faithfulness*, not *faith*. This is evident in that it is linked with *agathos* ("good servant"). Goodness is a character quality as is faithfulness. In addition, to be *faithful* "in a very little" fits the work he did in investing his master's money.

mitment leads to a lack of praise from his master. Rather than hearing, "Well done, good servant," he hears, "You also will be over five cities" (Luke 19:19). That he is given authority to reign with Christ in the age to come shows that he too endured. But clearly his effort was lacking.[13]

The third servant showed no profit and is given no cities to rule over. Rather than hearing, "Good servant," he hears, "Wicked [*ponēre*] servant" (Luke 19:22). While some conclude that this servant represents an unbeliever, there are strong reasons for thinking otherwise.

First, Scripture occasionally uses disparaging language to describe believers elsewhere. Jesus' disciples are described as "wicked" (*ponēroi*) (Matt. 7:11), the Corinthians as "unrighteous" (1 Cor. 6:8), the Hebrew Christians as "dull of hearing" (Heb. 5:11), and the church at Laodicea as "lukewarm" (Rev. 3:16). Obviously Christians can fail to endure, fall away, and prove to have been wicked. However, salvation is based on *faith in Christ*, not *faithful service for Christ*. Therefore we should not doubt this third servant's salvation simply because he is called "wicked."[14]

Second, the third servant is not part of the group that hated the nobleman. Jesus clearly makes a distinction between "the servants" who received ten minas (Luke 19:13) and the citizens who hated the nobleman (19:14). Take note: the third servant is called a *servant*, not a citizen. Furthermore, he does not call himself a servant. Jesus calls him a servant. That is quite telling. The citizens who hated the nobleman represent unbelieving Israel while the servants who received money represent believing disciples.

Third, Jesus uses a reflexive pronoun to emphasize the fact that all three of these servants belonged to the nobleman: "So calling ten *of*

---

13. However, Darrell L. Bock, *Luke 9:51 – 24:53* (BECNT; Grand Rapids: Baker, 1996), 1537, says, "Jesus really only needs two figures to make his point that some are faithful and 'others' are not." The problem with this is that Jesus chose *three* figures to make His point. While it is true that there is a difference between a faithful servant (servant no. 1) and an unfaithful servant (servant no. 3), there is also a difference between a faithful, wholehearted servant and a faithful, halfhearted servant. Why give the first servant twice as many cities to reign over if he was no more faithful than the second servant? More is going on here than distinguishing between servants who will and won't rule in the life to come—namely, how much authority the faithful servants will have.

14. The reasoning sometimes used, though simple, is suspect: *Believers are not wicked servants. The third servant is a wicked servant. Therefore the third servant is not a believer.* This simply does not stack up with other examples in Scripture (e.g., King Saul, Solomon, Hymenaeus, and Demas). Note too the fleshly believers in Corinth (1 Cor. 3:1 – 3; cf. 11:30).

his own [*heatou*] servants, he gave to them ten minas" (19:13). These servants belong to Jesus.

Fourth, the judgment of the third servant (19:20–26) stands in marked contrast to the judgment of the citizens who hated the nobleman (19:27). The third servant's mina is taken from him and given to the servant who had ten minas (19:24–26), meaning that he will not rule with Christ in the age to come.[15] However, this servant does not suffer the fate of the unbelievers: "But bring here those enemies of mine, who did not want me to reign over them, and slay them before me" (19:27). Significantly, the third servant is not slain as the enemies are.

Leon Morris agrees that the distinction between the third servant and the enemies is significant:

> The story finishes on a note of frightening severity. Those who rejected the nobleman and sent their embassy after him (14) are not forgotten. Safely installed in the kingdom and with accounts with his trading partners finalized, the nobleman commands the destruction of those he calls plainly *these enemies of mine*. They have set themselves in opposition to him; they must take the consequences.[16]

Morris implies that *all* of Jesus' servants are "safely installed in the kingdom" since he does not put the third servant in the same category as Jesus' enemies.

Even clearer on the importance of this distinction is Marvin Pate:

> Even though the action taken toward the disobedient servant was severe (even as it will be on Judgment Day for the unfaithful Christian), there is no hint in the text that the salvation of the faithless servant of the Lord was in jeopardy. Not so for the enemies of the nobleman, i.e., Christ, according to v. 27. The strong adversative "however" (*plēn*) seems to contrast the punishment of the unprofit-

---

15. See Leon Morris, *Luke* (TNTC, rev. ed.; Grand Rapids: Eerdmans, 1974, 1988), 302, and C. Marvin Pate, *Luke* (Moody Gospel Commentary; Chicago: Moody Press, 1995), 357–58. Admittedly some commentators see the loss of the mina to mean that the third servant will not be with Christ in His kingdom; see, e.g., John Martin, "Luke," in *Bible Knowledge Commentary* (NT ed.; Wheaton: Victor, 1983), 253.

16. Morris, *Luke*, 302 (italics original).

able servant with that of the master's enemies (cf. v. 14) who did not want him to rule over them. [17]

All this suggests that the first judgment (of the servants) is the Judgment Seat of Christ while the second judgment (of the enemies) is the Great White Throne Judgment. At the first judgment *believers* are judged according to their *works* to determine their *rewards* (Rom. 14:10–12; 1 Cor. 3:5–15; 4:1–5; 9:24–27; 2 Cor. 5:9–10; 1 John 4:17–19). At the second judgment *unbelievers* are judged according to their *works* to determine their degree of eternal *torment* (Rev. 20:11–15). The first judgment concerns only believers, but not their eternal destiny, which has already been decided. They "will not come into judgment" (John 5:24).

This parable shows that believers and unbelievers will appear at separate judgments. Once the servants (i.e., believers) are judged, the nobleman asks that his enemies be brought to him to be slaughtered (Luke 19:27). Thus servant judgment precedes enemy judgment. We should not miss the fact that the third servant escapes being slain. This indicates that perseverance is not a condition for "final salvation." However, perseverance *is* a condition for ruling with Christ.

Salvation by Grace versus Rewards by Works

While eternal life comes to the believer as a gift, the same cannot be said of rewards. According to Paul, Christians are to work hard to win the *prize* (*brabeion*) (1 Cor. 9:24). The term *brabeion* is "an award for exceptional performance, *prize, award*." [18] It comes to those who compete. [19] Fighting and running are vital athletic illustrations. As Paul's execution drew near, he confidently declared that he had run well and would soon obtain "the crown of righteousness" (2 Tim. 4:6–8). But he was not so confident some ten years earlier when he penned 1 Corinthians. He realized he would need to discipline his body and bring it into subjection if he was to avoid being disqualified (1 Cor. 9:27).

---

17. Pate, *Luke*, 358.

18. Walter Bauer, William F. Arndt, and F. Wilbur Gingrich, *A Greek-English Lexicon of the New Testament and Other Early Christian Literature* (3rd ed.; rev. Frederick William Danker; Chicago: University of Chicago Press, 2000), 183 (italics original).

19. Ibid.

We must be clear on this. Salvation is a free gift that comes through faith in Jesus Christ (e.g., Rom. 4:1–8; Gal. 2:16; Eph. 2:5, 8–9; Phil. 3:9; 2 Tim. 1:9; Titus 3:5), but rewards come as a result of work and perseverance (e.g., 1 Cor. 3:14–15; 9:24–27; Jas. 1:12; Rev. 3:11). "And whatever you do, work from the soul, as to the Lord and not to men, since you know that you will receive from the Lord the reward of the inheritance; for you serve the Lord Christ" (Col. 3:23–24).

What is remarkable is that the *same* speaker/writer can speak of salvation as a free gift on the one hand and rewards earned by works on the other.[20] (See chart on p. 33.)

Not All Believers Persevere

Reformed theologian Louis Berkhof responds to some common objections to the doctrine of perseverance. One objection states, "There are also exhortations urging believers to continue in the way of sanctification, which would appear to be unnecessary if there is no doubt about it that they will continue to the end." Berkhof counters this objection with, "But these are usually found in connection with warnings [against apostasy] ... and serve exactly the same purpose. They do not prove that any of the believers exhorted will not persevere, but only that God uses moral means for the accomplishment of moral ends."[21]

But this is no answer at all. If God guarantees that believers will persevere, then they will persevere with or without warnings. Even if they tried, they would not be able to fall away.

A much better way to approach this dilemma is simply to admit that appeals to persevere in the New Testament are legitimate warnings. By their very nature warnings suggest that believers may in fact fail to persevere. Therefore they should not be twisted into promises guaranteeing that saints will persevere. We do not find such promises, nor do we find salvation dependent on perseverance.

---

20. Other examples could be given beyond those listed in the chart. For example, John also spoke of the free gift of everlasting life in John 4:10 and Rev. 22:17, and he spoke of rewards for work done in John 4:33–38 and Rev. 2:7, 11, 17; 3:5, 12, 21; 22:14. Paul also spoke of the free gift in Rom. 3:24; 5:15; and 6:23, and he spoke of rewards for work done in Rom. 14:10–12 and Gal. 6:7–9.

21. Louis Berkhof, *Systematic Theology* (4th rev. ed.; Grand Rapids: Eerdmans, 1939, 1941), 548–49.

	Salvation by Grace	Rewards by Works
Matthew	"Come to Me, all you who labor and are heavy laden, and I will give you rest." (Matt. 11:28)	"For the Son of Man will come … and then He will reward each one according to what he has done." (Matt. 16:27)
Luke	"Believe in the Lord Jesus, and you will be saved, you and your household." (Acts 16:31)	"Blessed are you when men hate you.… Rejoice in that day and leap for joy! For indeed your reward is great in heaven." (Luke 6:22–23)
Paul	Not by works of righteousness … but according to His mercy He saved us. (Titus 3:5)	If we endure, we shall also reign with Him. If we deny Him, He also will deny us. (2 Tim. 2:12)
James	Every good gift and every perfect gift is from above.… Of His own will He brought us forth by the word of truth. (Jas. 1:17–18)	Indeed we count them blessed who endure. (Jas. 5:11)
Peter	Peter … said to them … "God … made no distinction between us and them, purifying their hearts by faith." (Acts 15:7–9)	But rejoice to the extent that you partake of Christ's sufferings, that when His glory is revealed, you may also be glad with exceeding joy. (1 Pet. 4:13)
John	"I am the Alpha and the Omega, the beginning and the end. I will give freely from the spring of the water of life to the one who thirsts." (Rev. 21:6)	"And he who overcomes and keeps My works until the end, to him I will give power over the nations." (Rev. 2:26)

Answering Biblical Objections

The Olivet Discourse (Matthew 24 - 25)

In his commentary on Matthew, D. A. Carson introduces chapters 24 by stating, "Few chapters of the Bible have elicited more disagreement among interpreters than Matthew 24 and its parallels in Mark 13 and Luke 21. The history of the interpretation of this chapter is immensely complex."[22] Indeed the way we interpret this discourse is crucial for how we understand Jesus' teaching on perseverance. Many contend that Jesus teaches perseverance as a condition for "final salvation." The context, however, shows otherwise.

He Who Endures to the End Will Be Saved (Matthew 24:13)[23]

Jesus' declaration that "he who endures to the end will be saved" (Matt. 24:13; cf. 10:22) would appear to put an end to the rewards view.[24] In truth, though, there is more to this verse than meets the eye. Context is everything, and we must clarify the context Jesus has in mind.

First, what "end" is in view? In short, it is the future (eschatological) tribulation. The Old Testament background for Jesus' statement can be found in Daniel. We see this from Matthew 24:15, where Jesus warns His hearers about "the abomination of desolation spoken of through the prophet Daniel." Daniel prophesied that history would run for another seventy sevens (or weeks) (Dan. 9:24–27), with an undisclosed gap between the sixty-ninth and seventieth seven. The last period consists of one seven/week (Dan. 9:27), which suggests that this time of tribulation will last seven *years*.[25] It is during this end-time period, according to Daniel, that "the abomination of desolation" occurs ("in the middle of the week he shall bring an end to sacrifice and offering. And on the wing of abominations shall be one who makes desolate," Dan. 9:27). The "end," then, is the "end of the age," a phrase that only occurs once outside Matthew (Matt. 13:39–40, 49; 24:3; 28:20; Heb. 10:26). This "end" will come after a period of tribulation unlike anything experienced since the beginning of the world (Matt. 24:21).

Second, what is this future salvation of which Jesus is speaking? The term "save" (*sōzō*) occurs twice in chapter 24, the latter being verse 22, where Jesus says that unless those days (of tribulation) were cut short,

---

22. D. A. Carson, "Matthew" (*EBC*, rev. ed.; Grand Rapids: Zondervan, 2010), 9:548.

23. For further discussion see David R. Anderson, "The Soteriological Impact of Augustine's Change from Premillennialism to Amillennialism, Part Two," *JGES* (Autumn 2002): 23, 26, 30–34, 36–38.

24. E.g., Schreiner and Caneday, *The Race Set before Us*, 151–52: "Jesus' words indicate that perseverance to the end is the necessary condition. Perseverance is a means that God has appointed by which one will be saved … in the final day. It is really this simple."

25. See, e.g., John F. Walvoord, *Daniel* (Chicago: Moody Press, 1971), 216–37; Charles C. Ryrie, *Basic Theology* (Wheaton, IL: Victor, 1986), 448, 465–66.

"no flesh would be saved." Jesus is not talking about eternal salvation. His point is that no one would *physically* survive the tribulation if God did not limit its duration. Since only enduring believers will survive, no unfaithful believers will be alive at the end of the tribulation. We find further support for this in Matthew 25:31–46 (to be discussed shortly).

The Destiny of Unfaithful Servants (Matthew 24:45 - 51) [26]

In this parable Jesus discusses a servant who was serving faithfully, but who lost faith in his master's soon return and then became an unfaithful and wicked servant:

> But if that bad [or wicked] servant should say in his heart, "My master is delaying his coming," and he should begin to beat his fellow servants and to eat and to drink with the drunkards, then the master of that servant will come on a day which he does not expect and at an hour which he does not know. And he will cut him in two and will appoint him a place with the hypocrites. There will be weeping and gnashing of teeth. (Matt. 24:48–51)

In this parable the servant is doing well and is in position to rule when his master returns. However, he gets tired of waiting and becomes reckless. As a result, his master "will cut him in two and appoint his portion with the hypocrites, where there shall be weeping and gnashing of teeth" (24:51). This refers to a painful experience in which the servant is *verbally* cut up at a future judgment (cf. Heb. 4:12; Rev. 1:16). Since this person is a servant of Christ, it is the Judgment Seat of Christ (the *Bema*) that is in view and not the Great White Throne Judgment. Believers are judged at the former and not the latter (cf. Rom. 14:10–12; 2 Cor. 5:9–10).

Furthermore, since faithfulness is the issue, not faith, eternal rewards rather than eternal destiny are at stake. The reference to weeping and gnashing of teeth is an oriental expression of grief and pain. [27]

---

26. Zane Hodges has a helpful discussion of this parable in his book *A Free Grace Primer: The Hungry Inherit, The Gospel under Siege, Grace in Eclipse* (Denton, TX: Grace Evangelical Society, 2011), 467–70.

27. See Gregory P. Sapaugh, "A Call to the Wedding Celebration: An Exposition of Matthew 22:1–14," *JGES* (Spring 1992): 30–32; Michael G. Huber, "The 'Outer Darkness' in Matthew and Its Relation to Grace," *JGES* (Autumn 1992): 14–16, 20–21; Joseph Dillow, *Final Destiny* (Monument, CO: Paniym Group, 2012), 767–73.

The New Testament elsewhere affirms that *unfaithful* believers will incur rebuke resulting in grief and pain at the *Bema* (cf. e.g., Luke 19:20–26; 1 Cor. 9:24–27; 2 Tim. 4:6–10; 1 John 2:28).

The Parable of the Ten Virgins (Matthew 25:1–13)

The second half of the parable of the ten virgins reads:

> At midnight a cry went out, "Behold, the bridegroom is coming! Go out to meet him!" Then all the virgins got up and trimmed their lamps. But the foolish ones said to the wise ones, "Give us from your oil because our lamps are going out." But the wise ones answered, "No, lest there not be enough for us and for you. Rather, go to the ones who sell and buy oil for yourselves." But as they were going away to buy oil, the bridegroom came. And those who were ready went with him into the marriage feast. Then the door was shut. Afterward the remaining virgins came, saying, "Lord, Lord, open for us." But he answered and said, "Truly I say to you, I do not know you." (Matt. 25:6–12)

The parable of the ten virgins is often understood to refer to the "final judgment."[28] Yet all ten are called virgins, an odd name for unbelievers (cf. esp. 2 Cor. 11:2; Rev. 14:4). All ten are expecting the bridegroom's soon return; again, this would be odd for unbelievers (cf. esp. 2 Tim. 4:8b). All ten have oil to light their torches, but only five have sufficient reserves of oil to keep their torches lit. The five with insufficient supply are not told that if they simply believe in the bridegroom, he will give them the needed oil. As Plummer points out, they were told to "go and buy" the needed oil themselves.[29]

So what does the presence or absence of sufficient reserves suggest? The midnight cry here refers to the "abomination of desolation" at the midpoint of the seven-year tribulation (Dan. 11:31; Matt. 24:15; see above). The point is that only tribulation believers who have stored up sufficient spiritual reserves in the first half will make it successfully

---

28. Commentators who express this view include R. T. France, *The Gospel According to Matthew* (NICNT; Grand Rapids: Eerdmans, 1985), 351–52; J. C. Ryle, *Matthew* (Wheaton: Crossway, 1993), 240–42; Leon Morris, *The Gospel According to Matthew* (PNTC; Grand Rapids: Eerdmans, 1992), 624–25.

29. Alfred Plummer, *An Exegetical Commentary on the Gospel According to St. Matthew* (Grand Rapids: Baker, 1982), 303.

through the persecutions of the second half. And those excluded from the torch dance[30] and other wedding festivities, while saved, will fail to rule with Christ in the life to come. It is a stretch to think exclusion from the torch dance equals spending eternity in hell.

The Parable of the Talents (Matthew 25:14 – 30)[31]

Jesus describes what was given to the first two servants and what they did with it.

> Then the one who had received five talents went and invested them and made another five talents. And likewise the one who had received two talents also gained two more. But the one who had received one went off and dug in the ground and hid the silver of his master. Then after much time the master of those servants came and settled accounts with them. (Matt. 25:16 – 19)

The Lord then explains the judgment of the third servant. This parable contains the last of the three New Testament "outer darkness" passages. Once again, since a servant of Christ is being judged, the *Bema* is in view. The fact that he is judged to be an unfaithful servant does not mean he is going to hell. Hell is not for believers (John 5:24).

> Then the one who had received the one talent came and said, "Master, I knew that you are a hard man, reaping where you did not sow and gathering where you did not scatter seed. And since I was afraid, I went off and hid your talent in the ground. Look, you have what is yours." But his master answered and said to him, "You wicked and lazy servant.... Therefore take from him the talent and give it to the one who has the ten talents. For to everyone who has more will be given, and he will have abundance. But from the one who does not have, even what he has will be taken away from him. And cast the useless servant into the darkness which is outside. There will be weeping and gnashing of teeth." (Matt. 25:24 – 26a, 28 – 30)

---

30. In Jewish weddings, young women would be chosen to provide a celebratory procession and dance with torches as part of the festivities. For more information see http://thirdmill. org/newfiles/kno_chamblin/NT.Chamblin.Matt.25.1 – 13.pdf, under A. 3. "The 'lamps.'"

31. For a detailed discussion of this parable and the three uses of *the outer darkness* in Matthew, see Michael G. Huber, "The 'Outer Darkness' in Matthew," 11 – 25. See also Dillow, *Reign of the Servant Kings*, 389 – 96.

The "outer darkness" is more literally "the darkness outside" (*to sko-tos to exōteron*). Jesus is alluding to a brightly lit banquet hall outside of which is darkness (cf. Matt. 22:1 – 14). Since this parable is parallel with the one discussed above (Luke 19:11 – 27), the fate of the third servant is the same. But recall that in Luke's parable the third servant is not slain, which means he is admitted into the kingdom. The same is true here in Matthew. Therefore though he is "in," that believer will miss out on the joys associated with ruling with Christ. The weeping and gnashing of teeth merely indicates that there will be shame at the *Bema*.

Elsewhere John urges believers to persevere so as to avoid shame at Christ's coming (1 John 2:28). Shame is a real possibility for believers when Christ returns. Indeed, we can understand why it is that those who belong to Christ and yet are found unfaithful would grieve and be ashamed at the moment they see the look of disapproval on their Lord's face.

The Sheep and the Goats (Matthew 25:31 - 46) [32]

In this passage we read of the judgment of the sheep and the goats.

> And He will place the sheep on his right, but the goats on His left. Then the King will say to the ones on His right, "Come, the ones blessed by My Father, inherit the kingdom which has been prepared for you from the foundation of the world. For I was hungry and you gave Me something to eat; I was thirsty and you gave Me drink; I was a stranger and you took Me in...." Then He will also say to the ones on His left, "Go away from Me, the cursed ones, into the everlasting fire which has been prepared for the devil and for his angels: for I was hungry and you did not give Me anything to eat; I was thirsty and you did not give Me drink...." And these will go away into everlasting punishment, but the righteous ones will go into life everlasting. (Matt. 25:33 – 35, 41 – 42, 46)

The judgment of the sheep and the goats will be an actual judgment following the tribulation (cf. Matt. 24:29 – 30; 25:31). All Gentiles who survive the tribulation will be judged. In his book, *Did Jesus Teach Salvation by Works?* Alan Stanley has a chapter entitled, "The Role of

---

32. For more details see Zane Hodges, *A Free Grace Primer*, 493 – 96.

Judgment in Salvation." [33] The entire chapter is devoted to Matthew 25:31–46. [34] He suggests that the goats "are cursed, though not because of their works per se, but because of their unfaithful actions toward Jesus [i.e., toward His emissaries]. Their lack of mercy has merely served to demonstrate their rejection of Him." [35]

Many would agree that there is a necessary connection between believing in Jesus and obeying His commandments. I would not. Before the judgment begins, the Son of Man will separate the sheep from the goats. He already knows which is which. The reason *the blessed* (Gentile believers) will inherit the kingdom is because of their good works (25:34–40). They aided Jesus' "brothers," that is, Jewish believers during the tribulation. [36] The reason *the cursed* (unbelieving Gentiles) receive eternal punishment is because they did not aid Jesus' brothers during the tribulation (25:41–46). If we recall Matthew 24:13 ("He who endures to the end will be saved") discussed above, the meaning of this judgment becomes clear. All believers, including those who did not befriend Jewish believers in the tribulation, receive eternal life and admittance into Christ's kingdom. The reason why we find no unfaithful believers here is because the only believers who will survive the seven-year tribulation will be those who endure in loving service until the end.

Note that the text does not say that these people *have eternal life* but that they *inherit the kingdom*. While many equate inheriting the kingdom with entering it, that is erroneous. Whenever inheriting the kingdom requires perseverance, it refers to more than spending eternity with Christ, namely, ruling with Him. [37] Jesus is saying that because they faithfully served Him during the tribulation, evidenced by their treatment of Jewish believers, they will be rewarded with the privilege of reigning with Him forever.

---

33. Alan P. Stanley, *Did Jesus Teach Salvation by Works?: The Role of Works in Salvation in the Synoptic Gospels* (ETSMS 4; Eugene, OR: Pickwick, 2006), 294–314.

34. See also ibid., 308–11, where Stanley offers a brief excursus on Jas. 2:14–26 since, in his mind "James … most likely explicates Matthew's teaching on the last judgment" (308). See also 332–33, where Stanley summarizes his understanding of Matt. 25:31–46 (and calls this "the final judgment").

35. Ibid., 314.

36. See ibid., 302–5, for an explanation of the five major views. Stanley defends the view that *Jesus' brothers* are Christian missionaries (cf. Matthew 10).

37. For more information on inheriting the kingdom see Robert N. Wilkin, "Christians Who Lose Their Legacy: Galatians 5:21," *JGES* (Autumn 1991): 23–27.

That not all believers will reign with Christ is brought out by texts like Romans 8:17; 1 Corinthians 9:24–27; 2 Timothy 2:12; 4:6–10; and Revelation 2:26. All believers *have* eternal life. Only persevering believers will *inherit* eternal life/the kingdom. The judgment of the sheep and the goats, which occurs immediately after the tribulation and *before* the millennium, cannot be the Great White Throne Judgment of Revelation 20:11–15 since that judgment occurs *after* the millennium (20:1–10). For the unbelievers at the judgment of the sheep and the goats, their judgment is merely an arraignment. They are sent off to Hades to await final judgment.[38] After the millennium, they will appear at the Great White Throne Judgment. At that judgment the book of life will be opened and they will not be found in it—because they never believed in Jesus. They will then be sent to a new place, the lake of fire (Rev. 20:15).[39]

We Reap What We Sow (Galatians 6:7–9)

"Do not be deceived, God is not mocked, for whatever a man sows, that he will also reap" (Gal. 6:7). Sowing and reaping are agricultural terms. Farming is hard work. Farmers do not reap a harvest based on faith alone. They must work hard in order to reap a crop (cf. 2 Tim. 2:6). Paul continues, "For he who sows to his flesh will of the flesh reap corruption, but he who sows to the Spirit will of the Spirit reap eternal life" (Gal. 6:8). The conclusion emphasizes the need to persevere, "And let us not grow weary while doing good, for in due season we shall reap if we do not lose heart" (6:9).

It is impossible to harmonize this text with Ephesians 2:8–9 if both are speaking of the same aspect of eternal life. Though both texts do speak of eternal life ("saved" in Eph. 2:8 clearly refers to the new birth, as v. 5 shows), Ephesians 2:8–9 refers to the *definite present possession* of it as a gift, whereas Galatians 6:7–9 speaks of the *possible future possession* of it as a reward for work done.

---

38. In light of Matt. 7:21–23, it is evident that some (many?) of those held in Hades for one thousand years will nonetheless feel they deserve to enter the kingdom because of the works that they did in Jesus' name.

39. For a discussion of the distinction between Hades and the lake of fire, see Robert N. Wilkin, *The Ten Most Misunderstood Words in the Bible* (Corinth, TX: Grace Evangelical Society, 2012), 91–93.

Galatians 6:7–9	Ephesians 2:8–9
Do not be deceived, God is not mocked, for whatever a man sows, that he will also reap. For he who sows to his flesh will of the flesh reap corruption, but he who sows to the Spirit will of the Spirit reap eternal life. And let us not grow weary while doing good, for in due season we shall reap if we do not lose heart.	For by grace you have been saved through faith. And this is not from yourselves; it is the gift of God, not from works, so that no one may boast.

Reaping is only for those who do not grow weary or lose heart while doing good (Gal. 6:9). The simple explanation is that reaping eternal life as a future reward refers to *inheriting* the kingdom and ruling with Christ, not simply to *inhabiting* the kingdom.[40] Donald Campbell adopts a similar view: "If a person sows to please his sinful nature, that is, if he spends his money to indulge the flesh, he will reap a harvest that will fade into oblivion. On the other hand, if he uses his funds to support the Lord's work, or sows to please the Spirit, and promotes his own spiritual growth, he will reap a harvest that will last forever."[41]

If You Continue in the Faith (Colossians 1:21 - 23)

This passage is often cited to prove that perseverance is a condition for "final salvation."[42]

And you who were once alienated and enemies in your mind by wicked works, yet now He has reconciled in the body of His flesh through death, in order to present you holy and blameless and irreproachable before Him, if indeed you continue in the faith, grounded and steadfast, and not drifting away from the expectation of the gospel which you heard. (Col. 1:21–23a)

Commentators often understand the condition in Colossians 1:23 ("if you continue...") to refer not to the near antecedent (the presentation

---

40. Ibid., 33–35.

41. Donald K. Campbell, "Galatians," in *Bible Knowledge Commentary* (NT ed.; Wheaton: Victor, 1983), 610; see also Dillow, *Reign of the Servant Kings*, 140.

42. See e.g., Stanley, *Did Jesus Teach Salvation By Works?* 253; Schreiner and Caneday, *The Race Set Before Us*, 192–93.

in 1:22), but to the far antecedent (reconciliation, mentioned earlier in 1:22). According to this view, one's reconciliation with God is not a settled matter, but hinges on perseverance in faith. The matter would then be settled at the Great White Throne Judgment; thus, the eternal destiny of the believer hangs in the balance. This view is well expressed by Peter O'Brien in his commentary on Colossians: "The prospect of the Colossians' standing irreproachable before him at the Great Assize is conditional upon their remaining firmly founded and established in the faith." [43] And, as Doug Moo asserts:

> Paul is genuinely concerned that the false teachers might "dis-qualify" the Colossian Christians (2:18). This being the case, Paul would clearly want his words here to be taken with great serious-ness. He wants to confront the Colossians with the reality that their eventual salvation depends on their remaining faithful to Christ and to the true gospel. Only by continuing in their faith can they hope to find a favorable verdict from God on the day of judg-ment. We have in this verse, then, a real warning. This warning, along with many similar ones, presents the "human responsibility" side in the biblical portrayal of final salvation. God does, indeed, by his grace and through his Spirit, work to preserve his people so that they will be vindicated in the judgment; but, at the same time, God's people are responsible to persevere in their faith if they expect to see that vindication. [44]

However, Charles Bing has argued that the condition more natu-rally refers to the believer's presentation rather than his reconciliation. [45] So yes, believers must indeed persevere, but not in order to attain "final salvation" or prove their reconciliation. Rather, believers must perse-vere to be found "holy and blameless and irreproachable before Him." This being the case, this presentation will not take place at the "Great Assize" (O'Brien), the "day of judgment" (Moo) (i.e., the Great White Throne Judgment), but rather at the Judgment Seat of Christ. Hence

---

43. Peter T. O'Brien, *Colossians, Philemon* (WBC; Dallas: 1982), 69.
44. Douglas J. Moo, *The Letters to the Colossians and to Philemon* (PNTC; Grand Rapids: Eerdmans, 2008), 144.
45. Charles C. Bing, "The Warning in Colossians 1:21–23," *BSac* (Jan.-Mar. 2007): 85–87.

what is at stake is not the eternal destiny of believers but their eternal rewards.

This interpretation is supported by the words Paul uses to describe believers at the time of presentation: "holy" (*hagios*), "blameless" (*amōmos*), and "above reproach" (*anenklētos*). These three words occur elsewhere to describe *mature* Christians. One of the requirements for *elders* (as opposed to all Christians), for example, is that they be "above reproach" (*anenklētos*) (Titus 1:6). *Blamelessness* is exemplified by the 144,000 who "stand without fault [*amōmos*] before the throne of God" (Rev. 14:4–5). [46] Finally, "holy" (*hagios*) is used frequently to describe the expected or actual *experience* of believers (e.g., Rom. 12:1; 1 Cor. 7:34; Eph. 1:4; 5:27; 1 Pet. 3:5; 2 Pet. 3:2; Rev. 20:6; 22:11). Peter, for example, reminds his readers that "as He who called you is holy [*hagios*], you also be holy [*hagios*] in all your conduct" (1 Pet. 1:15–16, citing Lev. 11:44). The point is that believers may indeed fall short of holiness, though that does not make them *un*believers.

These three terms ("holy," "blameless," and "irreproachable") do not necessarily describe the experience of all believers. Therefore, Bing defends and sums up the rewards view:

> When Colossians 1:21–23 is studied in the context of the entire epistle, it is clear that Paul wrote to believers who were in danger of having their assurance undermined by the false and legalistic doctrines of certain teachers. If they moved away from the truth of the gospel and the hope that is based on it, they would lose the prospect of a good presentation and therefore a good evaluation before the judgment seat of Christ, because hope is inexorably related to the believer's practical relationship to God and others. [47]

Persevere to Receive the Promise (Hebrews 10:36)

Here is another verse that many understand to refer to "final salvation" at the last judgment when endurance is taken into account. "For you

---

46. See, e.g., Robert L. Thomas, *Revelation 8–22: An Exegetical Commentary* (WEC; Chicago: Moody Press, 1992), 197–98.

47. Bing, "Warning," 88.

have need of endurance, so that after you have done the will of God, you may receive the promise." However, the promise cannot refer to "final salvation" for these readers are already eternally secure. They are "holy brothers, partakers of the heavenly calling" (Heb. 3:1); they "have a great High Priest ... Jesus Christ" (4:14), and "by this time ... ought to be teachers" (5:12). Hence they are "partakers of the Holy Spirit" (6:4) who "have been sanctified through the offering of the body of Jesus Christ once for all" (10:10).

The promise, then, rather than referring to "final salvation," refers to being Christ's partners (*metochoi*) in the life to come (cf. 1:9, 14). This, however, is not automatic. Only believers who persevere will be partners (*metochoi*) with Christ (3:14) — a matter to be decided at the Judgment Seat of Christ (cf. 10:39). Thus J. Paul Tanner writes, "The Lord's return should mean good news for believers, but for some it could mean shame (cf. 1 John 2:28)."[48] Tanner rejects the *final salvation* option:

> Any thought, however, that [Heb.] 10:39 might have *soteriological faith* in view must certainly be rejected in light of the fact that the author clearly portrays in chap. 11 that the faith he has in mind is *a life of walking by faith* in which one pleases God.[49]

Jesus Will Praise Believers Who Overcome (Revelation 3:5)

In light of His imminent return Jesus commands the church at Sardis to "be watchful" (cf. Matt. 24:42; 25:13; 1 Thess. 5:6, 10) and to persevere: "He who overcomes shall be clothed in white garments, and I will not blot out his name from the book of life; but I will confess his name before my Father and before His angels" (Rev. 3:5). The book of life contains everyone who will escape the lake of fire (20:15). However, there are major differences between 20:15 and 3:5.

Revelation 20:15 does not mention the term "name" (*onoma*), overcomers, blotting out names, or confessing names before the Father. But in 3:5 the term "name" is emphasized by both the repetition of the

---

48. J. Paul Tanner, "The Epistle to the Hebrews" (*GNTC*; Denton, TX: Grace Evangelical Society, 2010), 2:1077–78.

49. Ibid., 2:1078 (italics original).

Revelation 3:5	Revelation 20:15
"He who overcomes shall be clothed in white garments, and I will not blot out his *name* from the book of life; but I will confess his *name* before My Father and before His angels."	And anyone not found written in the book of life was cast into the lake of fire.

word itself and its connection with Jesus' confession. Jesus affirms that He will not blot out the overcomer's name from the book of life. He promises to confess the name of the overcomer before His Father and the angels.

Note that Jesus does not say that He *will* blot anyone's name out of the book of life. Many regard this as *litotes*, a figure of speech in which an affirmative is expressed by negating its opposite. If I say, "It is no big deal," then I mean, "It is a little deal." If this is litotes, then what Jesus is saying is that He will exalt the name of the overcomer. Another option, resulting in essentially the same conclusion, is that the term "name" (*onoma*) does not mean *name* here but *reputation*. Thus J. William Fuller suggests that verse 5 is a promise:

> God will remember and preserve the *onoma* [name/reputation] of the Christian who overcomes, implying a particularly close relationship between God and this believer. But the implicit warning is that the Christian who denies the faith will lose that privileged position and identity and relationship, even though that Christian will enter eternal life. The concept of an honorable name versus a shameful one is somewhat foreign to the western mind. The difference in perception, however, may be the very reason this verse has been misunderstood for so long.[50]

This does not mean that the believer who fails to persevere is no longer found in the book of life. It means that his "name" (i.e., his exalted reputation) has been blotted out. The point is that Jesus will praise the overcomer at the Judgment Seat of Christ, but He will not praise those who fail to overcome (cf. 1 Cor. 3:15; 4:5). It is important to remember

---

50. J. William Fuller, "'I Will Not Erase His Name from the Book of Life' (Revelation 3:5)," *JETS* (September 1983): 305.

that Christ will save all believers, even those who do not overcome. However, He will only exalt the names of those who overcome.

This fits perfectly with what Jesus said in Matthew 10:32–33. He will confess before His Father those who confess Him before others, whereas the ones who deny Jesus before others He will also deny before His Father. It is precisely along these lines that we should understand Paul's words in 2 Timothy 2:12: "If we endure, we shall also reign with Him. If we deny Him, He will also deny us." What is at stake in all these passages is not the believer's eternal destiny at the final judgment but rather the believer's praise, or lack of it, at the Judgment Seat of Christ.

The Great White Throne Judgment (Revelation 20:11 - 15)

Revelation 20:11–15 delineates the Great White Throne Judgment and is a key passage in this discussion.

> And I saw a great white throne and the One who sat on it, from whose face the earth and the heaven fled. And there was found no place for them. And I saw the dead, the great and the small, standing before the throne. And books were opened. And another book was opened, which is the book of life. And the dead were judged by the things which had been written in the books, according to their works. And the sea gave up the dead who were in it and death and Hades gave up the dead who were in them. And they were judged, each one according to his works. And death and Hades were thrown into the lake of fire. This is the second death, the lake of fire. And if anyone was not found having been written in the book of life, he was cast into the lake of fire.

Some think this judgment is for both believers and unbelievers.[51] However, I maintain there are actually two eschatological judgments: one for believers, called the Judgment Seat of Christ (2 Cor. 5:9–11), and one for unbelievers, called the Great White Throne Judgment (Rev. 20:11–15). Yet even if we were to grant that there is but one

---

51. E.g., G. K. Beale, *The Book of Revelation: A Commentary on the Greek Text* (2nd ed., NIGTC; Grand Rapids: Eerdmans, 1999), 1032–33; Leon Morris, *Revelation* (TNTC; Leicester, UK: Inter-Varsity Press, 1987), 234.

eschatological judgment, Revelation 20:11–15 does not support the contention that works determine one's eternal destiny. Zane Hodges comments:

> At the Great White Throne Judgment (Rev 20:11–15) people are temporarily released (paroled!) from hell (Hades) and the issue of their permanent eternal abode becomes a legal matter in the presence of their Judge (Jesus Christ: John 5:22). They are first judged according to their works to see if these works justify their permanent release from eternal judgment (Rev 20:13). As we know, there will be no justification based on works (Rom 3:20). Next, search is made in the Book of Life to see if they qualify for release because they have eternal life. They do not and are therefore placed in an eternal abode (the Lake of Fire) in separation from their Judge forever.
>
> Although the outcome of this whole process is a foregone conclusion, the justice of God requires the process to take place. Even in our own society, a man caught red-handed in the act of murder (or some other crime) must have his day in court. Every unsaved person will have his or her day in God's court. [52]

There is no hint in this passage that persevering in good works is the condition for escaping the lake of fire. In fact, if we carefully observe what the text says, being found in the book of life is the only requirement. Since the sole condition of having eternal life, and thus being found in the book of life, is faith in Christ (e.g., John 3:16; 6:35), the Great White Throne Judgment underscores the promise of life to all who simply believe.

Exegetical Problems with the View That Christians Will Appear at the Final Judgment

Eternal Life Is Everlasting

Charles Ryrie famously said, "Everlasting life is *ever-lasting life*. If everlasting life could be lost, then it has the wrong name." Jesus made it

52. Zane Hodges, "The Sin of Unbelief," *Grace in Focus* (Nov.-Dec. 2007): 2–3, available at www.faithalone.org.

crystal clear that eternal life can never be lost. The one who believes in Him shall *never* hunger or thirst (John 6:35), shall *never* die (11:26), and shall *not* come into judgment (5:24). Once a person has eternal life, he or she has it *forever.*

Eternal Life Is by Faith Alone

We look in vain in the New Testament for any condition pertaining to eternal life other than faith in Jesus Christ. Perseverance and works are excluded. [53] The only requirement is faith (cf. John 3:16; 5:24; 6:35; 11:26).

Eternal Life Is Not of Works

We are saved by grace through faith. Salvation is a gift of God and not of works (Eph. 2:8–9). Jesus himself taught that eternal life is a gift (John 4:10) and not from works (6:28–29). And since perseverance is work, perseverance is not a condition for salvation. Christians *should* work hard, but not for eternal salvation (e.g., 1 Cor. 9:24–27; 2 Tim. 2:3–6; 4:6–8).

Eternal Life Is Decided at Conversion

John 5:24 refutes the notion that believers will appear at the final judgment. That is where eternal destinies are decided, and Jesus specifically taught that believers "shall not come into judgment [*krisis*]." The eternal destiny of believers has already been decided. Unfortunately, many commentators maintain that believers *will come into* judgment (*krisis*). For example, many say that references to judgment (*krisis*) in James 2:13 and to salvation in 2:14 mean that brothers and sisters in Christ who are without works will be condemned at the final judgment. [54] But none

---

53. Contra Stanley, *Did Jesus Teach Salvation by Works?* In his concluding chapter he writes, "Eschatological [= final, see p. 335] salvation then, in the Synoptic Gospels, is indeed by works.... Thus, even though works are necessary for [eschatological] salvation, the works themselves are only possible 'with God'" (334).

54. See Peter H. Davids, *The Epistle of James: A Commentary of the Greek Text* (NIGTC; Grand Rapids: Eerdmans, 1982), 120; George M. Stulac, *James* (IVPNT Commentary Series; Downers Grove: InterVarsity Press, 1993), 107–9; Douglas J. Moo, *The Letter of James* (PNTC; Grand Rapids: Eerdmans, 2000), 134–35; Craig L. Blomberg and Mariam J. Kamell, *James* (ZECNT; Grand Rapids: Zondervan, 2008), 129 fn.13, 136; Scot McKnight, *The Letter of James* (NICNT; Grand Rapids: Eerdmans, 2011), 247.

of these commentators attempt to show how this can be so in light of John 5:24.

Practical Problems with the View That Christians Will Appear at the Final Judgment

Assurance Is Impossible [55]

If perseverance is a condition for "final salvation," and if we cannot be sure we will persevere (e.g., 1 Cor. 9:27), then assurance concerning "final salvation" is ultimately impossible. But imagine being convinced of hell and yet uncertain as to whether you will be there. That's a terrible way to live, and it's not of God. Even Reformed theologian Michael Horton acknowledges, "If my faith is too weak to have full assurance based on an unconditional promise, how on earth can I expect to get any better handle on my assurance by turning inward and taking inventory?" [56]

Evangelism Is Garbled [57]

It's strange that when many Christians share their faith, they don't simply call people to believe in Jesus; rather, they call them to give their lives to Him. Commitment, rather than faith, is presented as the condition for having everlasting life. Yet the Lord Jesus said that whoever *believes in Him* has everlasting life (e.g., John 3:16).

Motivation Is Marred

What would your motivation be to serve God if you believed that the verdict on your salvation awaited the final judgment? Would you not be motivated by fear rather than love (cf. 2 Cor. 5:14)? This is what I find among Christians who believe they must persevere until the end to be saved. Fear of hell motivates them to give money, to attend church, to

---

55. For more discussion of assurance and perseverance, see Robert N. Wilkin, *Secure and Sure: Grasping the Promises of God* (Irving, TX: Grace Evangelical Society, 2005); see esp. pp. 107–111.

56. Michael Horton (ed.), *Christ the Lord: The Reformation and Lordship Salvation* (Grand Rapids: Baker, 1992), 146. Horton, though not holding my view, is a Calvinist who believes it is dangerous to look for assurance by means of introspection.

57. For a handy evangelistic tool I recommend, *Living Water: The Gospel of John with Notes* (Glide, OR: Absolutely Free, 1996).

try hard to please God. Gratitude goes out the window, and some even quit the faith under the pressure of having to perform.

The Bible Is Unintelligible

There is no sense in teaching that Jesus died for helpless sinners, only to leave them with the crushing burden of having to attain "final salvation" by persevering in good works. If we do not recognize the difference between the free gift of eternal life, which is received by faith apart from works, and the rewards that are earned by persevering in faithful works, the Bible will seem needlessly paradoxical and self-contradictory. Distinguishing between the two allows us to maintain both the freeness of everlasting life, and the importance of good works.

Conclusion

No one can be sure that he or she will persevere in faith and good works. If Paul thought he could be disqualified for the prize (1 Cor. 9:27), then so should we. But that uncertainty concerns only the "prize," not eternal life. If we believe the promise of everlasting life (e.g., John 3:16), then we are assured; it's that simple. We do not look to our works for assurance. We do not harbor hidden fears that we will appear at the final judgment only to find we were never saved. Rather, we believe Jesus' promise that the one who believes in Him "has everlasting life [present tense], shall not come into judgment [future tense], but has passed from death into life [past tense]" (John 5:24). We rejoice in this security. Let us not go through life fearful of the final judgment. Believers will *not* be judged there.

THOMAS R. SCHREINER

Agreements

Robert Wilkin makes a valiant attempt to defend the notion that works are assessed for rewards only, so that they play no role in whether one receives eternal life. Unfortunately, his exegetical support for his thesis is singularly unconvincing. Let me step back, however, and point out where Wilkin and I agree. Like Wilkin, I understand the New Testament to teach that eternal life is irrevocable. Those who have eternal life will never perish (John 10:28–29). Those whom the Father has given to the Son and who believe in the Son will never be lost. Jesus will raise them on the final day (6:37–40). Or, as Paul puts it, God will complete the saving work he began in believers (Phil. 1:6; cf. 1 Thess. 5:24). Nothing will ever separate believers from the love of God in Jesus Christ (Rom. 8:35–39).

Wilkin is also correct in saying that faith alone saves. The work God requires is to believe in the sent one, Jesus Christ (John 6:29). Luther interpreted Romans 3:28 correctly in adding the German word *allein* (which means "alone"), so that the verse teaches that justification is obtained through faith alone. I point out in my essay that the outstanding Roman Catholic scholar Joseph Fitzmyer sides with Luther here.

Disagreements

The Nature of Saving Faith

Yet while Wilkin and I agree that faith alone saves, we disagree on the nature of faith and on its relationship with works. Here is where James comes in, for James teaches that a genuine and living faith always produces good works (Jas. 2:14–26). Yes, justification is by faith alone, but such faith is never alone.

Space is lacking to engage the texts fully here, but there is a kind of faith that isn't saving. Mental agreement with propositions doesn't mean someone has saving faith. Believing that there is one God doesn't save, for demons believe such but they don't belong to God (Jas. 2:19). Similarly, demons rightly identified Jesus as "the Holy One of God" (Mark 1:24), but they remained his opponents. Saving faith embraces, prizes, and treasures Jesus Christ for salvation. A full study of the gospel of John would be illuminating, for John teaches us that faith comes to Jesus, follows him, obeys him, and receives him. The dynamism of faith is communicated with other metaphors as well: faith eats and drinks of Jesus' flesh and blood respectively. Faith receives Jesus and abides in him.

Wilkin defines faith as mental assent, but such a definition does not accord with the biblical witness, with the breadth and depth of faith as we find it in the Scriptures. We can think of Hebrews 11, where faith functioned as the wellspring for Abel's sacrifice, Noah's building of the ark, Abraham's migration to Canaan, and Moses' identification with pitiful Israel instead of powerful Egypt. The relationship between faith and works is conveyed well by Hebrews 11:8, "By faith Abraham obeyed." Despite Wilkin's protestations, the scenarios in John 2:23–25 and 8:31–59 illustrate the truth that there is a kind of faith that isn't saving. There is a false faith that must be distinguished from genuine faith. Not everyone who speaks in Christ's name belongs to him (Matt. 7:21–23).

Theological Paradigms

Dispensational theology. Another weakness of Wilkin's essay is its inextricable tie with a certain kind of dispensational theology. I say a "certain kind" since there is diversity in dispensationalism today. But here is the problem. If his kind of dispensationalism collapses, so does Wilkin's interpretation. I don't have space to unpack all that could be said here. But it must be said that the dispensational reading offered is artificial and strained. When I first encountered solutions like Wilkin proposes regarding the judgment, I found it impossible to remember in the judgment passages whether the judgment of believers or unbelievers was in view. For example, the judgment of the sheep and goats is allegedly restricted to Gentiles and placed at the end of the tribulation (Matt.

25:31–46), whereas the judgment at the great white throne is supposedly limited to unbelievers (Rev. 20:11–15). I would suggest it is difficult to remember such distinctions because they have no textual warrant. The most natural way to understand the sheep and goat judgment in Matthew 25:31–46 and the great white throne judgment in Revelation 20:11–15 is as the judgment of *all* people. I won't linger on this point, since I will argue Wilkin's reading fails even if one grants his dispensational scheme. Still, many today widely acknowledge the weakness of his dispensational paradigm, even those nurtured and raised in that tradition.

Extraordinary presuppositions. Now I come to the fundamental and most serious problem with Wilkin's essay: he forces every text to fit his paradigm. All of us, of course, bring our theology to the text. None of us, if we're honest, are free from presuppositions. There is no neutral reading of the text. Nevertheless, there would be no point in doing exegesis if our preconceptions could not be altered. We must be willing to listen to the text and ask ourselves if we have adopted a system that is alien to the scriptural text.

Weeping and gnashing of teeth. In reading Wilkin, I sincerely wonder if there is any evidence that could ever overturn his convictions. Let me illustrate the point. It is patently clear in Matthew that those who weep and gnash their teeth are cast into hell. They won't sit at the banquet with Abraham and the patriarchs (Matt. 8:11–12). Those who do evil are removed from God's kingdom, thrown into the fiery furnace, and weep and gnash their teeth (13:41–42). Similarly, "at the end of the age" angels will segregate "the wicked from the righteous" and cast the wicked "into the blazing furnace, where there will be weeping and gnashing of teeth" (13:49–50). So too, the man without the wedding garment is thrown out of the banquet hall into outer darkness, where there is weeping and gnashing of teeth (22:11–13). Jesus makes clear he wasn't among the chosen (22:14). So it is astonishing to read Wilkin say that the unfaithful servant who is among the hypocrites who weep and gnash their teeth and is "cut ... to pieces" (24:51) is simply losing his reward. What language would convince Wilkin to say that hell is in view if being cut to pieces and placed among the hypocrites doesn't refer to eternal punishment?

Colossians 1:21–23. Wilkin argues that the condition in 1:23 that demands perseverance in the faith does not pertain to reconciliation but to the eschatological presentation. He may very well be right about this, but it is a distinction without a difference for the discussion we are having, for holiness is necessary to obtain the final reward, to receive eternal life.

Other texts in the New Testament confirm this judgment. For instance, in Philippians 2:15 "without fault" (amōma), which must not be confused with sinlessness, is necessary to belong to the "children of God." Being a child of God is not a reward above and beyond eternal life. Being a child of God is another way of saying that one belongs to God, that one is a member of his people. So too, in Jude 24 "without fault" (amōmous) does not refer to a reward but represents the character of those who stand before God. Such a theme fits with Hebrews 12:14, which affirms that no one will see the Lord without holiness. Seeing the Lord isn't a reward for a few but is the privilege that will belong to all those who are in the heavenly city. Entrance into the city is granted only to those who are holy, only to those who do the will of God and do good works. Hence, the eschatological presentation in Colossians 1:22 doesn't refer to rewards above and beyond eternal life, but to the necessity of perseverance in faith to stand before the Lord.

Galatians 6:7–9. These verses serve as another example of a jaundiced reading of the text. Paul asserts that those who sow to the Spirit "will reap eternal life," while those who sow to the flesh "will reap corruption [*phthoran*]." This seems to be a clear example of the necessity of good works and life in the Spirit to obtain everlasting life. "Corruption" is the antithesis to "eternal life" (Gal. 6:8), and thus it must refer to final judgment, to exclusion from eternal life. Wilkin dissents. Eternal life, he claims, can't have the same meaning in Galatians 6:8 as it does in Ephesians 2:8–9 since in the latter instance it is a past gift and in the Galatians text it is a future reward. Hence, eternal life in Galatians "refers to *inheriting* the kingdom and ruling with Christ, not simply inhabiting the kingdom" (p. 41).

Once again, what can be said in response? First a minor quibble. Contrary to Wilkin, Ephesians 2:8–9 doesn't speak of eternal life. Paul refers to God's past saving work here and doesn't use the expression "eternal life." That brings me to the second point, which is more substantive. Notice how Wilkin's argument works. Paul can't mean by the term "eternal life" in Galatians 6:8 the same thing meant by this term in other texts, for then eternal life would require works, and we know from other texts, according to Wilkin, that he would never say such a thing.

Hence, the main problem with Wilkin's essay surfaces again. Yes, we all have presuppositions. We all interpret texts in light of other texts. Scripture interprets Scripture, and so it is fitting to consider other texts in interpreting any particular passage of Scripture. Nevertheless, there comes a point where a doctrine needs to be revised because other texts speak so clearly against the doctrinal formulation. I would suggest that Galatians 6:8 is such a text (and it isn't a rare exception!). Those who do not sow to the Spirit will experience eschatological corruption. To put it another way: they will go to hell. Wilkin rejects this reading, claiming that eternal life can't mean inhabiting the kingdom since that would contradict other texts.

I ask again: What could ever convince Wilkin and those who support him that they are wrong? If the text says good works are necessary for eternal life, then (according to Wilkin) the eternal life is different from the eternal life that brings salvation. His reading is unfalsifiable. He has already decided that works aren't necessary for eternal life, so if the text says that works bring eternal life, then we have a different kind of eternal life. I truly hope I am not being unkind, but this seems like a can't-lose proposition. No evidence could ever be adduced that would prove the contrary. For even if the Bible were to say, "Good works are necessary for eternal life and to escape hell," it seems that Wilkin would say, "Eternal life and hell have a different meaning here."

Hebrews 10:36. The same pattern plays itself out in the entire essay. Hebrews 10:36, for example, states that one must do God's will to receive the promise. The promise is clearly eschatological rescue, for it is contrasted a few verses later (10:39) with a typical word for eschatological destruction (*apōleia*). Wilkin waves aside such a reading by saying, "However, the promise [in 10:36] cannot refer to 'final salvation' for these readers are already eternally secure" (p. 44). The necessity of works for final salvation is ruled out dogmatically and presuppositionally from the outset.

Revelation 3:5. Wilkin says that Revelation 3:5, where Jesus threatens to blot out a person's name from the book of life, refers to their reputation but not their identity. In other words, they will experience eternal life but will not enjoy rewards and privileges granted to those who obeyed. But in Revelation 3:5 John draws on Jesus' words, "But whoever disowns me before others, I will disown before my Father in heaven" (Matt. 10:33 NIV). Paul picks up the same saying in 2 Timothy 2:12. The one who denies Jesus will be denied by him. It is not merely the reputation of the person that is denied but the person himself. The text doesn't say that they will not be given rewards but that Jesus himself will deny them. So too, in Revelation 3:5 being blotted out of the book of life most naturally means that those who defile their garments by pursuing a life of sin will not be in the book of life.

Conclusion

To sum up, Wilkin rightly sees that eternal life is a gift that the elect never forsake, and he is right in affirming that it is received by believing. Furthermore, I sympathize with his ultimate goal. He wants to protect the purity of the gospel so that salvation is by grace alone through faith alone and in Christ alone. But his exegesis of texts that demand good works for final salvation is forced and unconvincing. A better approach would be to integrate the necessity of good works for final salvation with the claim that eternal life is a gift of God.

RESPONSE TO ROBERT N. WILKIN

JAMES D. G. DUNN

Major Disagreements

A Canon within the Canon

Robert Wilkin's essay is a classic case of a solution to various problem texts drawn from an unequivocal reading of one or two texts and imposed on the problem texts with the sole justification that they resolve the problem. In this case the problem is that so many New Testament texts envisage that Christians will be subjected to divine judgment before the throne of God or of his Christ. These seem to conflict with other texts that give assurance to believers, that they (already) have eternal life, and since they already have it, it cannot be taken away (otherwise it wouldn't be "eternal"). In this case the solution-providing texts, the texts on which everything else turns, are John 5:24 and Revelation 20:11–15. This is interpretation by "canon within the canon"— the "canon within" in this case being these two verses. Expressed less provocatively, this is an extreme case where the perspicacity of Scripture hangs on a particular interpretation of two verses being allowed to determine that many other verses should be interpreted in a way that seems to run counter to their most obvious sense.

Some people find it hard to accept that their reading of a text is an interpretation of the text. They may think and claim that their understanding of the text accords with the "plain sense" of the text. But they do need to acknowledge that what they take the text to mean is an *interpretation*, an interpretation that has to be justified. The debates about the authority of Scripture are never going to be finally resolved by arguments about its inspiration. The actual authority of Scripture depends on its interpretation. And when conclusions about a particular text are then applied to or enforced on other Scriptures, the responsibility to justify the procedure is even greater. Are the various texts speaking the same language? Are they theologizing in the same way? Is one chalk and the other cheese? If they are singing even slightly different tunes, do they harmonize quite so readily?

The "Already/Not Yet"' Tension Is Neglected

In the case of John 5:24, it would be generally agreed that John's presentation of the gospel can be well characterized as "realized eschatology," and that John 5:24 is one of its strongest expressions — indeed, probably the strongest affirmation of realized eschatology in the New Testament. That is to say, that in the already/not yet understanding of the process of salvation characteristic of most of the New Testament writings, John gives special emphasis to the "already" aspect of the process. In John's gospel the coming into the world of the light is decisive; everything depends on how one responds to that light. The light of Jesus is the critical factor (*krisis* as a separating force as well as judgmental force). The judgment is the separation of those who respond to the light from those who turn away from it, those who believe and those who do not (John 3:17–21; 9:39).

Quite how this "judgment," which marks the decisive beginning of the process of salvation, correlates with the final judgment at the resurrection of the dead (John 5:28–29) is not clear, or at least, John does not make it clear. The beginning of the process is clear, since that is where the emphasis is placed in John's gospel. How it should be correlated with those Scriptures that have greater focus on the end of the process, on the final judgment, is not clear. Paul, for example, strongly emphasizes the decisiveness of the "already" (Rom. 6:2–4; 7:4–6; 8:1–10), but he goes on to indicate that the "not yet" completion is not yet assured (6:12–19; 7:14–25; 8:12–13). In the light of Paul's treatment of the issue, one might well ask whether John's gospel overemphasizes the "already" and underemphasizes or even neglects the "not yet."

The point becomes still clearer when Wilkin turns to "what the Bible says" (p. 27). He picks up immediately on the strong words of assurance in John 3:16 ("will not perish"), 6:35 ("will never hunger and ... will never thirst"), and 11:26 ("will never die"). Doesn't he recognize hyperbole when he sees it? To take such expressions as literal statements of fact runs so counter to the experience of Christians from day one as to undermine any belief in them. A literary pedancy makes such biblical language less credible, not more credible.

Revelation Mentions Only One Judgment

So far as Revelation 20:11–15 is concerned, it is clear that the throne of judgment is in view; references to "judgment" in Revelation usually refer to judgment of condemnation. But did John conceive of an earlier judgment, involving only "the elect and faithful," a judgment where they receive varying rewards? None of that seems to be in view in the promises to the faithful in chapters 2–3, or to those with their robes washed white in the blood of the Lamb (7:14). The only judgment in view is that of 20:11–15, in which, it would appear, all the dead will be judged "according to their works," and those whose names are not in the book of life will be thrown in the lake of fire. The emphasis is still on judgment of condemnation, but the implication is that those whose names are in the book of life will be judged favorably.[58] Since no other judgment is mentioned in Revelation, that would seem to be the plainest of senses.

Neglecting the Distinct Emphases of Biblical Authors

What we have, in other words, in these two passages are emphases being placed at quite different points in the range of New Testament teachings on believing and judgment. It is not realistic to draw *both* elements of Wilkin's reconstruction from *either* of the writings in view (John and Revelation). It can only be achieved by taking the emphasis from one and reading it into the other, inserting an apocalyptic emphasis into a nonapocalyptic writing, and vice versa. Is that fair to either? I question the legitimacy, and wisdom, of taking verses from different New Testament writings and blending them into a system, as though they are all written in straightforward prose and all make propositional statements for a rule of faith. But even if it was appropriate, surely we

---

58. What a contrived interpretation of Rev. 3:5 is offered by Wilkin: to have one's name blotted out from the book of life "means that his 'name' (i.e., his exalted reputation) has been blotted out" (p. 45). But the most obvious (plain sense) reading of the Revelation references is that to have one's "name (in) the book of life" (3:5), to have one's "name written in the book of life" (13:8), and to be "found written in the book of life" (20:15) are all alternative ways of saying the same thing, that is, a way of affirming, particularly for those suffering for their faith, that they will be vindicated in the final judgment.

should first inquire whether the system is fully rooted in and true to *each* of the writings being drawn on. Can a systematized treatment such as that of Wilkin be genuinely described as *New Testament* teaching when it cannot be shown to be the teaching of each, or any, of the particular New Testament writings being drawn on?

Paul Envisioned Only One Judgment

When we try to bring Paul fully into the discussion, Wilkin's resolution/interpretation becomes even more questionable. Is there any indication whatsoever that Paul envisaged different judgments—one for believers judged for their lives and doings as believers, the other for unbelievers whose doom is already sealed, simply because they are unbelievers? Paul obviously envisaged that judgment would be "according to each one's deeds" (Rom. 2:6–11); there is not even the barest hint either that this would be a judgment exclusively for believers, or that believers would be excluded from it, having already been judged. And the following paragraph speaks of "the day when, according to my gospel, God through Jesus Christ will judge the secret thoughts of all" (2:16)—that is, the normal, traditional concept of a day of judgment, a final judgment when *all* will be judged. Likewise 1 Corinthians 3:13 envisages a "day" of judgment; anyone hearing that read would naturally think of the traditional concept of a day appointed by God for final judgment;[59] the judgment of believers and of what they had done would be part of that day—as clearly implied also, we might note, in 1 John 4:17.

Returning to Paul: Are we to argue that the appearance "before the judgment seat of God" (Rom. 14:10) is different from the appearance "before the judgment seat of Christ" (2 Cor. 5.10)? Are we to interpret Paul as envisaging a judgment for believers before Christ, quite different and separate from a judgment for everyone else before God (before the Great White Throne of God)?[60] But both clearly have in view the judgment of believers ("we will stand before the judgment seat of God"—Rom. 14.10; "all of us must appear before the judgment seat of Christ"—2 Cor. 5.10). And there is no hint whatsoever that Paul

---

59. Elsewhere in the New Testament—Matt. 10:15; 11:22, 24; 12:36, 41–42; 2 Pet. 2:9; 3:7; Jude 6.

60. Wilkin seems to go down this road in his interpretation of Col. 1:21–23 (pp. 41–43).

would have wanted the audience to whom each letter was read to think of anything other than the same final judgment, as in Romans 2.

Galatians 6:7-9 Is So Clear

I have probably said enough in my own essay about Paul's warnings about possible failure of believers to persevere (to use Wilkin's language). But I cannot fail to respond to his treatment of Galatians 6:7–9. It is clear that Paul directs his exhortation to the Galatian believers ("you" and "us"). It is equally clear that "corruption/destruction" (*phthora*) is the opposite of "eternal life." The conclusion can hardly be avoided, then, that Paul envisages the possibility that believers may indeed "sow to their own flesh" and in consequence be excluded from "eternal life." This presumably ties into Paul's usual concept of salvation as a process of being saved, a process of which salvation is the end result. So, Paul envisages the possibility of the process not being completed, that is, of a final judgment that goes against those who once believed but did not "persevere." Does Wilkin really think that when people first believe, they believe forever, so that it can be said finally and for every case that "eternal life is decided [that is, finally and irrevocably decided] at conversion" (p. 48)?[61] Surely the history of Christianity, and probably Wilkin's own experience, have known many cases where those who once believed no longer believe.

Jesus' Warning Parables

Finally, I cannot really let Wilkin's interpretations of Jesus' warning parables pass without comment. The warning of Matthew 24:48–51 seems clear beyond doubt: that the returning master "will cut him [the reckless servant] in two and appoint his portion with the hypocrites, where there shall be weeping and gnashing of teeth" (24:51). Can Wilkin really think that this means merely being "verbally cut up at a future judgment" (p. 35)? And in 25:1–13 the warning is equally clear: the unprepared bridesmaids will be shut out from the wedding banquet, and the bridegroom will tell them, "I never knew you" (25:10–12). Can Wilkin really think this means simply that they will be "excluded from

---

61. "If God guarantees that believers will persevere, then they will persevere with or without warnings. Even if they tried, they would not be able to fall away" (p. 32).

the torch dance and other wedding festivities" (p. 37), but otherwise will "eat with Abraham and Isaac and Jacob in the kingdom of heaven" (8:11–12)?

Equally feeble, I would have to say, is Wilkin's interpretation of Matthew 25:14–30. The "worthless slave" is to be "thrown into the outer darkness, where there will be weeping and gnashing of teeth" (25:30). Does Wilkin really ask us to believe that Jesus meant simply to contrast "the darkness outside" with the "brightly lit banquet hall outside of which is darkness" and that the worthless slave really was "in" after all (p. 38)? Matthew uses the same phrases several times in his gospel—"thrown into outer darkness" (8:12; 22:13; 25:30), equivalent to being "thrown into the fire" (3:10; 7:19), the "unquenchable fire" (3:12), "the hell of fire" (5:22; 18:9), thrown into "the furnace of fire" (13:40, 42, 50), "the eternal fire" (18:8; 25:41), "where there will be weeping and gnashing of teeth" (8:12; 13:42, 50; 22:13; 24:51; 25:30). Since this is the lot of those thrown out from the kingdom (8:12; 13:42), for "the evil" as distinct from "the righteous" (13:50), for the man without the wedding robe (22:13), and for "the devil and his angels" (25:41), there isn't really any room for a nice softer interpretation that allows something much less fierce and less eternal for "worthless" believers, is there? Or should we revive a belief in purgatory?[62]

Summary

Exegesis that consists of special pleading and is guilty of *petitio principii* is never going to prove satisfactory.

---

62. But in reference to Matt. 25:31–46, Wilkin thinks that for *unbelievers* the judgment of the sheep and goats will be "merely an arraignment. They are sent off to Hades to await final judgment" (p. 40). So the first judgment will be of everyone after all?

MICHAEL P. BARBER

I am grateful to Robert Wilkin for his essay. His approach springs from an effort to affirm truths reiterated numerous times in the New Testament, namely, that God is faithful to his promises and that salvation is the result of God's free gift of grace. As those who read my article will see, as a Catholic I affirm these beliefs. I am grateful to his commitment to proclaim the gospel.

Notwithstanding this common ground, I find his specific interpretation of various biblical texts unconvincing. In this response, I cannot offer a point-for-point response to all of his claims. I will therefore focus my attention on four major areas.

Are Grace and Good Works Really Antithetical Categories?

Wilkin's attempt to distinguish between "salvation" and "rewards" in various passages ultimately flows from his commitment to the belief that salvation is by grace alone. I echo that affirmation. I would, however, challenge the dichotomy he seems to assume exists between God's gift of grace and the believer's response to it. For grace to be grace, Wilkin seems to insist it must be isolated from all human effort.

I take a different view. It is true that no good work prior to the reception of God's grace can save a person (Eph. 2:8). However, once united to Christ by grace, the believer is empowered to do good works (2:9–10). The good works accomplished by believers are recognized as the work of Christ. Just as saving faith is the "work of God" (John 6:29), the good works accomplished by the believer are really and truly likewise the work of God in the believer; they are *Christ's* work (cf. Gal. 2:20; Phil. 2:12–13; Eph. 3:20). Church fathers such as Jerome explained things in this way. [63] These works are meritorious *not* because of human effort,

---

63. See, e.g., Jerome's explanation of Ephesians 2:8 (*PL* 26:469A–470A [575–76]).

but *because of grace*. This is why the New Testament speaks of the salvific value of good works (e.g., Jas. 2:24–26)—and why we do not need to engage in exegetical gymnastics to explain such passages away.

Salvation and Rewards

Wilkin's attempt to link good works to "rewards" distinct from salvation is fraught with difficulties. Tom Schreiner does a fine job in his essay highlighting New Testament passages that link salvation to good works.[64] In fact, Wilkin seems to almost rule out a priori the possibility that salvation is described metaphorically in the New Testament, e.g., as a "reward," "prize," or "crown." This becomes especially problematic when one is dealing with something like the parables of Jesus, since, by virtue of their genre, they speak of spiritual realities *allegorically*.[65] This leads Wilkin to idiosyncratic interpretations.

For example, Wilkin takes the parable of the ten virgins (Matt. 25:1–13) as referring not to the final judgment but as a teaching about endurance in the tribulation. According to him, those excluded from the feast are those who will fail to gain rewards ("ruling"). His reading strikes me as implausible. Significantly, he cites no commentator who agrees with his view. As we find elsewhere in Matthew (22:1–10), Jesus specifically likens the kingdom of heaven to a wedding feast (25:1)— not to ruling with Christ.

The last judgment imagery is also hard to miss. When the virgins who are left outside cry out, "Lord, Lord, open to us," the bridegroom replies, "Truly, I say to you, *I do not know you*" (Matt. 25:11–12; emphasis added).[66] Jesus elsewhere explains that many who call out "Lord, Lord," will not "enter the kingdom" (7:21–23). These will be told, "*I never knew you*; depart from me, you evildoers." In light of such contextual parallels, Wilkin would seem to be suggesting something startling: that one can be saved and yet not know the Lord!

---

64. See, e.g., Schreiner's treatment of Romans 2:6–10 (pp. 78-79), Galatians 6:8 (p. 82), 2 Peter 1:5–11 (p. 94).

65. The allegorical nature of Jesus' parables has been underscored by recent scholarship. See Klyne Snodgrass, *Stories with Intent: A Comprehensive Guide to the Parables of Jesus* (Grand Rapids: Eerdmans, 2008), 15–17; Arland J. Hultgren, *The Parables of Jesus: A Commentary* (Grand Rapids: Eerdmans, 2002), 12–14.

66. See, e.g., David L. Turner, *Matthew* (BECNT; Grand Rapids: Baker Academic), 596; Donald Hagner, *Matthew* (WBC 33; Dallas: Word, 1998), 729.

Wilkin also parses out other terms that are best understood as synonymous. He writes that it is "erroneous" to equate "inherit the kingdom" with "have eternal life" (Wilkin, p. 39). Yet a look at the Gospels reveals a fluidity of terminology. An example of this is found in the Sermon on the Mount. The section of the Sermon typically identified as the "six antitheses"[67] (Matt. 5:21–48) follows from Jesus' statement, "Unless your righteousness *surpasses* [*perisseusē*] that of the scribes and Pharisees, you will in no way *enter the kingdom of heaven*" (5:20; emphasis added). Others have noted that the language here is picked up in the final part of this section of the Sermon, namely, the instruction to love one's enemies (5:43–48).[68] Once again, the language of "surpassing" appears, but this time in connection with a statement regarding gaining a "reward":

> "If you love those who love you, what *reward* [*misthon*] do you have? Do not also the tax collectors *do the same thing*? If you greet your brothers only, what *surpassing* [*perisson*] thing do you do? Do not also the Gentiles *do the same thing*?"[69] (emphasis added)

Here receiving a "reward" and doing something "surpassing" are obviously linked together as having a synonymous meaning. Since Matthew 5:20 links "surpassing righteousness" with the language of "enter the kingdom," it is hard to believe that "entrance into the kingdom" and "reward" should be seen as relating different ideas.

Likewise, the use of different language to communicate the notion of salvation also appears in Matthew 19, a passage I treat in my article. Jesus answers a question about what is necessary to "have eternal life" (Matt. 19:16) with a statement about "entering life" (19:17). After the man walks away, Jesus explains that it is difficult for a rich man to "enter the kingdom of heaven," using that particular phrase two times (19:23–24).

---

67. The language of "antitheses" (i.e., teachings "antithetical" to the law) is not exactly representative of the section but I employ it simply because it represents the conventional language used to describe this section of the Sermon.

68. See Ulrich Luz, *Matthew 1–7* (Hermeneia; trans. J. E. Crouch; Minneapolis: Fortress, 2007), 289; Alan Stanley, *Did Jesus Teach Salvation by Works? The Role of Works in Salvation in the Synoptic Gospels* (ETSMS; Eugene, OR: Wipf & Stock, 2006), 274; E. M. Sidebottom, "'Reward' in Matthew 5.46, etc.," *ExpTim* 67 (1956–57): 219.

69. Here I use the translation in Alan P. Stanley, *Did Jesus Teach Salvation by Works?*, 274.

That salvation is in view is clear from the disciples' question that follows: "Who then can be saved [*sōthēnai*]?" (19:25). Jesus never corrects them by explaining to them that he is not speaking about salvation. Instead, the passage ends with Jesus describing who will "inherit eternal life" (19:29).

Are these terms ("have eternal life," "entering life," "entering the kingdom," "be saved," "inherit eternal life") really meant to indicate different realities? While someone like Wilkin might attempt to argue that the meaning of Jesus' teaching shifts back and forth from salvation to something else (and back again?), such would be a forced interpretation. The man received a direct call from the Lord, which he clearly understood and flatly rejected. His rejection entails something more than the loss of rewards, as the disciples' response clearly indicates (Matt. 19:25). To be clear: it would be wrong to conclude that a rich man cannot be saved. Jesus goes on to say, "with God all things are possible" (19:26). The parable that follows in 20:1–16 further stresses God's mercy. Still, there can be little doubt within the context in Matthew 19 that what is at stake is salvation itself.[70]

Is Perseverance Necessary?

Wilkin holds that perseverance is not necessary for salvation. He points to passages that indicate that those having faith will receive eternal life. For example, in the famous passage in John 3:16, we read, "For God so loved the world that he gave his only Son, that whoever believes in him should not perish but have eternal life." Yet as even Protestant scholars have noted, the present tense of the Greek word for "believe" (*pisteuōn*) is best read as indicating that salvation depends not on a single act of faith but rather that "whoever *continues to believe* in him ... shall have eternal life"[71] (emphasis added).

Wilkin also seems to ignore the fact that salvation is spoken of as past, present, and future realities in Scripture (e.g., his treatment of Gal

---

70. Protestant interpreters agree. See, e.g., the treatment of the passage in W. D. Davies and Dale C. Allison, *Matthew* (3 vols.; ICC; London: T&T Clark, 1988–1997), 3:47–48; D. A. Carson, "Matthew" (*EBC*; ed. Frank E. Gaebelein; Grand Rapids: Zondervan, 1995), 8:423–24.

71. See Alan P. Stanley, *Salvation Is More Complicated Than You Think* (Downers Grove, IL: InterVarsity Press, 2012), 164–65, citing Craig Keener, *The Gospel of John: A Commentary* (Peabody, MA: Hendrickson, 2003), 1:570; George Beasley-Murray, *Gospel of Life: Theology in the Fourth Gospel* (Peabody, MA: Hendrickson, 1991), 107.

6:7–9 and Eph 2:8–9). I treat this aspect of Scripture's teaching more fully in my essay. Suffice it here to observe that there is nothing inconsistent in affirming that one might experience salvation in the present and then not attain it in the future.

Scripture is clear that this is a real possibility. Dunn highlights numerous passages that teach as much in his essay (cf., e.g., Gal 5:4). I think, however, the clearest text in this regard is John 15. Here Jesus describes himself as the "true vine" and believers as "branches." Yet he indicates that some branches can be *removed* from the vine:

> I am the vine, you are the branches. He who abides in me, and I in him, he it is that bears much fruit, for apart from me you can do nothing. If a man does not abide in me, he is cast forth as a branch and withers; and the branches are gathered, thrown into the fire and burned. (John 15:5–6)

Jesus describes those who "abide" or "remain"[72] in him as branches and yet goes on to indicate that some of these same branches may be "cast forth" (*eblēthē*), "wither" (*exēranthē*) and be "thrown into the fire and burned" (*eis to pyr ballousin kai kaietai*).

Wilkin fails to mention this passage in his article, but offers a discussion on it in print elsewhere.[73] He suggests that this passage speaks of *temporary judgment* on believers. While it is true that the disciplining of believers is described in terms of being "tested by fire" elsewhere in the New Testament (e.g., 1 Pet 1:6–7), that does not seem to be the meaning here. Wilkin claims, "Since the Lord did not use the verb *to be burned up*, but rather the less intense verb *to be burned*, He is holding open the possibility that the unproductive believer may respond to the burning and return to fruitfulness."[74]

This is a tortured reading. First, it is hard to see how the viticultural imagery would make sense if "burning" does not refer to destruction. Why would a vinedresser cut off and "burn" a branch in order to restore it? As Keener observes, the natural implication of the burning of the

---

72. The Greek word *menō* can be translated either "abide" or "remain." See the treatment in George Beasley-Murray, *John* (WBC 36; 2nd ed.; Dallas: Word, 1999), 272.

73. Robert N. Wilkin, "The Gospel According to John," in *The Grace New Testament Commentary* (ed. R. N. Wilkin; Denton, TX: Grace Evangelical Society, 2010), 357–479.

74. Ibid., 450.

branches is destruction.[75] Second, contrary to Wilkin's claim, there is nothing in the Greek that suggests temporary judgment is in view. Note the burning that is referred to in Matthew 13:30, where Jesus teaches that the wicked will be "burned" (*katakaiō*) with fire at the final judgment.

Thus, as many Protestant commentators agree, John 15 makes it clear that some who are united to Christ can in fact be cast forth from him. This makes sense of Jesus' insistence on *remaining* in him—it is possible to *not* remain in him, that is, to be separated from him.[76] Attempts to explain the branches that are cast off as simply those who "appeared" to be Christians (e.g., Calvin)[77] are likewise not convincing. As Whitacre writes, "Jesus does not say, 'those who appear to be in me' but every branch *in me*."[78]

Assurance of Salvation

I would like to close by addressing the issue of "assurance of salvation." In Catholic teaching believers have the assurance not of certainty but of "hope."[79] Hope, not absolute certainty, is the language of Scripture (e.g., Rom. 8:24–25; Gal. 5:5; Eph. 4:4; Col. 1:5). As Aquinas explains, the object of the believer's hope is not in what one has attained—e.g., by virtue of his act of faith—but in God's mercy and faithfulness to his promises.

This should not lead us to be paralyzed by anxiety. Attempts to portray the Catholic view of this matter in such terms are wide of the mark.[80] Yes, nowhere in divine revelation is it stated that I, Michael Barber, am among the elect who will persevere. Yet Catholic teaching recognizes that in Scripture the promise of salvation is linked to

---

75. Keener, *The Gospel of John*, 2:1002. See also Schreiner's essay in this volume: "Burning most naturally refers to the final judgment" (p. 93).

76. Ibid., 2:998–1002.

77. John Calvin, *The Gospel according to St. John: Part Two, 11–21 and the First Epistle of John* (trans. T. H. L. Parker; Grand Rapids: Eerdmans, 1959), in loc.

78. Rodney A. Whitacre, *John* (IVPNTC; Downers Grove, IL: InterVarsity Press, 1999), 373–74.

79. See Thomas Aquinas, *Summa Theologiae* II-II, q. 18, art. 4. A fine treatment is found in Stephen Pfurtner, *Luther and Aquinas on Salvation* (trans. E. Quinn; New York: Sheed and Ward, 1964), 51–116.

80. See Michael Schmaus, *Justification and the Last Things* (Dogma 6; London: Sheed and Ward, 1977), 114–15.

the sacraments (e.g., 1 Pet. 3:21). While we do not have indubitable assurance that we are among the elect, we do have confidence in his promises (Heb. 10:23). There is no need to psychoanalyze oneself to determine whether one has truly authentic faith. *Christ* is the object of faith, not the knowledge of one's own salvation. It is he who is acting in the sacraments. Because I am weak and fickle, I may turn away from God and reject his salvation—and he will respect my choice to do so. Nonetheless, if I remain in him, I know he will not disappoint me and will continue to remain in me (John 15:1–10).

JUSTIFICATION APART FROM AND BY WORKS: AT THE FINAL JUDGMENT WORKS WILL *CONFIRM* JUSTIFICATION [1]

THOMAS R. SCHREINER

I should say up front the title of this article is a bit misleading, for I am not restricting myself to justification but will also consider the role of works with regard to salvation. [2] Justification and salvation don't mean the same thing, of course, but they are closely related. Though space is lacking to defend the definitions offered here, I define justification as being acquitted before the divine judge. [3] Those who are justified are declared to be "not guilty" before God. In addition, justification is understood in this essay to be an eschatological reality. Hence, the verdict of "not guilty," which believers receive now by faith, is confirmed at the final judgment before the whole world. Salvation, by contrast, means that one has been rescued or delivered; here the focus is on being rescued from God's wrath or punishment on the last day.

I have attempted to show elsewhere that justification is a soteriological term, [4] and thus justification and salvation both address the question

---

1. I want to thank Alan Stanley for his comments on this essay and his many helpful suggestions. Although I did not incorporate all his suggestions, I am convinced that this essay is better than it would have been otherwise.

2. In fact, other soteriological realities will be included here and there as well.

3. For a recent work on justification, see *Justification: Five Views* (ed. James K. Beilby and Paul R. Eddy; Downers Grove, IL: InterVarsity Press, 2011). See my review in *Credo* 1 (2011): 78–79 (see www.credomag.com/issues/October%20Spread%202011.pdf).

4. See Thomas R. Schreiner, "Justification: The Saving Righteousness of God in Christ," *JETS* 54 (2011): 22–28.

of the human being's standing before God on the day of judgment, whether one stands in the right before him or is saved, or whether one is condemned before him or destroyed. I should also say that I am not trying to be overly technical in the use of the words "apart from" and "by." In the essay below I also say that we are not saved or justified "by" works, so the prepositions in the title are not used technically. The meaning of the title should not be gleaned by the prepositions but by the content of this essay.

Another preliminary word should be added. Given the space constraints of this essay, I will mainly limit myself to the Pauline letters and to James. At the close of the essay I will briefly refer to other texts since they speak to the issue before us as well, but there is no pretense here of offering an exhaustive word on the topic. My goal is to take soundings from Paul and James and a few other New Testament texts so that we can navigate our way through the controversy on the role of works in justification. Finally, I am assuming that all the letters in the New Testament are authentic. Even if some dissent from this opinion, the argument would not be affected greatly as long as one believes that the letters in question are authoritative as Scripture.

The structure of the essay is as follows. First, I examine the texts in Paul that teach that justification or salvation cannot be obtained by works. Second, I move to texts where works are said to be necessary for justification or salvation. The same basic outline is then pursued in James. James teaches that all fall short of perfection so that all need mercy on the day of judgment. At the same time, he insists that good works are necessary for justification. It is imperative to reflect on both sets of texts to achieve a balanced perspective on the role of works in both Paul and James. If we restrict ourselves to texts that say works are necessary for justification, or even if we focus on such texts, we will lack the necessary perspective for interpreting what Paul and James mean. Within the constraints demanded by the format of the present work, both dimensions ("justification *apart from* and *by* works") must be explored and explicated. Otherwise, the tension between both sets of statements may not be fully appreciated.

After examining Paul and James, I include a brief section where the contribution of other New Testament writings is briefly examined. I conclude with a section entitled "theological reflection." I propose here a solution to the dilemma posed in the teaching of both Paul and James and other New Testament writings, arguing that works are necessary for justification, but they should not be considered the basis or foundation of justification. Instead, they constitute the necessary evidence or fruit of justification.

Justification apart from Works in Paul

Justification and Works of Law in Galatians

On eight occasions in his letters Paul teaches that justification or the reception of the Spirit is not obtained through works of law. Three times in Galatians 2:16 he affirms that human beings are not justified by works of law but only through faith in Jesus Christ.[5] The importance of this verse can scarcely be exaggerated, for it occurs in the part of the Galatian letter that Betz calls the *propositio*, representing the thesis of the letter.[6] Boundary markers (i.e., observing that part of the law that particularly set Israel apart from the other nations: e.g., Sabbath, circumcision, purity regulations) are the impetus for Paul's declaration since Peter was in effect compelling Gentiles to abide by the food laws in order to belong to the people of God (2:11–14). Furthermore, the burning issue in Galatians is whether circumcision is mandatory for salvation (cf. 2:3–5; 5:2–6; 5:11–12; 6:12, 13, 15). Hence, the new perspective rightly sees that the inclusion of Gentiles is a major concern in Pauline theology.[7] Nevertheless, the debate in Galatians is not restricted to boundary markers since "works of law" encompass the whole law.[8] Indeed, the question in Galatians includes the larger issue of whether observance of the law is necessary for justification (2:21).

Justification cannot be gained by works of law, for the law demands perfect obedience to stand in the right before God. Galatians 3:10 is

5. For a full discussion of faith in Jesus Christ, see *The Faith of Jesus Christ: Exegetical, Biblical, and Theological Studies* (ed. Michael F. Bird and Preston Sprinkle; Peabody, MA: Hendrickson, 2009). I think those who support the objective genitive ("faith *in* Christ") are more persuasive.

6. See his commentary for his outline of the letter. Hans Dieter Betz, *Galatians: A Commentary on Paul's Letter to the Churches in Galatia* (Hermeneia; Philadelphia: Fortress, 1979).

7. Many sources could be cited, but see James D. G. Dunn, *The New Perspective on Paul: Collected Essays* (WUNT 185; Tübingen: Mohr Siebeck, 2005).

8. Cf. Thomas R. Schreiner, *Galatians* (ZECNT; Grand Rapids: Zondervan, 2010), 157–61.

clear here.[9] One must abide by *everything* in the law to be justified if one opts for circumcision and adherence to the Mosaic law. There is a salvation historical argument here as well, for the Sinai law offered forgiveness through the sacrifices when one transgressed. But such sacrifices are no longer valid, according to Paul, now that Christ has come and offered the definitive and final sacrifice for sins.[10] The *only* way to escape the curse is through the cross of Christ, for he took the curse upon himself that human beings deserved (3:13). Those who place themselves under the law and rely on circumcision for salvation cut themselves off from Christ (5:2–4), and hence their only recourse is to keep the entire law for salvation (5:3). But no one can keep the law perfectly, and thus turning to the law is a vain and hopeless endeavor.

Galatians clearly teaches that human works cannot justify. Righteousness comes by faith instead of by the law (Gal. 3:11–12).[11] Paul opposes circumcision and the desire to live under the law (4:21), for the law, instead of curbing sin, increases it. Those who live "under the law" (3:23; 4:4, 5, 21; 5:18)[12] are "under a curse" (3:10), "under sin" (3:22), "under a pedagogue" (3:25), and are "enslaved under the elements of the world" (4:3). The law exposes the wickedness of the human heart, the selfishness and self-worship that consumes every one of us. Works do not lead to the verdict "justified," for the law opens the floodgates of sin instead of restraining sin. Paul reiterates this thesis in Romans 7. Sin as a deceptive power takes control of the law, using it as its ally in producing even more sin (cf. Rom. 5:20; 7:8–11). As Paul says in 1 Corinthians 15:56, "the power of sin is the law."

In Galatians justification is not obtained by the law but through faith in Christ (cf. Gal. 3:8, 11, 24). It is not surprising, then, that the cross of Christ plays a central role in Galatians.[13] Believers have been

---

9. For further discussion, see ibid., 203–7.

10. See esp. A. Andrew Das, *Paul, the Law, and the Covenant* (Peabody, MA: Hendrickson, 2001), 113–44.

11. In defense of the notion that righteousness in Galatians is forensic, see Douglas J. Moo, "Justification in Galatians," in *Understanding the Times: New Testament Studies in the 21st Century: Essays in Honor of D. A. Carson on the Occasion of His 65th Birthday* (ed. Andreas J. Kostenberger and Robert W. Yarbrough; Wheaton: Crossway, 2011), 160–95.

12. Christ is the exception who proves the rule, for he lived under the law and won redemption for those under law.

13. For the centrality of the cross in Galatians, see Robert A. Bryant, *The Risen Crucified Christ in Galatians* (SBLDS 185; Atlanta: Society of Biblical Literature, 2001), 163–94.

delivered from "this present evil age" (1:4) through Christ's giving of himself over to death. There is no middle ground; righteousness is either gained through the cross of Christ or the law (2:21). Those who turn to the law for justification have had a spell cast over them that obscures the cross from their vision (3:1). The curse hanging over human beings is only removed through Christ's taking the curse that human beings deserved (3:13), liberating them from the law via his death (4:4–5). Relying on circumcision denies the scandal of the cross (5:11), for circumcision centers on the work of the human subject, so that praise goes to human beings rather than God (cf. 1:5!). Hence, Paul boasts only in the cross (6:14), while his opponents boast in their own accomplishments (6:12–13). Justification cannot be obtained through the law, for human beings are radically sinful, needing redemption and not merely reformation. We need deliverance, not a slight makeover of our evil inclinations.

Justification and Works in Romans

Romans flies in the same orbit as Galatians. Justification is not obtained through works of law (Rom. 3:20, 28). Again, works of law include the boundary markers, and Paul is concerned about the inclusion of Gentiles as the new perspective has reminded us. Still, the fundamental complaint against the Jews is not their exclusion of the Gentiles. Paul focuses on their failure to keep the law they treasured and taught (2:21–24). Their *moral* failings are the focus of his indictment (stealing, adultery, and robbing temples), showing that they, like the Gentiles, were unrighteous. Despite their salvation historical advantages, they, like the Gentiles, did not seek God or do his will (3:10–18). Every mouth is shut before God because of human sin (3:19), and justification cannot be obtained by works of law, for the law discloses human sin (3:20).

Righteousness is, therefore, available only through the atoning work of Jesus Christ (Rom. 3:21–26), just as we saw in Galatians. Jesus has satisfied God's wrath on the cross, taking the punishment we deserved. Justification, then, is a gift given and received, so that there is no basis for human boasting (3:27–28), and the offer of salvation is extended to all of humanity. Both Jews and Gentiles are righteous in the same way, by believing in Jesus Christ, not by working to obtain a reward (3:29–30).

In Romans 4, Paul brings up Abraham, the progenitor of the Jewish people, to confirm his teaching on justification (cf. also Gal. 3:6–9).

Here the discussion is no longer on "works of law" but "works." This is scarcely surprising, for Abraham did not live under the Mosaic law, and thus "works of law" do not fit the era in which he lived. Now this is not to say that ethnic issues are absent from the discussion, for the role of circumcision relative to Abraham arises in Romans 4:9–12, showing that one does not have to be Jewish to belong to the people of God.

Nevertheless, ethnic issues are not at the forefront of Romans 4:1–8, for here Paul addresses the matter of works and justification in general. Hence, he says in 4:2 that if Abraham did the works required for justification, he would have a reason for boasting. The term "works" is used in the broadest sense here, referring to what human beings do (cf. 9:11–12) and explaining that they would provide a basis for righteousness if they were observed. Abraham did not meet the test, however, for he lacked the necessary works before God (4:2).

Romans 4:4 constitutes a further explication of verse 2. Those who do the necessary works are like someone who works for an employer. If one does what is required, he or she receives a reward; wages are the payment. So too, if human beings do the works God requires, they will receive the reward of justification. If human beings keep all that God demands, they will indeed be rewarded and declared to be in the right before God. Abraham, however, is indicted as "ungodly" (4:5; cf. Josh. 24:2). Hence, righteousness is not gained by doing but by believing, as Genesis 15:6 affirms (Rom. 4:3). The justification of Abraham represents the justification of the ungodly, demonstrating that righteousness is apart from works.

Paul introduces David as a second witness (Rom. 4:6–8). David received the blessing of justification, which is defined in terms of the forgiveness of sins. David could not be righteous on the basis of his works, for his adultery with Bathsheba and murder of Uriah reveal that he needed forgiveness. Nor can we say that David was justified on the basis of his postconversion works, for the sins David committed were after his conversion. Hence, when we say that justification is apart from works, we cannot limit the works to preconversion works.[14] Justification is apart from all works, for perfection is required, and all people, even the most devoted saints, fall short in significant ways (cf. 9:30–10:13).

---

14. Against Paul A. Rainbow, *The Way of Salvation: The Role of Christian Obedience in Justification* (Waynesboro, GA: Paternoster, 2005), 216–17.

The Contribution of Other Pauline Letters

What Paul teaches is confirmed in other letters. The heart of the gospel, what is of first importance, is the forgiveness of sins that is secured only through the death and resurrection of Jesus Christ (1 Cor. 15:1–11). The fundamental need for human beings is forgiveness.[15] What believers need is to be rescued from God's end-time wrath, and Jesus is the one who will save believers from God's eschatological wrath (Rom. 5:9–10; 1 Thess. 1:10; 5:9).

Paul's later letters communicate the same truth.[16] Salvation is not secured by works but by faith. "For by grace we are saved through faith; this is not of ourselves but it is the gift of God, not of works so that no one should boast" (Eph. 2:8–9). If human beings do the works demanded by God, they can legitimately claim that they have fulfilled what God demanded and should receive the reward of salvation. But salvation is not received on such a basis, for human beings are "dead in trespasses and sins" (2:1, 5). They carry out the desires of the flesh, following the pattern of the world and the dictates of the devil (2:1–3). Thus, salvation cannot be on the basis of works. It is granted by God as a gift, as a witness to his astonishing love (2:4; cf. 3:18–19).

We find the same teaching in Titus 3:3–7. Human beings are radically evil, as is witnessed by our cruelty toward and hatred of one another. But God has showered his extraordinary kindness on us. He has saved us through Jesus Christ. Paul emphasizes again that humans are not saved by works. In fact, his definition of works here is "works done ... in righteousness." Human works don't pass muster; they don't meet the bar of God's righteous standard. And we know just what Paul means from the previous verses. Human beings have lived wickedly and foolishly, pursuing sinful desires so that they have failed to do God's will.

Still, human evil is not the last word, for God has poured out his mercy on sinners. He has showered his grace on those who trust in Jesus Christ, renewing and regenerating them through the Holy Spirit. Hence, those who belong to Jesus are justified, not on the basis of their

---

15. It is evident from Romans 4:6–8 that justification and forgiveness of sins are, if not identical, closely related. See Thomas R. Schreiner, *Romans* (BECNT; Grand Rapids: Baker, 1998), 219.

16. Cf. I. Howard Marshall, "Salvation, Grace and Works in the Later Writings in the Pauline Corpus," *NTS* 42 (1996): 339–58.

own work but by virtue of the saving work of the Father, the Son, and the Spirit (cf. also 2 Tim. 1:9–11).

Conclusion

When we consider the role of works in final justification, we must begin where Paul does. Human beings cannot be justified or saved on the basis of their works, for they are sinners and fail to meet God's standard. They need to be rescued, redeemed, and reconciled. They need to be justified and saved. They need to be cleansed and washed to be adopted into God's family. Justification must be apart from works, for human beings do not and cannot do what God demands. Hence, their righteousness is not in themselves but in Jesus Christ their Lord.

Justification by Works

Romans 2

Works in Romans 2:6-10

The previous discussion seems to be the end of the story, but there are more verses to this song than the first one. Paul disavows justification by works in some texts, but then in other verses he teaches that we are justified by works. Paul's teaching about works in Romans 2 is remarkable, for this text is nestled within 1:18–3:20, where Paul affirms that no one is justified by works. In 2:6 Paul articulates the thesis for all of 2:6–11, namely, that God "will repay each one according to his works." Verses 7–10 unpack the meaning of this statement in a chiastic arrangement:

> A   He will grant "eternal life to those who seek glory and honor and incorruptibility by patiently enduring in a good work" (2:7).
> B   Conversely, he will pour out his "wrath and anger" on those who pursue evil (2:8).
> B' Those "who carry out evil," whether they are Jews or Greeks, will experience "affliction and distress" (2:9).
> A' But "the one who does what is good" will enjoy "glory and honor and peace" (2:10).

Paul is certainly not talking about rewards above and beyond eternal life here. Verse 7 demonstrates without doubt that "eternal life" is at stake in whether one does good or evil. Indeed, in the context of Romans 1–3 the entire issue is whether one will escape the final judgment "on the day of wrath and the revelation of the righteous judgment of God" (2:5). The doing of the law is not optional but necessary on the day that "God judges the secrets of human beings" (2:16), for "the doers of the law will be justified" (2:13).

Romans 2:26 – 27

Many interpreters, of course, think that Paul speaks hypothetically in Romans 2:6 – 10 since the final conclusion of his argument is that no one is justified by works of law (3:19 – 20).[17] Such a reading resolves the tension between the two texts, but it fails as satisfying exegesis because of what Paul writes in 2:26 – 29.[18] A hypothetical reading fails in 2:26 – 29, confirming that 2:6 – 10 should not be read hypothetically either, since both texts address the same issue and are in the same context. We read in vv. 26 – 27:

> If the uncircumcised person keeps the ordinances of the law, will not his uncircumcision be counted as circumcision? And the one who is uncircumcised from birth who keeps the law will judge you who are a transgressor of the law despite the advantages of the letter and the circumcision.

We have a conditional statement in verse 26, and hence verses 26 – 27 on their own could be construed as hypothetical. Paul considers a situation where an uncircumcised person, a Gentile, observes what is commanded in the law, which is an astonishing statement in its own right since circumcision was commanded in the law! In any case, if the uncircumcised person does what the law requires, he will be counted as circumcised. In other words, he would be considered a covenant member, a part of the people of God, since he observes what the law requires. Paul takes the argument a step further. Not only will the uncircumcised person be

---

17. E.g., see Douglas J. Moo's exposition of Romans 2 (*Romans* [NICNT; Grand Rapids: Eerdmans, 1996], 125 – 77).

18. Whether Paul refers to saving obedience in Rom. 2:13 – 15 is intensely debated. Because of the space constraints of this essay and the especially controversial nature of 2:13 – 15, I have focused on what I think is the clearer text (2:26 – 29) instead of including a discussion of 2:13 – 15.

counted as a covenant member, but since he keeps the law, he will judge so-called Jewish covenant members who possess the law and circumcision but fail to do what the law says.

The New Covenant Character of Romans 2:28-29

Since Romans 2:26–27 is conditional, we could interpret it hypothetically, but such a reading runs aground on the rocks of 2:28–29, where Paul says:

> For a Jew is not a Jew outwardly, neither is circumcision outward in the flesh, but a Jew is a Jew in secret, and circumcision is circumcision of the heart, by means of the Spirit not the letter, and the praise of such a person is not from human beings but from God.

The "for" (*gar*) linking verses 28–29 to verses 26–27 indicates that the former provides the ground or reason for the latter. The logic runs like this: the uncircumcised person (the Gentile) who keeps the law will be counted as a covenant member (as a Jew) and will judge disobedient Jews on the last days, for true Jewishness and true circumcision are not outward and physical matters. They are matters of the heart and are the result of the Spirit's work in a human being.

Paul doesn't leave readers in the land called *hypothetical*. He brings them into a land called *actual*, speaking of the Spirit's new covenant work of transforming hearts. Paul contrasts in 2:29 "the Spirit" and "the letter." We find the same contrast on two other occasions in Paul (Rom. 7:6; 2 Cor. 3:6). In both texts Paul does not speak hypothetically. He refers to new covenant realities actualized by the Holy Spirit. There is no reason to think that Paul has something different in mind in Romans 2:26–29.

It was tempting for the Jews to think that true Jewishness and true circumcision were outward and physical realities, but Paul punctures such illusions here. A true Jew is one "in secret" (*en tō kryptō*, v. 29). Paul picks up in verse 29 the language of the final judgment when "God will judge the secrets [*ta krypta*] of human beings" (2:16). Gentiles who are Jews in secret will pass the final test, for they are circumcised in heart. The circumcision of the heart was what Israel lacked (Deut. 10:16), but the Lord promised in the last days to circumcise the hearts of his people (30:6). Jeremiah laments the uncircumcised heart of Israel in his day (Jer. 4:4; 9:25–26), but hope is not extinguished, for he looks forward to a future day, to a new covenant, when the Lord will write his law on the hearts of his people (31:31–34).

Paul almost certainly reflects on that promise here, and he combines it with Ezekiel's prophecy that anticipates the day when the Lord will put his Spirit within his people so that they will walk in his statutes (Ezek. 36:26–27). The new covenant echoes throughout Romans 2:26–29, which shows that the fulfillment here is not hypothetical. God has fulfilled his covenant with Israel and Judah, and shock of shocks, Gentiles who are circumcised in heart and recipients of the Spirit's work are part of the true Israel.

The obedience of the Gentiles (Rom. 2:26–27), then, is not merely hypothetical but actual (vv. 28–29). Their obedience, however, stems from the new covenant work of the Holy Spirit. There is no suggestion that the Gentiles have observed the law in their own strength, as if they autonomously do God's will. They have been transferred from darkness to light through faith in Christ and are the recipients of the Spirit's transforming work. Their Spirit-wrought obedience warrants eschatological reward. The will receive "praise" (*epainos*) from God for being true Jews and circumcised in heart. Paul uses the same word in 1 Corinthians 4:5 to speak of the end-time reward that will be given to those who faithfully carry out the ministry of the Lord.

To sum up, Paul teaches here that works play a role in the final judgment. They are necessary for final salvation. But how does that fit with Paul saying that justification cannot be obtained by works of law? Clearly, he doesn't think the necessary works *merit* salvation. What he does mean will be answered before this essay concludes.

Why would Paul introduce the Spirit-produced obedience of Gentiles into a section that has as its major theme universal sinfulness? Often in Romans Paul anticipates a matter that he takes up later in the letter (e.g., Rom. 3:1–8 in chapters 6 and 9 or 5:20 in chapter 7). Hence, in Romans 2 the obedience of Gentiles anticipates 10:19 and 11:11, 14, where the inclusion of the Gentiles into God's saving promises is intended to provoke the Jews to jealousy. Thus, Paul does not stray from his main theme in referring to Gentile obedience, for their inclusion underscores the sins of the Jews, demonstrating that they need to turn to Christ for salvation.[19]

The Necessity of Obedience in Galatians

The necessity of obedience for salvation is not restricted to Romans 2. In fact, it is a common theme in Paul (cf. also 2 Cor. 11:15; Eph. 2:10; 2 Tim. 2:21; 4:14; Titus 1:16; 3:8, 14), but for space reasons I will focus on Galatians. As noted above, the letter to the Galatians features the gospel of grace. Paul emphasizes that righteousness and the reception of the Spirit are not obtained via the works of law but through faith in Jesus Christ (Gal. 2:16; 3:2, 5, 10). But the Pauline emphasis on grace (cf. 1:3, 6, 15; 2:9, 21; 5:4; 6:18) does not preclude the importance of good works. In fact, the grace of God is the foundation and basis for good works (cf. also 1 Cor. 15:10; Titus 2:11–12). Faith alone does not, to paraphrase a popular saying, mean that faith is alone, for "faith expresses itself in love" (Gal. 5:6).

Believers are called upon to walk in the Spirit (Gal. 5:16), be led by the Spirit (5:18), march in step with the Spirit (5:25), and sow to the Spirit (6:8), and thereby to manifest the fruit of the Spirit (5:22–23). "The one who sows to his own flesh will reap corruption from the flesh, but the one who sows to the Spirit will reap eternal life from the Spirit" (6:8). The contrast between "corruption" (*pthoran*) and "eternal life" (*zōēn aiōnion*) shows that eschatological salvation is at stake in whether one sows to the flesh or sows to the Spirit. The phrase "eternal life" represents the life of the age to come. It will hardly do to say that eternal life refers to "rewards" here.[20] Such an interpretation betrays special pleading, which does not accord with the way the term is used elsewhere (Rom. 2:7; 5:21; 6:22–23; 1 Tim. 1:16; 6:12; Titus 1:2; 3:7). Sowing to the Spirit and walking in the Spirit are not optional, for the one who fails to do so will experience eschatological judgment and destruction. It is hard to imagine a statement that could be clearer than this: those who sow to the flesh will not experience final salvation.

---

19. Paul has already shown that Gentiles are sinners (Rom. 1:19–32) and need the saving work of Christ, so there is no need to return to that theme here. His point is that Gentiles who have put their faith in Jesus Christ belong to the people of God.

20. So Michael Eaton, *No Condemnation: A New Theology of Assurance* (Downers Grove, IL: InterVarsity Press, 1995), 113.

We find a similar statement in Galatians 5:19–21, which features "the works of the flesh." After listing the works of the flesh, Paul makes a most interesting statement in 5:21. "I am telling you in advance, just as I told you before, that those who practice such things will not inherit the kingdom of God." It is likely that Paul regularly warned believers about the consequences of turning toward evil since he informs the Galatians that he had instructed them about these matters previously. The "kingdom of God" refers here to God's end-time kingdom (cf. Matt. 5:20; 7:21; 8:11–12; 19:23–24; 25:34; John 3:3, 5; Acts 14:22; 1 Cor. 6:9, 10; Eph. 5:5; 1 Thess. 2:12; 2 Tim. 4:18). Practicing the works of the flesh is not a minor matter, for those who pursue evil will not enter the kingdom.

The book of Galatians celebrates the grace of God in Christ, but God's grace is effective grace. Grace transforms human beings so that they live a new life. Paul is not talking about perfection, nor does he advocate works-righteousness. But there is a significant change in the lives of those who are indwelt and empowered by the Holy Spirit. Believers have been liberated from "this present evil age" through Christ's self-giving death (Gal. 1:4). They are freed by his death from slavery to the elements of the world (4:3–5). They have died to the law since they are crucified with Christ (2:19) and now Christ lives in them (2:20). They are children of the free woman, not the slave woman (4:21–31), and thus they are to stand in the freedom they have in Christ (5:1). Through the Spirit they are now enabled to serve one another in love (5:13–14). The world and its evil have been crucified for believers through the cross of Jesus Christ (6:14), for believers are transferred into a "new creation" (6:15).

Galatians knows nothing, then, of autonomous works or of works produced by the virtue of the human being. Good works are energized and accomplished by the Holy Spirit, being rooted in the cross-work of Jesus Christ by which believers have been freed from the old creation and have been inducted into the new creation. Galatians makes it clear that these works are necessary for eternal life. Those who don't sow to the Spirit will not experience eternal life. Those who practice the works of the flesh will be excluded from the kingdom. Clearly Paul did not think emphasizing the necessity of works compromised his gospel of grace, and if he did not think so, neither should we.

A Peek into 1 Corinthians and Philippians

The necessity of good works is also emphasized in 1 Corinthians 6:9–11. In 6:1–8 Paul addresses the problem with lawsuits in the congregation. What annoys him is not that the lawsuits per se, for he understands that conflicts arise among Christians. What he finds outrageous is that the believers called on unbelievers to resolve their problems, that they were unable to adjudicate the matter among themselves. Such behavior brings a stain on the gospel they proclaim, and hence on the name of Christ. The believers should surrender their own rights so that they don't grumble about "being wronged" (*adikeisthe*) or "defrauded" (*apostereisthe*). Actually, the believers are not forgiving the sin of others but committing sin themselves. They "wrong" (*adikeite*) and "defraud" (*apostereite*) others (1 Cor. 6:7–8). The link between 6:7–8 and 6:9 is forged by the word "unrighteous" or "wrongdoers" (*adikoi*) in 6:9. And Paul says, "And don't you know that wrongdoers will not inherit the kingdom of God?" The link between 6:7–8 and 6:9 demonstrates that he is addressing believers in 6:9. His words are not directed to unbelievers but to the redeemed community.[21]

The Corinthians' behavior in the matter of lawsuits was not trivial, for it showed a grasping and selfish spirit that does not accord with new life in Christ. Hence, Paul warns them that they are drifting into danger, for those who practice evil will not inherit the kingdom. The language is similar to Galatians 5:19–21, where those who practice the works of the flesh are threatened with exclusion from the kingdom (cf. also Eph. 5:5–6). Indeed, Paul is worried that the Corinthians will blithely ignore his warning, so he proceeds to warn them against deception:[22] "Do not be deceived. Neither the sexually immoral, nor idolaters, nor adulterers, nor homosexuals, nor thieves, nor coveters, nor drunkards, nor revilers, will inherit the kingdom of God" (1 Cor. 6:9–10). Once again, what Paul says here should not be interpreted as

---

21. Other verses draw the parallel as well. Note that in 6:1 Paul laments that they are going before "the unrighteous" (*adikōn*) to have the matter resolved. Such behavior does not accord with being "justified" (*edikaiōthēte*, v. 11).

22. Garland (quoting Godet, 1886), says that the command to "not be deceived" suggests that "the Corinthians seemed to imagine that their religious knowledge and Christian talk would suffice to open heaven to them, whatever their conduct otherwise might be." See David E Garland, *1 Corinthians* (BECNT; Grand Rapids: Baker, 2003), 209.

teaching perfection. Still, those who give themselves over to evil and fail to repent of their sin will not be members of the kingdom. One must embrace and practice what is good to be included in the final reward.

Some worry that the necessity of good works for final salvation denies the grace of the gospel, but we must be careful that we are not more Pauline than Paul! Paul did not think his words contradicted the gospel of grace (see again Titus 2:11–12). Indeed, the centrality of grace is underscored in this very context. After listing the sins that exclude from the kingdom, Paul remarks, "And some of you used to be like this" (1 Cor. 6:11 HCSB). The grace of God, however, has invaded their lives, so that Paul says, "But you were washed, but you were sanctified, but you were justified in the name of the Lord Jesus Christ and by the Spirit of our God" (6:11).

The verbs "washed," "sanctified," and "justified" all refer here to the conversion of the Corinthians. They were cleansed from their sins when they were baptized. They were placed in the realm of the holy when they were sanctified. The verb "sanctified" here does not denote progress in holiness but the definitive or positional sanctification that occurs when one is saved. Justification means that they were declared to be in the right and were counted as righteous via their union with Christ. Another way of putting it is that these three verbs signal the grace of God in Jesus Christ and by the Holy Spirit. Believers are new, for they are washed, holy, and righteous before God.

What Paul argues in 1 Corinthians 6:9–11 is that those who have received the grace of Christ — those who are washed in baptism and who are holy and righteous before God — must live a new way. They contradict their baptism, sanctification, and justification if they practice the vices listed in 6:9–10. The grace received in conversion is not an abstraction separated from everyday life and behavior. God saves the whole person so that those who have received his grace are transformed by that grace.

Certainly we must beware of an overrealized eschatology since believers live in the period between the already and not yet. Christians still experience in part what Paul describes in Romans 7:14–25.[23] Transformation is not the same thing as perfection, and believers still

---

23. Cf. Schreiner, *Romans*, 371–96.

battle the flesh (Gal. 5:13–6:10). Believers are no longer slaves to sin (Rom. 6), but there is still a battle with sin (Gal. 5:17). Our bodies are still mortal and hence believers await the final resurrection (Rom. 8:10–13). Until that day of resurrection believers are not yet perfected, and thus they struggle with sin (Phil. 3:12–16). Transformation should not be confused with what is sometimes called "victorious Christian living" or with a passive "let go and let God" mentality.[24] The Christian life is a war (see Eph. 6:10–19; cf. 1 Cor. 9:26; 2 Cor. 10:4; 1 Tim. 1:18; 6:12; 2 Tim. 4:7), and there are plenty of failures along the way.

There is a danger, then, with being too optimistic and with being too pessimistic. On the one hand, there are streams in Protestantism that have taught a kind of perfectionism that is contrary to everyday experience and is deeply discouraging to believers who are keenly aware of their defects. On the other hand, some overemphasize Romans 7:14–25, reading that text as if it is the only text in Paul about the Christian life. Such an enterprise ignores the role of Romans 6 and 8 in the argument. According to Romans 6, believers have died to sin and have been liberated from the tyranny and dominion (not the presence!) of sin. Romans 8 teaches that the Holy Spirit empowers believers to live in a new way, a way pleasing to God. The fundamental melody in the life of the Christian should be optimism, not pessimism, but optimism is not the same thing as perfectionism.

The above comments bring us back to 1 Corinthians 6:9–11. Those who have been converted must show the newness of their life by rejecting evil and pursuing what is good. Vice and virtue lists are common in Paul (e.g., Rom. 1:29–31; 12:9–16; 13:13; 1 Cor. 5:9–10; 2 Cor. 12:20–21; Gal. 5:19–23; Eph. 4:31–32, 5:3–5; Col. 3:5, 8–9, 12–13; Titus 3:3), showing that Paul expected believers to forsake evil and to live in a way that pleases God. Indeed, as we have seen, Paul makes it clear that those who give themselves over to evil, those whose lives are dominated by evil, will not inherit the kingdom of God.

Another remarkable text on the necessity of obedience is Philippians 2:12–13. "So then, my beloved, just as you have always obeyed, not in my presence only but now much more in my absence, accomplish

---

24. Andrew David Naselli, *Let Go and Let God? A Survey and Analysis of Keswick Theology* (Logos Bible Software, 2010).

your own salvation with fear and trembling, for God is the one working in you, both to will and to do for his good pleasure."[25] The verb "accomplish" (*katergazesthe*) means to work, do, or accomplish (cf. Rom. 1:27; 2:9 7:8; 15:18; 1 Cor. 5:3; 2 Cor. 5:5; Eph. 6:13), and in Philippians 2:12 it is parallel in meaning with the verb "obeyed" (*hypēkousate*). What Paul says here is striking. The Philippians must "obey" and "work" in order to be saved! There is no salvation apart from obedience or good works. Indeed, Paul emphasizes that believers must accomplish their own salvation.

Such a statement may cause us to worry that Paul has forgotten about the gospel of grace, but we can put that idea to rest. Paul emphasizes in Philippians 3 that his own righteousness will not qualify him to stand before God on the last day. A righteousness that hails from obedience to the law will not save him (3:9). Instead, his righteousness is a gift from God (*tēn ek theou dikaiosynēn*), granted to him by faith. No autonomous righteousness here! No conception that our goodness ultimately saves us. Indeed, 2:12 is immediately followed by 2:13. Every desire and act of obedience comes from God himself, and hence any good works are the result of his grace and power (cf. 1 Cor. 15:9) and cannot be attributed to the nobility or virtue of the human being.

The Contribution of James[26]
The Need for Mercy on the Day of Judgment

James clearly teaches that good works are necessary for justification. Unfortunately, Luther made some rash statements about James, failing to see how James cohered with Paul. Even in James, however, the necessity of good works for justification may be underemphasized or overemphasized. Some underemphasize what James teaches by suggesting that the words "justify" (*dikaioō*) and "save" (*sōzō*) do not refer to salvation.[27] Such a reading should be rejected, for it posits meanings for these terms that do not square with the remainder of the New Testament and the

---

25. The verse relates to individual salvation and is not merely sociological. See Peter O'Brien, *The Epistle to the Philippians* (NIGTC; Grand Rapids: Eerdmans, 1991), 276–80.

26. For further discussion of James's view of justification, see Thomas R. Schreiner, *New Testament Theology: Magnifying God in Christ* (Grand Rapids: Baker, 2008), 599–605.

27. Earl D. Radmacher, "First Response to 'Faith According to the Apostle James' by John F. MacArthur Jr," *JETS* 33 (1990): 35–41.

most natural reading of the text. Few commentators support such exegesis since it constitutes special pleading and is an obvious attempt to force the text to fit a predetermined theological grid.

Nevertheless, we must beware of overreading what James says as well. Good works must be present, but they must not be confused with perfection. What James says in James 3:2 is remarkable. "For we all stumble in many ways." The word "stumble" (*ptaiō*) means "sin" as in 2:10, where James says, "for whoever keeps the entire law, but stumbles [*ptaiō*] in one point, has become guilty of all." Notice how emphatic 3:2 is. James emphasizes that all are sinners and no one is excluded ("all") from the ranks of sinners. Furthermore, he includes himself as a transgressor ("we all"). Nor does he say that the sin of believers is rare, for we all sin "in many ways." Now this does not detract from the insistence that good works are necessary for justification, but it does spare us from thinking that good works signify perfection. The direction and orientation of a believer's life are toward righteousness, even if we sin regularly. We must balance the tension found in the New Testament to express accurately the role of good works in final justification, so that we do not deny the necessity of good works and so that we do not lurch into perfectionism.

James 2:12–13 is significant as well. Mercy will be the portion of those who show mercy. On the one hand, believers must be merciful. Those who don't show mercy will not receive mercy (cf. Matt. 18:21–35); they will face God's wrath in the final judgment. On the other hand, James recognizes that believers need God's mercy when the judgment arrives! Their works do not qualify them to stand before God and to claim salvation on the basis of their deeds. Their only hope for salvation is the mercy of God. The notion that mercy is needed to stand before God accords with Paul's claim that no one is justified by works of law. James doesn't emphasize to the same extent as Paul that God's grace saves, and yet a careful examination of the letter shows that he repudiates the idea that good works are the basis of righteousness.

Nor does James attribute goodness to the human being, as if we have the inherent strength to do what is pleasing to God. Believers have new life, they experience the new birth, because of God's will, since "he gave us birth by the word of truth" (Jas. 1:18). Similarly, the "implanted word" (*emphyton logon*, 1:21) probably refers to the new covenant work of God by which he inscribes the law on the hearts of believers (Jer. 31:31–34).[28] Indeed, the "implanted word" (1:21) is linked to "the word of truth" (1:18), suggesting that the "word" here is the gospel.[29] Believers do good works because they have been grasped and changed by the gospel. God has chosen them as the poor "to be rich in faith" (2:5), and we know from 2:14–26 that genuine faith results in works; hence, the good works are the fruit of God's grace.

Justification by Works in James

What James teaches in James 2:14–26 needs to be examined more closely. I have already noted that the words "save" and "justify" are soteriological. The notion that James refers to a fruitful life on earth can be safely dismissed. Often scholars have argued that the word "justify" (*dikaioō*) in James means "prove to be righteous," in contrast to Paul where it means "declare righteous." I suggest that such a solution confuses the meaning of the passage as a whole with the lexical meaning of the word "justify." There is scant evidence supporting the meaning "prove to be righteous" for the verb *dikaioō*. The verb regularly has a forensic sense ("declare to be righteous"), and it should be understood to have this meaning in 2:14–26 as well. Nevertheless, James is *not* teaching that works are the *basis* of justification, for as we have already seen, believers need *mercy* on the day of judgment.

Still, James teaches that human beings are declared to be righteous by works. So, if the works are not the basis of justification, how should we understand their role? Perhaps James thinks about justification eschatologically. After all, "save" is typically an eschatological word, and it seems James uses the word "save" eschatologically as well (Jas. 1:21; 2:14, 4:12; 5:20).[30] Furthermore, the word "save" is used in the same text with "justify" (2:14), suggesting the eschatological character of justification. James is infused with eschatology, promising an eschatological exaltation for the poor (1:9; cf. 4:10), a crown of life for those who endure testing (1:12), an inheritance for those who love God

---

28. E.g., Richard J. Bauckham, *James: Wisdom of James, Disciple of Jesus the Sage* (New York: Routledge, 1999), 146.

29. E.g., Sophie Laws, *A Commentary on the Epistle of James* (HNTC; San Francisco: Harper & Row, 1980), 82.

30. The one exception may be Jas. 5:15, but that text may refer to physical healing.

(2:5), mercy for those who show mercy (2:13), judgment for those who oppressed the poor (5:1–5), and vindication for those who patiently wait for Jesus' return (5:7–11). Since eschatology and the notion of the final judgment permeate James and since justification has to do with God's verdict, it makes sense to understand justification in 2:14–26 eschatologically.

Most scholars also agree that James draws significantly on the words of Jesus. In Matthew 12:37 Jesus declares that human beings will be "justified" (*dikaiōthēse*) or "condemned" by the words they speak. The future tense here certainly refers to the day of judgment (cf. 12:36!) when human beings will be assessed for the words they have spoken. The point for our discussion is this: just as Jesus refers to a future justification in accordance with words spoken, so James refers to a future justification in accord with the deeds performed.

Another feature of James's argument in James 2:14–26 should be noted. James does not deny the Pauline teaching that faith alone justifies (Rom. 3:28), though this will need some explanation.[31] What James rejects is a faith that is devoid of works. Faith that does not produce good works is "dead" (Jas. 2:17, 26) and "useless" (2:20). Faith without any corresponding works is not saving faith (2:14). What is the flaw with such faith? It lacks vitality and life and energy. Notional and doctrinal agreement do not constitute saving faith. One can sign off on the idea that "God is one" and be no better off than the demons (2:19).

Another way of putting this is that there are two kinds of faith. Saving faith is living and active; it feeds the hungry and clothes the naked (Jas. 2:15–16). It demonstrates its reality by the deeds that flow from it (2:18). "Faith is completed by works" (2:22). Faith alone saves, but it is never faith that is alone (2:24), for genuine faith inevitably leads to works.[32] Saving faith embraces a new reality and lives within it. But mere intellectual faith—notional acceptance of truths and doctrines—does not save and should not be confused with saving faith. If

---

31. The Roman Catholic scholar Joseph A. Fitzmyer agrees that Paul teaches in Rom. 3:28 that faith alone justifies (*Romans: A New Translation with Introduction and Commentary* [AB; New York: Doubleday, 1993], 360–62).

32. Timo Laato says, "Good works subsequently brought into effect the living nature of faith" ("Justification according to James: A Comparison with Paul," *TrinJ* 18 [1997]: 69). He goes on to say "that faith *only subsequently* (but nevertheless inevitably) will yield fruit" (70, italics original).

our behavior is not changed, we have not truly embraced and prized the glorious Lord Jesus Christ (2:1).

Does Paul teach that justification is by faith when one enters into the people of God, whereas James teaches that one is justified by works at the final judgment? There is some truth in this formulation, but we saw in the case of David that postconversion works are not sufficient for justification either. Furthermore, the initial verdict of justification upon belief is also an eschatological verdict. The verdict of the final day is announced in advance for those who trust in Jesus. It is not convincing to distinguish between initial and final justification, as if the latter is eschatological and the former is not. Or, to put it another way, we could easily fall into the mistake of segregating justification into two distinct acts where the first justification is by faith and the second is by works, which in effect suspends the first act of justification upon the second. Such a move would mean that there is no assurance of justification until the final day, when it will be revealed by our works whether we really believed.

The justification that is ours when we believe guarantees final glorification so that believers are assured that they are right with God when they believe (Rom. 8:30). In both Paul and James faith and works are inseparable. Faith and works can be distinguished logically, but in life they are inseparable. So, how should we understand the logical relationship between justification by faith and justification by works? I will suggest a way forward at the conclusion of the essay.

Conclusion from Paul and James

Paul clearly argues that good works are necessary for eternal life. Only those who sow to the Spirit will enjoy eternal life, and those who practice evil will not inherit the kingdom. James also teaches that justification is by works. No one will be justified if he or she fails to do good works. Such works are not autonomous but are the result of the new covenant work of the Holy Spirit. Nor are the works perfect. Believers still sin regularly, so that the good works constitute a new direction or a new orientation in their lives. Believers inhabit the already but not yet, and live, as some have said, "in an eschatological war zone." Hence, the power of the Spirit is evident in their lives, but they still struggle against sin.

Other Texts Emphasizing the Necessity of Good Works

Space precludes a full examination of the remainder of the New Testament, but a quick survey of other writings in the New Testament demonstrates that good works are necessary for eschatological salvation. I will comment on these texts rather quickly, for they indicate that what we have found in Paul and James coheres with other New Testament writings. The necessity of good works for salvation is pervasive; it is not an isolated theme!

For instance, in Matthew 7:15–20 false prophets are recognized by the evil fruit in their lives. Trees that bear rotten fruit are thrown into the fire (7:19); that is, they are cast into hell. The text does not say that the fruit is burned but that the tree itself is burned. The tree represents the person practicing evil. The false prophets do not merely lose rewards; they are deprived of eternal life because of the evil they practice.

The very next paragraph in Matthew confirms the interpretation just advocated (Matt. 7:21–23). Claiming that Jesus is one's Lord does not guarantee entrance into the kingdom of heaven. Indeed, one may prophesy in the Lord's name, expel demons, and do many miracles and still be excluded from the kingdom. The reason such people are excluded is because they did not do the Father's will. There is no doubt that they are removed from God's presence because of their evil, for Jesus declares to them, "Depart from me, you lawbreakers" (7:23).

The same theme surfaces in Matthew 25:31–46 in the parable of the sheep and goats. The issue here is who will "inherit the kingdom" (25:34). Those who show mercy to fellow believers (25:45) and practice good works will experience "eternal life" (25:46), but those who refuse to show mercy will be "cursed" and enter "the eternal fire prepared for the devil and his angels" (25:41); as a consequence they will suffer "eternal punishment" (25:46). The necessity of good works to receive a final reward accords with Jesus' words 16:27; when he returns, "he will repay each person according to what he has done."

The gospel of John emphasizes, as is well known, that those who believe will enjoy eternal life (cf. John 20:30–31). If we look at one paragraph (5:24–29), we see that Jesus clearly teaches that the one who believes enjoys eternal life (5:24). The centrality of belief, however, does not contradict or cancel out the necessity of works for final salvation. In the same paragraph Jesus speaks of the final resurrection (5:28–29). The reference is clearly to the physical resurrection of the dead since he speaks of those who come out of their tombs. On this final day a great division between the evil and the righteous will be apparent, for those who have practiced what is good will enjoy "the resurrection of life," whereas those who have done what is evil will experience "the resurrection of judgment" (5:29). Eschatological life belongs to believers, but their belief expresses itself in a life of goodness, for "belief" without a changed life is a charade.

Such a reading fits with John 15:6. Those who do not abide in Jesus are like a branch that is "thrown away" and "withers." Such branches are "thrown into the fire and burned." Scholars debate what is meant here, but being cut off from the vine almost certainly means that one is cut off from Jesus himself. Burning most naturally refers to the final judgment. Those who don't continue to abide in Jesus will perish in the judgment. What it means to abide is to keep the commands of Jesus and the Father (15:10). Abiding in Jesus' love manifests itself in doing what he enjoins. Those who are Jesus' disciples bear fruit (15:8). Indeed, the text says they "bear much fruit" (15:8). There is no room here for saying that one can be saved without being a disciple, for those who don't bear fruit are cut off from the vine.[33] They don't belong to Jesus at all and will be destroyed as unfruitful branches.

The necessity of good works is also found in the book of Acts. Those who preached the good news about Jesus called on people to believe in order to be saved (cf. Acts 16:31). At the same time, however, and with no sense of contradiction, people are called on to repent and turn to the Lord in order to receive life and forgiveness of sins (2:38; 3:19; 5:31; 11:18; 17:30). Indeed, repentance and faith are placed together, for they are really two sides of the same coin (20:21). The genuineness of repentance is evident when believers do "deeds in keeping with their repentance" (26:20). Believing the good news about Jesus Christ, turning to

---

33. I don't believe genuine believers will ever apostatize, but space is lacking to explain why here. See Thomas R. Schreiner and Ardel B. Caneday, *The Race Set before Us: A Biblical Theology of Perseverance and Assurance* (Downers Grove, IL: InterVarsity Press, 2001); Thomas R. Schreiner, *Run to Win the Prize: Perseverance in the New Testament* (Nottingham, UK: InterVarsity Press, 2009/Wheaton: Crossway, 2010).

God in repentance, and doing good works as an expression of repentance are a seamless web in Acts. The notion that one can repent without a genuine change of life would have been incomprehensible to Luke.

In 1 Peter we read that on the last day God will judge fairly and impartially according to the work one has done (1 Pet. 1:17). Only those who pursue what is good and put it into practice will experience eschatological life (3:10–12). Peter takes a text that refers to life on earth in the Psalms (Ps. 34:12–14) and applies it typologically to eschatological life, which is a common feature of the use of the Old Testament by New Testament writers.

Similarly, in 2 Peter 1:5–11 Peter itemizes the godly qualities that believers must diligently practice. One's calling and election are confirmed and validated by godly behavior, for those who don't practice such virtues will not enter the "the eternal kingdom of our Lord and Savior Jesus Christ" (1:11). The issue isn't rewards but whether one will enter the kingdom at all. Indeed, this is the problem with the false teachers in 2 Peter. They professed to know Jesus Christ, but they were destined for eschatological judgment because of their ungodly lives (2:1–22; cf. also Jude 4–23).

The first epistle of John emphasizes the importance of belief. The author wants readers to be assured that they have eternal life because they have believed in Jesus and confessed him as the Christ (1 John 2:21–23; 3:23; 4:2, 15; 5:11–13). Such assurance, however, is not given apart from obedience. Those who truly know Jesus keep his commands (2:3–6). Those who regularly practice sin have not truly seen Christ, nor do they know him in a saving way (3:6). John could scarcely make it clearer, for he affirms that those who practice sin are of the devil (3:8). Those who are "born of God" (i.e., those who are truly Christians) are not sinless (1:8), but their lives aren't characterized by sin (3:9; 5:18). They live in a new way. They show they are "children of God" by their righteous lives (3:10). In other words, those who fail to love one another don't really know God (4:7–8). John makes it clear that those who are "born of God" and believe in Jesus keep his commands as a result of their new life (5:4–5).

The book of Revelation calls on believers to overcome and conquer (Rev. 2:7, 11, 17, 26; 3:5, 12, 21; 12:11; 21:7). Overcoming is not optional. Only those who overcome will eat of the tree of life in paradise (2:7), and only those who overcome will avoid the second death (2:11).

If someone's name is in the book of life, he or she will overcome and conquer and persevere to the end (3:5). Those who conquer will enjoy the final inheritance, but those who follow the course of evil and pursue murder, lying, sexual sin, and the like will burn in the lake of fire and face the second death (21:7–8). Only those who do good works will receive the final inheritance.

The text is clear on this matter. Certainly the lake of fire doesn't refer to loss of rewards! And John tells us specifically that those who practice evil will experience it. But there is another remarkable feature in the context as well. The verse right before Revelation 21:7–8 promises that the thirsty will be given "the spring of the water of life without payment" (21:6). Eternal life is free! It is given to all who long for it. It is not merited or earned but is given as a gift. But then John immediately says that only those who overcome will enter paradise, and those who practice evil will be sent to the lake of fire. There is no contradiction here or denial of God's grace, for those who receive the water of life are changed by it. They don't remain the same. They are not perfect in this present evil age, but they are transformed and changed so that they live in a way that pleases God. Those who continue to follow an evil path reveal that they never received the water of life.

John emphasizes in Revelation how important it is for believers to endure and be faithful (Rev. 13:10). Those who worship the beast and receive his mark will be tormented forever (14:9–11)—hence the need for believers to endure to the end (14:12). It fits with the message of Revelation as a whole, then, that the dead are judged by their works (20:11–15). Those who have practiced evil are cast into the lake of fire, whereas those whose names are in the book of life are rescued. It seems clear that those whose names are inscribed in the book of life are in the book because they did good works, and yet John tells us that life is a gift given to those who thirst for it, and hence good works do not merit or earn life.

Theological Reflection

What we have seen in our study is remarkable. On the one hand, New Testament writers teach that justification and salvation cannot be gained by works. On the other hand, they declare that works are necessary for justification and salvation. Let's think about Paul in particular. Has he become mixed up while writing his letters? Has he been derailed at some point along the way so that he actually ends up contradicting himself by teaching that justification is apart from works and also by works? That Paul trips over his own feet here is unlikely. It is implausible that he was unaware of what he was doing in writing his letters. The so-called "contradictory" statements stand close to each other (cf. Rom. 2:1–3:20!), and even the most biting critic has to admit that the structure and rhetoric of the Pauline epistles are impressive.

When we add to this that Paul regularly affirms both themes (works can't gain salvation and yet they are necessary for salvation), it is even more unlikely that we have a contradiction, for both themes are a staple of Pauline theology. Positing that a writer is contradictory should be a matter of last resort, especially when we are talking about sacred Scripture. We can make the same point regarding James and other New Testament writers. They teach that justification and salvation are by works, but they also teach that we need mercy from God on the day of judgment and that salvation is a gift.

Still, the matter is difficult. New Testament authors do not specifically explain how both sets of statements relate to one another. They affirm both truths without explaining to us precisely how they cohere. Hence, the debate! We are called upon, then, to be virtuous and discerning readers, readers who are sympathetic with the aims and teaching found in the New Testament canon. We could simply say that any resolution is inherently distorting, that we must let both sets of statements stand without trying to explain how they fit together. I would suggest, however, that readers of Scripture are invited to go deeper than this, that the Scriptures summon us to a profound reading of the text, to a theological reading. Some worry that theological readings inevitably lead to distortion. But at the end of the day, we all engage in a theological reading of the text, and so the issue rests on which reading is most faithful to all that Paul and James and the other New Testament writers teach.

To put it another way, clues and hints are given as to how we are to read the text. The obedience necessary for salvation and justification can't be perfect obedience, for both James and Paul clearly teach that all human beings without exception are sinners. And we saw from the example of David (Rom. 4:6–8) that even after conversion, believers may fall into serious sin and yet still be forgiven and justified. So, the blemish of human disobedience cannot be restricted to one's preconversion life. Human works cannot be the *basis* of right standing with God since all sin and all fall short of the glory of God.

The saving righteousness of God given to us in Jesus Christ is the foundation and basis of our right standing with God. But if works aren't the basis, what are they? They are surely necessary, for one is not saved without them. But they can't be the necessary basis since God demands perfection and all fall short of what God requires (Rom. 3:23). It seems legitimate to say that works are the necessary evidence and fruit of a right relation with God. They demonstrate, although imperfectly, that one is truly trusting in Jesus Christ.[34]

I will restrict myself to two texts that seem to confirm this view. The first is Ephesians 2:8–10. I have already written briefly about 2:8–9, which clearly and emphatically teaches that believers are not saved by works. Works can never be the basis of salvation, for human beings are radically sinful, enslaved to the world, the flesh, and the devil and dead in trespasses and sins (2:1–5). However, believers are a new creation in Jesus Christ (2:10). And the consequence of being a good creation is that believers do "good works." When we put 2:8–10 together, it seems legitimate to say that all those who are a new creation will and must do good works. Still, given what Paul says in 2:8–9, these good works cannot be the basis of salvation. Instead, they are the necessary fruit or consequence of being a new creation.[35]

---

34. See here Richard B. Gaffin, *"By Faith, Not By Sight": Paul and the Order of Salvation* (Waynseboro, GA: Paternoster, 2006), 102–3. Gaffin rightly notes (98) that there are not two justifications: "one present, by faith and one future, by works; or, present justification by faith alone, future justification by faith plus works, the former based on Christ's work, the latter based on our works, even if seen as Spirit-empowered; or, yet again, present justification based on faith in anticipation of future justification on the basis of a lifetime of faithfulness." Instead, Gaffin finds the solution in the already–not yet character of Paul's theology, in the truth that faith works through love (Gal. 5:6). Future justification, then, is the manifestation of present justification. It is not as if present and future justification operate on different principles. Works "are not the ground or basis. Nor are they (co-)instrumental, a coordinate instrument for appropriating divine approbation as they supplement faith. Rather, they are the essential and manifest criterion of that faith, the integral 'fruits and evidences of a true and living faith.'"

35. Luther expresses this truth well, "Works are necessary to salvation, but they do not cause salvation, because faith alone gives life. On account of the hypocrisy we must say that good works are necessary to salvation. It is necessary to work. Nevertheless, it does not follow that works save on that account, unless we understand necessity very clearly as the necessity that there must be an inward and outward salvation or righteousness. Works save outwardly, that is, they show evidence that we are righteous and that there is faith in a man which saves inwardly.... Outward salvation shows faith to be present, just as fruit shows a tree to be good" (Martin Luther, *Works*, 34:165).

The second text is James 2:14–26. A careful look at the passage reveals that James doesn't teach that works in and of themselves justify and save. What he teaches is that "faith" that does not issue in works is not genuine faith. Faith that is merely intellectual (2:19)—that is, faith that embraces theological propositions without corresponding works—does not save or justify. There is a kind of faith that does not save. But James also indicates that there is another kind of faith, the kind of faith exhibited by Abraham and Rahab, that results in good works. This faith is living, active, and vital. James isn't teaching that works are the basis of justification. Instead, he teaches that authentic faith expresses itself in good works, contrasting authentic faith with an "intellectual" faith that is actually "dead" and "useless" (2:17, 20, 26).

Now what is remarkable about this reading of James is that it accords with Paul. Paul also teaches works are a result of faith, referring to "the obedience of faith" (Rom. 1:5; 16:26) and "work of faith" (1 Thess. 1:3). It is abundantly clear in 1 Thessalonians 1:3 that faith produces works, for the same verse speaks of a labor that springs from love and an endurance rooted in hope. In every case, the genitive is the source of the action or work that occurs. Paul, like James, believes that works are necessary at the final judgment, but the works are the fruit of the faith, the result of a faith that embraces and rests on Jesus Christ. I conclude, then, that the New Testament witness is consistent. Works are necessary for justification, but they are not the basis of justification or salvation since God requires perfection and all human beings sin. Hence, works constitute the necessary evidence or fruit of one's new life in Christ. We can even say that salvation and justification are through faith alone, but such faith is living and vital and always produces works.

ROBERT N. WILKIN

Three Contradictions

If our interpretation of the Bible leaves us with serious contradictions, we should take that as evidence that somehow, somewhere, our reading of the text has gone wrong. I suggest that Schreiner's interpretation collapses under the weight of three contradictions.

First, he has both Paul and James teaching forensic justification before God by faith *apart from works*, while also teaching forensic justification before God *by works*. On the one hand, Schreiner is admirably clear on Paul's doctrine of justification by faith apart from works. There can be no question that for Paul our eternal salvation cannot be accomplished by our works but only by faith in Christ. Regarding James he writes, "Their only hope for salvation is the mercy of God" (p. 88). On the other hand, Schreiner seems to think that Paul and James also taught a doctrine of salvation from hell by works righteousness. Concerning Philippians 2:12 Schreiner boldly says, "Indeed, Paul emphasizes that believers must accomplish their own salvation" (p. 87). Similarly he writes concerning James 2:13 that James insists "that good works are necessary for justification" (p. 87). Later he writes on this passage, "Those who don't show mercy ... will face God's wrath in the final judgment" (p. 88).

However, both propositions cannot be true in the same sense. Forensic justification before God is either once and for all by faith apart from works, or it is not once for all and is by faith plus works.

Second, throughout his essay, Schreiner insists that Paul and James both teach that works are *necessary* for eternal salvation. Yet he ultimately concludes that what they really mean is that works are only the necessary *evidence* for eternal salvation. But this, too, is contradictory, because saying that we must persevere in good works *in order to be eternally saved* is not at all the same thing as saying that *if* we are saved, *we will* persevere in good works. The former says that good works are *a cause* of our eternal salvation. The latter says that they are *an effect*.

Third, in either case, Schreiner appeals to the necessity of works as *evidence* of our salvation, while also teaching that our works are imperfect and rightly deserve God's condemnation. We are left to wonder how sinfully imperfect works could possibly confirm either justification or regeneration. Only Christ is perfectly sinless. No matter how godly, believers are still sinners who fall short of God's glory (Rom. 3:23). Not a single work believers do can be considered unreservedly good, untainted by any sin. For every good work we do that "confirms" our salvation, there will be a sin that denies it.

Even the idea that our works will confirm that we have been justified by faith in the first place does not make sense, for if justification is by faith alone, apart from works, then how could works confirm it? Would not *faith* confirm that one had been justified by faith?

Schreiner's theological paradigm makes it seem as though the biblical text is hopelessly confused. But these interpretive knots can be untied by paying careful attention to several biblical themes whose nuances Schreiner does not adequately address.

Biblical Themes That Need to Be Addressed
The Concept of Salvation Receives Inadequate Explanation

Schreiner reads the New Testament somewhat monochromatically. For instance, he usually interprets the words *save* and *salvation* as though they routinely refer to eternal salvation from hell. But why think that? The vast majority of biblical references to salvation have nothing to do with hell or regeneration at all, but refer instead to deliverance from enemies (Ps. 18:2–3), trouble (50:15), poverty (12:5), death (Matt. 8:24–25; 14:30; Acts 27:31), persecution (Phil. 1:19, 28), illness (Matt. 9:21), false teachers (1 Tim. 4:16), and many other calamities. Salvation is a fully orbed concept, and it can apply to many different kinds of afflictions. So while it is true that Paul teaches both salvation (justification) by faith apart from works and salvation by faith plus works, it is clearly not true that he is speaking about the same kind of salvation in both instances. Paul's thought only seems contradictory if we assume that he *has only one kind of salvation in mind*, namely, salvation from hell.

The truth is, hell is not the only calamity we need to be saved from. There are many different kinds of salvation available to the Christian, and while salvation from hell is by faith alone apart from our works, deliverance from temporal troubles often requires repentance and perseverance in good works.

This flattened reading of salvation [36] is especially evident in Schreiner's treatment of James. When discussing James 2:14, he says that "the words 'save' and 'justify' are soteriological" (p. 89). He then adds, "The notion that James refers to a fruitful life on earth can be safely dismissed." Why? We are not told. What of the other four uses of *sōzō* in James (1:21; 4:12; 5:15, 20)? To his credit he does mention the other four uses (p. 89). However, he does not discuss any of them other than to say in a footnote: "The one exception [to eschatological salvation in James] may be Jas. 5:15, but that text may refer to physical healing" (p. 89 n.30).

May refer? What else could be in view? Is Schreiner implying that eschatological salvation from the lake of fire may be in view *in James 5:15*? The prayer of faith will eschatologically save from eternal condemnation the believer who is physically ill? *All four* uses of *sōzō* outside of James 2:14 clearly refer to salvation from physical death (1:21; 4:12; 5:20) and from physical illness that could culminate in death (5:15). The condition for being saved from afflictions such as illness or temporal punishment is different from the condition for being saved from hell. See my essay for more details.

The Concept of Judgment Receives Inadequate Explanation

Schreiner also interprets all the verses relating to judgment as if they referred to a single, final judgment, where the eternal destiny of all people, Christian and non-Christian alike, will be decided. So, for instance, regarding James 2:13 he writes, "Those who don't show mercy ... will face God's wrath in the final judgment" (p. 88). But James 2:13

---

36. For more on the breadth of salvation in the Bible see Robert N. Wilkin, *The Ten Most Misunderstood Words in the Bible* (Corinth, TX: Grace Evangelical Society, 2012), ch. 3 (33–51).

does not actually mention a *final judgment*. The word used for *judgment* in James 2:13 is *krisis*, and in John 5:24 the Lord Jesus used the exact same word when he said that believers "shall *not* come into judgment [*krisis*]." The context of John 5:24 ("has everlasting life ... has passed from death into life") makes it clear that the Lord was promising that there will be no judgment of believers *in reference to their eternal destiny*.

The biblical evidence is more nuanced than what Schreiner suggests. What we find is that the New Testament refers to at least three different kinds of judgment, namely, judgments of sin this life, the Great White Throne Judgment, and the Judgment Seat of Christ. Each kind of judgment has its own set of conditions. For instance, God can judge the believer's sin in this life anytime and anywhere, chastening us for our disobedience (1 Cor. 11:30–32; Heb. 12:7). By contrast, the Judgment Seat of Christ will be for believers, regarding their rewards in the life to come and not regarding their eternal destiny, which was decided the moment they believed in Jesus for everlasting life (John 5:24). Finally, unbelievers will be judged at the Great White Throne judgment. If James 2:13 does not look at the Judgment Seat of Christ and the rewards judgment and instead looks at some judgment whereby the eternal destiny of believers will be determined, then James 2:13 is a direct contradiction of John 5:24.

The Most Important Evidence Is Not Discussed

Like Barber and Dunn, Schreiner barely mentions John's gospel. His emphasis is on Paul and James. In a section entitled, "Other Texts Emphasizing the Necessity of Good Works [for Final Salvation]," he devotes little more than a page to John's gospel (pp. 92–95). And surprisingly he does not discuss John 5:24 (though he mentions it) and the promise that the believer "shall not come into judgment" (which he does not quote or discuss). Rather, Schreiner focuses on 5:28–29, concluding that the Lord taught that "those who have practiced what is good will enjoy 'the resurrection of life,' whereas those who have done what is evil will experience 'the resurrection of judgment' (5:29). Eschatological life belongs to believers, but their belief expresses itself in a life of goodness, for 'belief' without a changed life is a charade" (p. 93).

Schreiner also has a paragraph on John 15:6–10, in which he says, "Those who don't continue to abide in Jesus will perish in the judgment"

(p. 93). This seems odd coming from a Calvinist. Possibly he means that the person who abides in Christ for a time and then does not continue to do so will prove that he was never truly born again in the first place. But then how can an unbeliever abide in Christ for a time? Is not abiding *in Christ* something only one who is "in Christ" can do?

Nor does Schreiner discuss the many texts in John that speak of everlasting life for all who simply believe in Jesus (e.g., John 1:12; 3:16; 5:24; 6:28–29, 35, 47; 11:25–27; 20:31). What of a text like John 6:28–29, in which the Lord says that the only *work* that the Father is seeking in terms of regeneration is *belief* in Jesus? Again, this is not discussed.

Why the only evangelistic book in Scripture receives only a cursory glance is hard to understand.

Has Paul Contradicted Himself?

After a brief discussion of justification and works of the law in Galatians, Schreiner turns to justification and works in Romans. He first discusses Romans 3:21–4:25 (and related texts elsewhere in Paul, such as Eph. 2:8–9) and then turns to Romans 2 under the heading "Justification by Works."

Note the opening sentence in his discussion of Romans 2: "The previous discussion [on Romans 3:21–4:25] seems to be the end of the story, but there are more verses to this song than the first one. Paul disavows justification by works in some texts, but then in other verses he teaches that we are justified by works" (p. 78). It sure sounds as if Schreiner is saying that Paul contradicts himself. Indeed, it is hard to arrive at any other conclusion based on what Schreiner says.

The way to harmonize Romans 2:7, 13 with 3:20 is by seeing the former as referring to what is hypothetically, but not actually, possible. Schreiner rejects such a view: "Many interpreters, of course, think that Paul speaks hypothetically in Romans 2:6–10 since the final conclusion of his argument is that no one can be justified by works of law (3:19–20)." He continues, "Such a reading resolves the tension between the two texts, but it fails as satisfying exegesis because of what Paul writes in 2:26–29" (p. 79). Then, in a bit of circular reasoning, he assumes that 2:25–27 refers to uncircumcised people who actually keep the commands of the law. Why not understand verses 25–27 as hypothetical as well?

Schreiner seems to answer by fiat: "Paul doesn't leave readers in the land called *hypothetical*. He brings them into a land called *actual*, speaking of the Spirit's new covenant work of transforming hearts. Paul contrasts in 2:29 'the Spirit' and 'the letter'" (p. 80, italics his). Yet Romans 2:28 – 29 does not say or imply that there are Gentiles or Jews who, by virtue of their works, have received the circumcision of the heart. All Paul is saying is that physical circumcision, like efforts at law keeping, cannot justify anyone.

Romans 2 shows that neither Gentiles nor Jews can be justified by works. "The Jews Are as Guilty as the Gentiles They Judge" (2:17 – 24) and "Circumcision *Per Se* Is of No Avail" (2:25 – 29) are the headings Hodges and Farstad provide for Romans 2:17 – 29 in *The Greek New Testament According to the Majority Text* (pp. 479, 480).

Why Not Resolve the Tension?

While I'd like to discuss 2 Peter 1:5 – 11 and other texts Schreiner discusses, I've run out of space.[37] Schreiner admits that the tension he embraces can be resolved by understanding justification before God by works as hypothetical and by recognizing that many texts speak of eternal rewards and not eternal salvation. Yet he believes "the tension" is what God intends.

Rather than accepting an impossible contradiction, we should embrace the free gift of everlasting life by faith alone apart from works and the related yet distinct promise of eternal (and temporal) recompense for work done. Jesus promised that the one who believes in him "shall not come into judgment" concerning his eternal destiny (John 5:24). It really is that simple.

---

37. For more information on 2 Peter 1:5 – 11, see Zane Hodges, "An Exposition of 2 Peter 1:5 – 11," www.faithalone.org/journal/1998i/Hodges.html. Articles are available at that website by me and others dealing with most of the passages discussed by Schreiner.

JAMES D. G. DUNN

A Breath of Fresh Air, but with Questions

Should We Give More Weight to the Contexts of Paul's Letters?

In what has been all too often a rather fractious dispute, with texts being marshaled on each side (different texts, of course) in full scale polemic, Tom Schreiner's essay is something of a breath of fresh air. He recognizes the complexity, or perhaps better, the full diversity of Paul's teaching on the subject of faith and works—justification apart from works and judgment by works—and he reflects on this diversity. He doesn't insist on the one and subordinate the other to it, though he does try to fit the two into a more coherent whole. The assumption is, I take it, that Paul himself recognized the seeming contradictions between the different things he said on the subject—that it was, indeed, a single subject that Paul had fully thought through, including the interrelationship of its different elements to one another and to the whole. I like to think the same myself, which is why I believe we can talk intelligibly about Paul's theology, rather than just the theology of each of his letters. But I still wonder whether we need to give more weight to the fact and influence of different contexts.

It should occasion no surprise, for example, that Marcion seems to have put Galatians as the first in his collection of Pauline letters. Galatians, as probably the most sustainedly polemical of his letters, could well encourage Marcion to see that an antithesis between gospel and law was the central and most fundamental feature of Paul's gospel and theology. Lutheranism has built its view of Paul's theology in a not dissimilar way round the same antithesis between law and gospel. But should Galatians be regarded as entirely typical of Paul's theology? Is Romans, perhaps, as some have suggested, a more mature and measured expression of his gospel? Should we abstract Galatians wholly from its context—an indignant response to Jewish Christian missionaries trying to make good what they regarded as the deficiencies of Paul's gospel—and universalize it to every and any context? We are already familiar with the Christian conviction that Old Testament rulings about circumcision, laws of clean and unclean, Sabbath, and so on, are no longer authoritative for Christians—that is, that their relevance was context related (required in the Old Testament, but not in the New Testament). Might something similar apply to particular emphases and rulings in the New Testament too?

Should We Expect Paul to Have Fully Reconciled the Tension between Faith and Works?

If we think in such or similar terms about the issue discussed by Schreiner—justification apart from works and judgment by works—should we allow that Paul might well have stressed different emphases in different situations, without necessarily having worked out fully how the different emphases can best be correlated (in some abstract compendium of theology)? In confronting traditionalist Jewish believers who were convinced that all members of the people of God were bound to observe laws of circumcision and of clean and unclean, Paul had no doubt and no qualms: faith alone, trust in God as Abraham did, faith in Christ, was, on the human side, the sole means and basis of a positive relationship (acceptance/justification) with God; to require more than that, works of the law, such as Peter seemed to be doing in Antioch, was to undermine the gospel and prevent that relationship from being actualized and fruitful (Gal. 2:14–16).

But there were other situations, notably in Corinth, where the warnings were about immoral conduct and social casualness and where the emphasis had to be placed on the necessity for obedience and to avoid the sort of behavior that the law condemned; when it was not enough just to be familiar with the law or to respect that law, the law had to be *done* (Rom. 2:13). The fact that Paul never actually addressed the question of how to hold the two emphases together in so many words at least leaves open the question that he didn't find it necessary to do so, and was content to bring out the different emphases in different situations as the situation demanded. We should be more willing to recognize that there is arguably as much place for contextual theology as there is for contextual ethics.

Are Certain Texts Being Squeezed into an Interpretive Grid?

Even so, Schreiner is quite right in arguing in effect that even if Paul never found it necessary to tie the two emphases together explicitly, commentators on Paul cannot avoid the challenge of trying to do so, whether with Paul or in spite of Paul! And Schreiner meets that challenge well. In fact, I don't find much to quibble about in what he has written. My queries don't really affect the main thrust of what he has written. For example, did Paul, who understood Jesus' death to be effective in dealing with sin because it was a sin offering (as provided in the law), think that Jesus' death had made such sacrifices "no longer valid" (p. 74)? Or is that reading Hebrews into Paul? (Schreiner seems to talk more about "forgiveness" than ever Paul did).

Again, is Schreiner right in reading Galatians 6:12–13 as referring to the Jewish Christian missionaries "boast[ing] in their own accomplishments"? That echoes the old Bultmann interpretation of "boasting" in Romans 2:17, 23 and 3:27–29 (boasting in works of self-achievement), whereas in both cases the boasting in view was more Jewish boasting in covenant status and privilege over against Gentiles. And Galatians 6:12–13 seems to be the same—Jewish Christian missionaries wanting the Galatians to be circumcised (in the flesh) "so that they may boast about your flesh."

I also find myself demurring at Schreiner's broadening out the reference to "works" too quickly from "works of the law" in the case of Abraham (Rom. 4:2) (p. 76). The issue Paul had introduced in Romans 3:27 for discussion through to the end of chapter 4 was whether "the law of works" or "the law of faith" excluded boasting. And Schreiner will know well that Abraham, even though the Sinai law had not yet been given, was regarded as the model of the pious, law-observant Jew. The issue was precisely whether Genesis 15:6 should be understood in terms of Abraham's faithfulness in undergoing circumcision or offering up his son Isaac in sacrifice. And I must confess to being somewhat surprised and puzzled in Schreiner's talk of "David's conversion" (p. 76), since I am far from clear as to what that was and when it happened. It may be a minor point, but if it reflects another case of trying to fit biblical texts into a particular interpretive grid, then I become uneasy.

Optimism versus Pessimism, or Realism?

When Schreiner turns to "justification by works," I find myself in large scale agreement with his exposition of Romans 2 (pp. 78–82). He leaves no doubt that, in his view, Paul was clear on "the necessity of obedience for salvation'" (p. 82). His treatment of Galatians 6:8 and 1 Corinthians 6:9–10 is exemplary (pp. 82–86): Paul's warnings that eternal life and inheritance of the kingdom of God are jeopardized by irresponsible and evil living cannot be minimized into an occasional rap on the knuckles. Schreiner's observation is apropos: "Some worry that the necessity of good works for final salvation denies the grace of the gospel, but we must be careful that we are not more Pauline than Paul! Paul did not think his words contradicted the gospel of grace" (p. 85).

To be honest, I wouldn't put Paul's argument and exhortation in Romans 6–8 quite as Schreiner does, as some sort of playoff between optimism and pessimism (p. 86). These chapters, in fact, come as close as Paul does to handling the tension between the "already" and the "not yet": a decisive beginning—"baptized into Christ" (Rom. 6:3), "died to the law and united with Christ" (7:4), "set free from the law of sin and death" (8:2); but also an ongoing demand—"do not let sin exercise dominion in your mortal bodies" (6:12), still "with my flesh ... a slave to the law of sin" (7:25), "if you live according to the flesh you will die" (8:13). I would not set the latter against the former as "pessimism" against "optimism," but rather describe the overall perspective as "realism." Paul never dealt merely with theory, but he always confronted what was often the all-too-harsh reality of discipleship, of living by faith while still "in the flesh."

The seriousness with which Schreiner takes the challenge of the varying emphases of Paul's teaching and exhortation is well illustrated by his comment on Philippians 2:1–13: "What Paul says here is striking. The Philippians must 'obey' and 'work' in order to be saved! There is no salvation apart from obedience or good works. Indeed, Paul emphasizes that believers must accomplish their own salvation" (p. 87). And the treatment of James is in like kind (pp. 87–89). This is refreshing.

Is Schreiner's Resolution to the Tension between Faith and Works Too Neat?

And how does it all come out? After posing the tension in Paul's teaching in particular, as clearly as he does, how does Schreiner resolve the tension? He hints at his resolution to the conundrum of how to relate justification by faith and judgment according to works at several points but reserves his full, but brief (too brief?) statement on the subject till the end. He confronts the apparent contradiction forthrightly: "Paul regularly affirms both themes (works can't gain salvation and yet they are necessary for salvation)" (p. 96). His solution is "that works are the necessary evidence and fruit of a right relation with God. They demonstrate, although imperfectly, that one is truly trusting in Jesus Christ" (p. 97). The solution is hardly new—this is not a criticism—and recalls teaching I remember from long ago that "good works are the fruit and not the root of justification." But it does have the smack of the teacher who has retired into his study to reflect on the conundrum and has thus come up with the solution. The trouble is that, as a solution, it takes us away from the harsh reality of a life lived between the "already" and the "not yet," the harsh reality of a discipleship lived out in a first-century Ephesus or Corinth or Rome.

Pastoral Implications

In such a situation, readily compared with situations today, there will often arise the need for the pastor or teacher to warn that such and such behavior and attitudes and political maneuvering are putting salvation in jeopardy. "Your faith must be expressing itself in love, otherwise it may actually be dead, whatever the words you confess or the hymns you sing." In such a case it may be bad, even fatal pastoral practice to affirm the one side of Paul's teaching: "the initial verdict of justification upon belief is also an eschatological verdict. The verdict of the final day is announced in advance for those who trust in Jesus" (p. 91). In other circumstances (e.g., of great depression, lack of confidence, or deep repentance), that might well be the message to give. But where faith is not manifesting or evidencing itself in love, in works of good and kindness, there it is that the warnings and exhortations, which characterize the other dimension of Paul's teaching, need to be preached and heard, to set necessary alarm bells ringing.

When we do so, there may well be those who find it necessary to criticize for abandoning the core message of "justification by faith" alone. But that should not stop us, any more than it did Paul or James. In the end of the day it is more important that Christians practice faith working through love than that they have a theology that sees its top priority to be wholly consistent and coherent with "justification by faith apart from works."

MICHAEL P. BARBER

I am grateful for the opportunity to respond to Thomas R. Schreiner's essay. I find myself essentially agreeing with most of his exegesis. I especially appreciate his insistence on taking passages that link salvation to good works seriously. In my contribution I make a similar case: the good works that are necessary for salvation are not merely the product of human effort, but are *the result of the working of God*.

It seems to me, however, that different understandings of the nature of justification and salvation lead us to part ways when it comes to the precise role of good works. Here we cannot offer a full account of these terms, as Schreiner acknowledges. But he has offered a fuller analysis of their meaning elsewhere. [38] Here I present only a brief sketch of a Catholic explanation that, admittedly, I cannot fully explicate or defend but which I nonetheless hope will help shed light on how our positions differ.

Paul's Multifaceted Terminology

First, I think it is important to recognize that the New Testament writers, including Paul, use multiple metaphors to speak of salvation. At points, these metaphors overlap. For example, as Michael Gorman demonstrates, Paul speaks of "justification" in terms of being united to Christ (Gal. 2:16–21). [39] Thus, while theologians might wish Paul had separated things such as "justification" from "sanctification," a careful look reveals that he does no such thing (cf. 1 Cor. 6:11). [40] We must

---

38. Thomas R. Schreiner, *New Testament Theology: Magnifying God in Christ* (Grand Rapids: Baker, 2008), 353–62; idem, *Galatians* (ZECNT; Grand Rapids: Zondervan, 2010), 155–57.

39. Michael Gorman, *Inhabiting the Cruciform God: Kenosis, Justification, and Theosis in Paul's Narrative Soteriology* (Grand Rapids: Eerdmans, 2009), 40–104.

40. See, e.g., Terence L. Donaldson, "The Juridical, the Participatory and the 'New Persepctive' on Paul," in *Reading Paul in Context: Explorations in Identity Formation* (London: T&T Clark, 2010), 229–41.

be cautious, then, to not view these metaphors as hermetically sealed categories. [41] While we can *distinguish* the concept of justification from other aspects of salvation, we should not *separate* it from the larger complex of Paul's soteriological doctrine.

Moreover, as Dunn points out in his essay, no single metaphor seems to fully capture the entirety of the soteriological message of Paul or, for that matter, the New Testament as a whole. With that in mind, we must be careful not to isolate justification from the other soteriological language employed (sanctification, adoption, salvation, redemption, etc.) and then attribute to it an absolute significance that is out of all proportion to the totality of Paul's message, to say nothing of that of the New Testament as a whole.

Justification and Righteousness

Having stated what we have above, I do think it is important to look at justification carefully. While Schreiner defines the term as "acquittal," I see it as involving much more than that. Indeed, the Greek term from which "justification" comes to us is notoriously difficult to translate. [42] The terminology is derived from language of *righteousness*. [43] The exact term translated "to justify" (*dikaioō*) has no perfect English equivalent. Protestant scholar Michael Bird explains that the term could be rendered "to rightify," "to be righteoused" (passive), or even with the archaic, "to rightwise." [44] Jewett also insists that "it is essential to render it, 'being set right.'" [45]

Of course, translating the term "to acquit" works well since the terminology carries a forensic meaning (cf., e.g., 1 Cor 4:4). For Schreiner, it is precisely the juridical nature of the terminology that constrains the meaning of "justification." Judges "do not 'make' a person righteous" but

---

41. See Luke Timothy Johnson's response to Schreiner in *Four Views on the Apostle Paul* (ed. M. F. Bird; Grand Rapids: Zondervan, 2012), 48–52.

42. See Michael F. Bird, *The Saving Righteousness of God* (Eugene, OR: Wipf & Stock, 2007), 6–7.

43. See Gorman, *Inhabiting the Cruciform God,* 56, who explains that righteousness and justification are "essentially synonymous for Paul."

44. Note K. Grobel's translation of *Rechtfertigung* as "rightwise" in Rudolf Bultmann, *Theology of the New Testament* (2 vols.; trans. K. Grobel; London: SCM, 1952), 1:253.

45. Robert Jewett, *Romans: A Commentary* (Hermeneia; Minneapolis, MN: Fortress, 2006), 280.

simply "pronounce what is in fact the case." Thus Paul must mean that justification involves a purely forensic declaration. [46]

However, it should be noted that after Schreiner bases his opinion of the meaning of justification on the constraints of human juridical authority, he goes on to explain that God obliterates such limitations. By declaring the guilty "righteous" because they trust in Christ, God's "verdict violates the normal and just procedure for a judge.... Judges who declare the guilty to be righteous violate the standards of justice." [47]

I agree with Schreiner that God is not limited to what human judges can do. Yet, in the Catholic view, God transcends the constraints of human juridical authority not by violating justice (which would be impossible, since it would be to violate his nature), but because he actually *makes* the wicked righteous. As John Henry Newman observed, God effects what he declares (cf. Isa. 55:10–11). [48] This is evident in creation: when God says, "Let there be light," there was light (Gen. 1:3). Likewise, in the "new creation," when God pronounces the sinner "justified," they are *made* righteous. Why? Because they are united to the Son.

Justification and Sonship

As we have seen, the Greek term "to justify" (*dikaoō*) is inextricably linked to "righteousness." Righteousness (*dikaiosynē*) in Paul is best read against the Hebrew notion of righteousness (*ṣdq*), which underscores the idea of right relationship. [49] Indeed, Paul speaks of "justification" in relational terms (Rom. 5:9–10). [50] Against this biblical backdrop, one can hardly avoid interpreting "righteousness" apart from a "covenantal" matrix. Indeed, the covenant was the "principle manifestation" and "norm" of God's righteousness. [51]

---

46. Schreiner, *Galatians*, 156.

47. Ibid.

48. John Henry Newman, *Lectures on the Doctrine of Justification* (3rd ed.; New York: Longmans, Green, and Co., 1990), 81–82.

49. Among others, see Ernst Käsemann, "The Righteousness of God in Paul," in *New Testament Questions of Today* (trans. W. J. Montague; London: SCM, 1969), 172; James D. G. Dunn, "The Justice of God: A Renewed Perspective on Justification by Faith," *JTS* 43 (1992): 16–17.

50. See Gorman, *Inhabiting the Cruciform God*, 55.

51. See, e.g., Richard B. Hays, "Justification," *ABD*, 3:1131. Some scholars have disputed understanding of "righteousness" as "covenant faithfulness." However, see the rejoinder in Bird, *Saving Righteousness*, 12. Likewise, see Tom Schreiner, *New Testament Theology* (Downers Grove, IL: InterVarsity Press, 1998), 353; idem, *Galatians*,156 n. 14 (citing Bird's treatment).

Yet once we place the language of righteousness against the backdrop of the covenant, we see that the terminology of justification ("rightification") points to more than mere acquittal. While covenants most certainly involved a legal/juridical dimension, they also involved another reality: family. As the eminent scholar Frank Moore Cross has demonstrated, in the ancient world, covenants were fundamentally understood as establishing kinship bonds. [52] The logic of the covenant, then, is *familial*.

The juridical rationale behind "justification" is therefore familial. The judge is not simply an anonymous tribunal, but the *Father*. The "righteousness" that defines his decree of "rightification" is nothing less than sonship and membership in the new covenant family. [53] "Righteousness" is thus understood relationally—one is made righteous because one receives the gift of adoption (Rom. 8:14–17; Gal. 4:5–7; Eph. 1:5).

For Paul, then, justification is not a concept employed in isolation from his larger salvation-historical scheme. [54] What has occurred in Christ represents the fulfillment of Israel's hopes—particularly, hopes for a new covenant. [55] Indeed, as Schreiner observes, it is precisely "new covenant" righteousness Paul is speaking about in Romans 2 (see Schreiner, pp. 80-82). Paul's teaching regarding "justification" should not be detached from this context. [56]

"Rightification" in the Divine Economy

Paul's language of justification is thus best viewed against the broader salvation-historical scheme presented in his letters. Through Adam's sin, death entered the world (Rom. 5:12–15). As is well known, there is little said about the significance of Adam's sin in ancient Jewish

---

52. Frank Moore Cross, "Kinship and Covenant in Ancient Israel," in *From Epic to Canon: History and Literature in Ancient Israel* (Baltimore, MD: Johns Hopkins University Press, 1998), 3–21.

53. See, e.g., Jewett, *Romans*, 281.

54. See Mary Sylvia C. Nwachukwu, *Creation-Covenant Scheme and Justification by Faith* (Rome: Pontifical Biblical Institute, 2002).

55. Note that the language of the new covenant promise in the programmatic passage in Jeremiah 31 includes *familial* language, e.g., nuptial language. See John Andrew Dearman, *Jeremiah-Lamentations* (NIVAC; Grand Rapids: Zondervan, 2002), 36–37.

56. See Gorman, *Inhabiting the Cruciform God*, 56.

works. [57] The full significance of the failure of the first Adam was only fully appreciated by Paul in meditating on the work of Christ, the new Adam (Rom. 5:12–14; 1 Cor. 15:21–22, 45; cf. Rom 5:14). In the Son we discover what God intended for humanity from the beginning: sonship.

This original design for humanity might even be detected in the text of Genesis itself. In Genesis 1, God creates humanity in his "image" and "likeness" (Gen. 1:26–27), terms later used in reference to "sonship" in Genesis (5:3). Given all of this, it is probably not surprising that Luke describes Adam as "the son of God" (Luke 3:38).

What was lost in Adam, then, is restored in Christ: divine sonship. Justification is more than simply being declared "not guilty." It truly is being "rightified," that is, reinstated in a standing of covenant "righteousness," i.e., sonship. As Paul writes, "for in Christ Jesus you are all sons of God, through faith" (Gal. 3:26).

I hasten to add that this righteousness—this sonship—must be understood in *christological* terms: Christ is "our righteousness" (1 Cor. 1:30). Thus the work of salvation is more than simply deliverance from wrath; it is communion with God through the divine Son. It is even what the fathers call *theōsis*. [58] To borrow language from 2 Peter, it is being made "partakers in the divine nature" (2 Pet. 1:4).

Justification apart from Works

To support his claim that justification merely constitutes a divine decree and that it does not *make* the sinner righteous, Schreiner turns to Romans 4:1–8. Here Paul is clear that God justifies apart from "works of law." Those who read my article will see that I wholeheartedly affirm that *initial* justification is received by faith and not by works (Eph. 2:8). Justification is realized through being united to Christ, something no one can merit by good works.

With Schreiner, following Paul's statement in places such as 1 Corinthians 6:11, I affirm that this union and its resulting justification is linked to baptism. Baptism constitutes union with Christ (cf.

---

57. An exception is found in *4 Ezra* 7:118.

58. See Ben Blackwell, *Christosis: Pauline Soteriology in Light of Deification in Irenaeus and Cyril of Alexandria* (Tübingen: Mohr-Siebeck, 2011).

Rom. 6:1–4; Titus 3:5–7).[59] Thus, one is truly justified by grace *prior* to doing any good works. Pope Benedict XVI thus writes:

> Being just simply means being with Christ and in Christ. And this suffices. Further observances are no longer necessary. For this reason Luther's phrase: "*faith alone*" is true, if it is not opposed to faith in charity, in love. Faith is looking at Christ, entrusting oneself to Christ, being united to Christ, conformed to Christ, to his life. And the form, the life of Christ, is love; hence to believe is to conform to Christ and to enter into his love. So it is that in the Letter to the Galatians in which he primarily developed his teaching on justification St Paul speaks of faith that works through love (cf. Gal 5:14).[60]

It is striking how similar this sounds to Schreiner's presentation.

Justification, Works, and Sonship

Yet while Schreiner holds that works are necessary for salvation, he has a hard time explaining *how* this is the case when it comes to certain passages. James 2 poses particular difficulties. James writes, "You see that a man is justified by works and not by faith alone" (Jas. 2:24). He recognizes that "James clearly teaches that good works are necessary for justification" (p. 87). However, Schreiner insists that what James really means is that it is "saving faith" that justifies; such faith is necessarily accompanied by good works and that is why faith alone does not justify.

That may harmonize James with Paul, but it is decidedly *not* James's point. The *works themselves* have justifying value for James. The statement about Rahab that immediately follows makes this clear: receiving the messengers and sending them out another way was what justified her (Jas. 2:25). The point here is the *instrumentality* of the works, not simply faith.

Are James and Paul hopelessly irreconcilable? I think not. The Catholic view accounts for all the data. Justification is sonship, specifi-

---

59. On the link between baptism and justification, see Gorman, *Inhabiting the Cruciform God*, 59–69. On the authenticity of the Pastorals, see Luke Timothy Johnson, *The First and Second Letters to Timothy* (New York: Doubleday, 2001), 55–90.

60. General audience of Pope Benedict XVI on November 19, 2008; see www.vatican.va/holy_father/.../hf_ben-xvi_aud_20081119_en.html.

cally sharing in the sonship of Christ. Those who are justified are "conformed to the image of his Son" (Rom. 8:29). At baptism, one receives the grace of justification, which imparts saving faith, itself "the work of God" (John 6:29). Thus one is truly justified initially *apart* from works!

Yet once one is justified through faith, the person is glorified and conformed to the Son's image through good works. As I explain in my essay, justification, like salvation, is thus not simply a moment but a process. Why? Because justification is sonship. Sonship entails growth. Salvation is not simply being saved from "wrath" but from "the power of death"; in Christ we are empowered with the "Spirit of sonship" (Rom 8:15; cf. Gal 4:5). We are saved from being "outside of the family of God." The gift of justification at baptism is sufficient, then, to be saved. As one is saved in baptism (1 Pet. 3:21), one is justified at baptism (1 Cor. 6:11), because baptism is linked to sonship (cf. Gal. 3:26–27).

Yet the sons also mature. They cooperate with God's grace working within them and go on to do good works, thus being conformed to the image of Son. Thus their works *are* meritorious and salvific because their works are the result of Christ living within them (Gal. 2:20). Thus Paul says, "work out your own salvation ... for God is at work within you" (Phil. 2:12–13).

Conclusion

Let me conclude by saying that Schreiner and I agree on much. In fact, Schreiner's view corresponds closely to that of Thomas Aquinas, a major representative of the Catholic interpretive tradition. In his commentary on Romans 4, Aquinas writes:

> A man's works are not proportioned to *causing* the habit of this righteousness; rather, a man's heart needs first to be justified inwardly *by God*, so that he can perform works proportioned to divine glory." [61]

---

61. Thomas Aquinas, *Lectures on the Letter to the Romans* (trans. Fabian Larcher, O.P.; available online at the website of *Nova et Vetera: The English Edition of the International Theological Journal*, http://nvjournal.net/files/Aquinas_on_Romans.pdf.), 4; lect. 1.

CHAPTER THREE

IF PAUL COULD BELIEVE BOTH IN JUSTIFICATION BY FAITH AND JUDGMENT ACCORDING TO WORKS, WHY SHOULD THAT BE A PROBLEM FOR US?

JAMES D. G. DUNN

One of the most troubling problems in writing on the theology of the New Testament, or on the New Testament's teaching on a particular theme or issue, is that we quickly find there is no single or uniform theology. There are some basic essentials, of course — the centrality of Christ, the call for faith/trust, for example. But when such basic essentials are elaborated or referred to different situations, the more diverse expressions of the teaching can quickly become difficult to hold together. I made this point in my *Unity and Diversity in the New Testament*,[1] when I noted that it was certainly possible to abstract a core kerygma or gospel from the different New Testament writings, a core on which the New Testament writers would agree; but as soon as the core was elaborated in the different writings and expressed in reference to different particular situations, it became diverse.[2] An obvious case is the gospel for the Gentiles and the gospel for the circumcision, as agreed in Galatians 2:9 — the same gospel, yes; but it only takes the next paragraph (Gal. 2:11–16) to show that the question of how this gospel

---

1. James D. G. Dunn, *Unity and Diversity in the New Testament* (3rd ed.; London: SCM, 2006).

2. Chap. 2, particularly §7; and in the third edition xxviii-xxx and the revised §76.

was understood and worked out was by no means agreed or an effective force for unity or unified mission.

I made a similar point in *The Theology of Paul the Apostle*, in reference to Paul's diverse "metaphors of salvation."[3] The range of experiences that Paul referred to in his metaphors meant that no single metaphor was adequate to capture that range, or indeed to express the depths of any particular experience. Metaphors like "liberation" or "reconciliation" can undoubtedly express aspects of the beginning or process of salvation, but hardly the whole of it. Paul could talk of his own experience as an "abortion" (1 Cor. 15:8), of becoming the Corinthians' father through the gospel (1 Cor. 4:15), of giving birth to the Galatians (Gal. 4:19). He uses the imagery of "adoption" twice within a few verses—first in connection with the beginning of Christian experience and second of its climax in the resurrection of the body (Rom. 8:15, 23). Becoming a Christian can be likened to an engagement with Christ (2 Cor. 11:2), or indeed to a marriage with Christ (1 Cor. 6:17), or to being put to death with Christ (Rom. 6:3–6). How can we hold these all together? How can we fit them all into a single, coherent narrative?

Of course, fundamental to the whole is the problem of language— that the language of everyday human experience is basically inadequate to express the less than tangible spiritual realities, including the language and imagery used for God, for the reality of the risen and exalted Jesus, or for the person and work of the Holy Spirit. In all these cases, if we are to speak about them at all, we must accept that the imagery is analogical, that the language is metaphorical. And this has to include the recognition that such language is *not* literal, and that to understand it as literal propositional statements is to misunderstand it and abuse it.

Such language we can believe with confidence is referential: it refers to actual realities. But it is allusive and aspectical rather than straightforwardly descriptive. Any attempts to coordinate the metaphors into some kind of *ordo salutis* (order of salvation) inevitably use a model of rationality into which the metaphors do not readily fit. The amazing

---

3. James D. G. Dunn, *The Theology of Paul the Apostle* (Grand Rapids: Eerdmans, 1998), 328–33.

difficulty that so many Pauline commentators have experienced in trying to hold together his language of justification and participation "in Christ" well illustrates the blind spot here [4]—amazing, since Paul himself seems to have found no difficulty in thinking together the two (to us) divergent models of the salvation process held out in his gospel.

Despite all this, the history of Christianity has seen repeated attempts to draw up a coherent *ordo salutis*, to settle on a particular formulation or metaphor (or structure) that provides the key or norm for all the others—one to which all the others can therefore be subordinated. For example, in the history of mainstream Christianity it quickly became the norm to make the bishop the focus of church and to rule out of order any alternative, despite the diversity of church order attested in the New Testament churches. Or again, notwithstanding a verse like John 3:8 and the record of the Spirit's uncontrollability in Christianity's beginnings, the work of the Spirit was compressed into sacrament and Bible where it could more easily be controlled—the Spirit's function restrained by being neatly fitted into good order.

Similarly, in Lutheranism the metaphor of "justification" became the article by which the church stands or falls, and all the other metaphors were subordinated to it. Today the metaphor of new birth ("born again") dominates the way in which many Christians envisage what becoming and being a Christian means. "Scholasticism" may refer primarily to the theological discussions of the Middle Ages, but it is also a useful label for attempts to conform the charismatic insights of a Luther or a Calvin into a formal and coherent structure where rational consistency is the determinative consideration.

An especially poignant example of the frustrating inability to organize the diverse New Testament material into a neatly consistent schema—frustrating, because it would make it so much easier to speak in propositional terms about the schema and so much easier to identify and label those who depart from its clear-cut terms—is the issue of what the New Testament writers taught about final judgment; particularly, how to reconcile Paul's talk of judgment by faith and *not by works* (of the law) and his teaching that judgment will be *according to works*.

---

4. Well illustrated by D. A. Campbell's *The Deliverance of God: An Apocalyptic Rereading of Justification in Paul* (Grand Rapids: Eerdmans, 2009).

How, to refer to an exquisitely poignant example, are we to integrate the wonderful assurance held out in Romans 8:31–39[5] with the sobering warning of 2 Corinthians 5:10? The issues do not arise solely from Paul's letters, but the issue of judgment according to works, especially how it relates to his teaching on justification by faith and not by works, is so pressing in the case of Paul and so acute for any adequate appreciation of his theology and his gospel, that I will have to make Paul's teaching on the point the principal focus of this essay.[6]

As our introductory observations imply, when we turn to Paul, we must bear in mind that his teaching comes in different letters, written to different churches and to differing situations. The issue even arises whether we can speak of a theology of Paul or have to limit ourselves to speaking about the theology of the individual letters. I am sufficiently confident that we can speak of Paul's theology,[7] but even so, the particularity of the individual statements and individual letters can never be ignored.

So far as "judgment according to works" is concerned, the issue can be considered under several heads.

The Two Justifications

It is easy to forget that Paul draws the metaphor of justification from the law court—justification as the judge's acquittal of the accused—and that the primary reference of the law-court imagery for Paul is the final judgment.[8] There are two features of his gospel that made it such wonderful "good news" for Paul: that *God justified the ungodly*, that is, those who were guilty, despite their guilt—including, and especially the law-less Gentiles; and that the verdict of justification can be pronounced *now*, already, to those who accept his gospel and believe in Jesus Christ.

This conviction that God is a God "who justifies the ungodly" (Rom. 4:5), of course, actually cuts across the law-court metaphor

---

5. P. Stuhlmacher, "Christus Jesus ist hier, der gestorben ist, ja vielmehr, der auch auferweckt ist, der zur Rechten Gottes ist und uns vertritt," in *Auferstehung—Resurrection* (ed. F. Avemarie and H. Lichtenberger eds.; WUNT 135 (Tübingen: Mohr Siebeck, 2001), 351–61.

6. I will draw particularly on my *Theology of Paul* §§14 and 18; also *The New Perspective on Paul* (Tübingen: Mohr Siebeck, 2005; rev. Grand Rapids: Eerdmans, 2008), ch. 1, from which I make use of various footnotes.

7. See Dunn, *Theology of Paul*, esp. 13–26.

8. As implied also in passages like Rom. 2:5 and 3:3–6, as well as 8:31–39.

(another warning not to press the metaphor too logically). For justification/acquittal of the wicked was abhorrent to one of the most basic canons of Jewish justice.[9] It would seem also to run counter to Israel's covenant with God. After all the ungodly person was by definition the law breaker, the one unfaithful to the God who had been faithful to the promises he made to the patriarchs and who had delivered his people from slavery in Egypt. The law breaker had put himself outside the law, outside the covenant, beyond the outreach of God's saving righteousness. And this applied to the Gentile all the more, who was, by definition law-less, an out-law, a sinner.

However, Paul takes his start from the fact that God gave his promise to Abraham without precondition, made his covenant with Abraham when he was ungodly.[10] For Paul, Genesis 15:6 made clear the character and terms of God's justification: "Abraham believed God (God's promise) and it was reckoned to him for righteousness"; he was acquitted before God, treated as righteous by God. So this initial act of righteousing/right-wising the ungodly, this definitive act of justifying the sinner, was an act of pure grace. Not only so, but God remained faithful to the descendants of Abraham embraced by his promise, even when they proved faithless (Rom. 3:3–6), so that the righteousness of God to Israel was displayed as saving righteousness, vindicating righteousness.[11] And Paul takes this up too in his gospel of God's saving righteousness to all who believe, Gentile as well as Jew (Rom. 1:16–17).[12] So God's acceptance/justification of the sinner lies at the heart of Paul's gospel, not as a corrective of Israel's salvation history but as an extension and further application of it.

---

9. Exod. 23:7; Prov. 17:15; 24:24; Isa. 5:23; CD 1.19.

10. In Jewish reflection Abraham could be seen as the type of the proselyte, the Gentile who turned away from his idolatry to the one true God (*Jub.* 12.1–21; Josephus, *Ant.* 1.155; *Apoc. Ab.* 1–8; Strack-Billerbeck, 3.195).

11. See particularly the Psalms (e.g., Pss. 51:14; 65:5; 71:15) and second Isaiah (Isa. 46:13; 51:5–8; 62:1–2). In Psalms 51:14 and 65:5 the NRSV translates *ṣedeq/ṣĕdāqâ* ("righteousness") as "deliverance"; in the others God's "righteousness" parallels his "salvation"; and in Isa. 62:2 the NRSV translates *ṣedeq* as "vindication." Elsewhere (e.g., in Mic. 6:5 and 7:9), the NRSV translates God's *ṣĕdāqâ* as his "saving acts" and his "vindication." See further BDB, *ṣĕdāqâ* 2 and 6a.

12. It was this discovery by Luther, that "the righteousness of God" in Rom. 1:16–17 referred not to God's *punitive* righteousness but to his *saving* righteousness, that became the basis and starting point for the Reformation.

The other striking feature of Paul's gospel of justification is that it can be experienced now. This is nowhere clearer than in the triumphant aorist tense opening of Romans 5: "Therefore, having been justified from faith ..." (Rom. 5:1). [13] Yet at the same time Paul retains the more basic thought of justification, acquittal as taking place at and awaiting final judgment, using the same verb "justify" (*dikaioō*) to look forward to that final judgment (Rom. 2:13; 3:20, 30). [14] Less typical of Paul's actual usage, but more typical of his theology, is his talk of "the hope of righteousness" (or hoped-for righteousness) as something "eagerly awaited" (Gal. 5:5). This recognition of the "not yet" dimension of justification by faith gives added force to Luther's *simul peccator et iustus* ("simultaneously sinner and righteous").

The issue raised, however, is how the two justifications relate to one another. Does the first justification ensure the second? And since the initial justification is justification of the ungodly, does that mean that the final justification will be similar? And if it is only the ungodly sinner who is justified, by divine initiative and grace, does that bind the doctrine of justification to a doctrine of election; that is, only those will be acquitted at the final judgment to whom God has made promise and stretched out his grace without precondition? Let us look more closely at the "not yet" aspect of Paul's gospel of salvation.

Beginning and Completing

In two places Paul speaks about beginning and completing the Christian life. In Philippians 1:6 it is a word of reassurance: "I am confident of this, that the one who began a good work in/among you will complete it by the day of Jesus Christ." But in Galatians 3:3 there is a warning note: "Are you so foolish? Having begun with the Spirit, are you now made complete with the flesh?" There is a process certainly already begun but yet still to be completed.

Similarly, we recall that the gift of the Spirit, which for Paul constitutes the beginning of the Christian experience (Rom. 8:9, 14), is the first stage in a lengthy process. The Spirit is the *arrabōn*, the "first install-

---

13. See also Rom. 4:2; 5:9; 1 Cor. 6:11; Titus 3:7.
14. But implicit also in the present continuous tenses in Rom. 3:24, 26, 28; 4:5; 8:33; Gal. 2:16; 3:8, 11; 5:4; and aorists of Rom. 3:4; 8:30; Gal. 2:16, 17; 3:24.

ment" of the whole process and "guarantee" of its completion (2 Cor. 1:22). It is the "pledge" of God's complete inheritance (Eph. 1:13–14). In 2 Corinthians 5:5 the Spirit is the *arrabōn* of the process described in 4:16–5:4, the process of outward wasting away and inner renewal that climaxes in the transition/transformation into resurrection body.

In the equivalent imagery of the *aparchē*, the "firstfruits," which is the first sheaf of the harvest being reaped, the Spirit is the beginning of the process destined to climax in "the redemption of the body" (Rom. 8:23). As Jesus' resurrection was the *aparchē* of the harvest of the resurrected dead (1 Cor. 15:20), so the gift of the Spirit begins a process that will climax in the resurrection of the body (Rom. 8:11), the *aparchē* of the eschatological harvest of resurrection/spiritual bodies patterned on Christ's resurrection (1 Cor. 15:44–49).

It is easy, then, to forget that for Paul "salvation" is a process. Indeed, Paul uses the term itself, "salvation," to speak of the end result of the process (particularly Rom. 13:11; 1 Thess. 5:8–9), and the verb "save" in the future tense as something still hoped for (Rom. 5:9–10; 10:9, 13; 11:26; 1 Cor. 3:15; 5:5). Christians most typically are "those who are (in process of) being saved" (1 Cor. 1:18; 15:2; 2 Cor. 2:15).

The question, then, is how these two tenses, the already beginning and the not yet completion, are related to each other in Paul's thought. Does the beginning guarantee the completion? A reading of Philippians 1:6 might suggest so: Christ will complete what he has begun. But a reading of Galatians 3:3 might as easily suggest much more caution: Is it possible that those who have begun with the Spirit will revert to the flesh — and so fail to complete? Could the guarantee fail, not because of the guarantee itself, but because of the failure of the one to whom it was given? Could the process of renewal not reach its intended goal? This leads directly to another aspect of Paul's teaching on the process of salvation.

The Conditionality of Salvation

A disturbing feature of Paul's theology of the salvation process is the degree of hesitation and concern he shows that it might not be completed — disturbing at least to anyone brought up theologically within a Calvinist systematic theology, as I was, where the perseverance/preservation of the saints is a fundamental tenet. The disturbing feature is that Paul regarded the possibility of apostasy, of failing to persevere, as a *real* danger for his converts. [15]

- Romans 8:13 — "If you live in accordance with the flesh, you will certainly die; but if by the Spirit you put to death the deeds of the body, you will live." Paul evidently envisaged the real possibility that believers might live *kata sarka* ("according to the flesh"), and if they did so they would die. That is to say, if they abandoned the struggle between Spirit and flesh and reverted to a wholly fleshly existence, they would not experience that daily renewal toward wholeness, but only the daily deterioration toward the destruction of the flesh in death.
- Galatians 6:8 — "Those who sow to the Spirit shall from the Spirit reap eternal life"; whereas "those who sow to their own flesh shall from the flesh reap corruption." The "corruption" referred to is evidently the opposite of "eternal life."

We are not surprised, then, at the equivalent warnings elsewhere:

- Paul envisages the possibility of "destroying" the work of salvation in a person (Rom. 14:15, 20; 1 Cor. 3:17; 8:11; 10:9–11).
- Paul is concerned lest his evangelistic work might have been in vain (2 Cor. 6:1; Gal. 2:2; 4:11; Phil. 2:16; 1 Thess. 3:5).
- Paul is concerned lest his converts be "estranged from Christ" and fall "away from grace" (Gal. 5:4).
- Paul is concerned lest he himself should be "disqualified" (1 Cor. 9.27).
- Paul warns regularly about the perils of moral failure (1 Cor. 3:17; 10:12; 11:27–29; 2 Cor. 12:21; 13:5; Gal. 5:4; Col. 1:22–23).
- Paul warns the Gentile Christians in Rome that they could be cut off from the olive tree of Israel just as easily as the unbelieving of Israel had been (Rom. 11:20–22).

We should also observe the qualifications that feature at a number of points in Paul's letters:

---

15. *Pace* the rather tendentious attempt of J. M. Gundry Volf, *Paul and Perseverance: Staying in and Falling Away* (WUNT 2.37; Mohr Siebeck, 1990), to weaken the seriousness of Paul's repeated warnings on this point. I. H. Marshall, *Kept by the Power of God: A Study of Perseverance and Falling Away* (London: Epworth, 1969; 3rd ed., Carlisle: Paternoster, 1995), 99–125, better reflects the "eschatological reserve" in Paul's overall treatment.

- "joint heirs with Christ *provided that* we suffer with him in order that we might be glorified with him" (Rom. 8:17)
- the gospel "through which you are being saved *if* you hold on to it" (1 Cor. 15:2)
- reconciled to be presented holy and blameless before God "*provided that* you remain in the faith established and steadfast and not shifting from the hope of the gospel" (Col. 1:22–23)[16]
- hence also the calls to carefulness and watchfulness (1 Cor. 3:10; 8:9; 10:12; Gal. 5:15) and to self-scrutiny (1 Cor. 11:29–30; 2 Cor. 13:5), and Paul's recognition that discipline is still necessary if the race is to be completed (1 Cor. 9:27; Phil. 3:12–14)

In the face of such a catalogue of concern, it is hardly possible to doubt that part of Paul's pastoral theology was his all-too-real concern that faith could once again be compromised and cease to be simple trust, that commitment could be relaxed and resolve critically weakened. The result would be an estrangement from Christ, a falling away from grace, a reversion to life solely "in accordance with the flesh," *and the loss of the prospect of resurrection life.*

Here the parallel with the history of salvation as it was understood within Israel and in Second Temple Judaism becomes somewhat uncomfortable. For if E. P. Sanders is correct and Israel's pattern of salvation can be summed up in terms of "covenantal nomism,"[17] then the parallel with what Paul seems to hold forth as the pattern of salvation according

---

16. F. F. Bruce, *The Epistle of Paul to the Romans* (Grand Rapids: Eerdmans, 1963), 219: "Throughout the New Testament continuance is the test of reality."

17. E. P. Sanders, *Paul and Palestinian Judaism* (London: SCM, 1977), 75: "Covenantal nomism is the view that one's place in God's plan is established on the basis of the covenant and that the covenant requires as the proper response of man his obedience to its commandments, while providing means of atonement for transgression" (see also pp. 236, 420, 544). In "The New Perspective on Paul," in *Jesus, Paul and the Law* (Louisville: Westminster, 1990), 183–214, I note that, though criticizing Sanders' methodology, J. Neusner accepted Sanders' representation of rabbinic Judaism at this point as a "wholly sound and … self-evident proposition" (204 fn. 16). It is worth noting that despite some criticisms of the way Sanders develops his argument, nevertheless Sanders' basic point has been taken in German scholarship: see, e.g., C. Strecker, "Paulus aus einer 'neuen Perspektive': Der Paradigmenwechsel in der jüngeren Paulusforschung," *Kirche und Israel* 11 (1996): 3–18 (note p. 7); F. Avemarie, "Bund als Gabe und Recht: Semantische Überlegeungen zu berît in der rabbinischen Literatur," in *Bund und Tora: Zur theologischen Begriffsgeschichte in alttestamentlicher, frühjüdischer und urchristlicher Tradition* (ed. F. Avemarie and H. Lichtenberger; Tübingen: Mohr Siebeck, 1996), 163–216 (note pp. 213–15); R. Bergmeier, "Das Gesetz im Römerbrief," in *Das Gesetz im Römerbrief und andere Studien zum Neuen Testament* (WUNT 121; Tübingen: Mohr Siebeck, 2000), 31–90 (note pp. 44–48).

to his gospel does begin to become uncomfortable for all who take it for granted that salvation in Judaism and Christianity are antithetical.

Traditionally, Paul's opposition to Israel's "pattern of religion" has been premised on his being opposed to the suggestion that Israel had to prove its worthiness of salvation by its obedience to the Torah. That is to say, Paul reacted negatively to the inference that Israel's salvation was conditional upon its obedience. The reaction against Sanders' emphasis on the election/covenant dimension of "covenantal nomism" was provoked by the uncomfortable suggestion in effect that Sanders was making Israel's hope of salvation unjustifiably dependent on God's prior and unmerited choice of Israel to be his special people.

It is true that Sanders had emphasized the nomism dimension of "covenantal nomism" — that the maintenance of Israel's position within the covenant was conditional on its obedience to the Torah — but evidently he had not emphasized it sufficiently for those who thought it essential rather to emphasize the conditionality of Israel's salvation on such obedience.[18] But now it would appear that Paul also saw the salvation that his gospel promised to be conditional, at least in some degree, on his converts' "obedience of faith" (Rom. 1:5). Morna Hooker was surprised that the pattern of salvation that Sanders saw in Palestinian Judaism fitted so exactly the Pauline pattern of Christian experience: "God's saving grace evokes man's answering obedience."[19] But the real surprise for many is that *Paul's* theology of salvation fits so well with *Judaism's* "covenantal nomism"!

Status Accorded or Person Transformed?

I refer here to the long-running dispute between Reformed and Catholic theology on this point, usually referred to as the issue whether righteousness is "imputed" or "infused." Is the righteousness of the Christian always an "alien righteousness," something that the Christian never "has"? Can the status of "righteous" never be affirmed of the sinner except as a status attributed to one who will never be less or other than

---

18. D. A. Carson, et al., *Justification and Variegated Nomism I: The Complexities of Second Temple Judaism* (WUNT 2.140; Tübingen: Mohr Siebeck, 2001); S. J. Gathercole, *Where Is Boasting? Early Jewish Soteriology and Paul's Response in Romans 1–5* (Grand Rapids: Eerdmans, 2002).

19. M. D. Hooker, "Paul and 'Covenantal Nomism,'" in *From Adam to Christ: Essays on Paul* (Cambridge: Cambridge University Press, 1990), 155–64 (here p. 157).

undeserving?[20] Or is the promise of the gospel that the believing sinner will *become* righteous, or the obligation of the gospel that the believing sinner will act righteously? In the one case, the Reformed concern is that any emphasis given to the believing sinner as "righteous" opens the door to the idea of salvation as something earned, to doctrines of merit. On the Catholic side, the case can be made that while the Christian life begins with faith and always depends on faith, it is never less than the divine intention that faith should be expressed also in faithfulness (*pistis* embraces both meanings),[21] that Paul always intended that faith should "operate effectively through love" (Gal. 5:6), and that James was correct in his insistence that "faith, by itself, if it has no works, is dead" (Jas. 2:17).

Here we find ourselves caught in the same dilemma as referred to in the opening section: that there are two emphases in Paul that his post-Reformation followers have found difficult to hold together. On the one hand, there is little doubt that Paul used the verb "justify" to refer to God's justifying the sinner, vindicating the ungodly, acquitting the guilty. The gospel for Paul was that God's saving righteousness reached out to and embraced all, Gentile as well as Jew, simply on the basis that they trusted and relied on him, not on anything they had done or achieved (Rom. 4:5, 16–22). Faith was what made it possible for the sinner to partake in that saving righteousness, and faith remained on the human side the only medium for reception of and response to God's grace; "whatever does not proceed from faith is sin" (Rom. 14:23).

On the other hand, however, we can hardly ignore Paul's equal emphasis on the transforming character of divine grace. In the present

20. A. McGrath, *Iustitia Dei: A History of the Christian Doctrine of Justification* (Cambridge: Cambridge University, 1986; 2nd ed., 1998), 189, summarizes "the leading primary characteristics of Protestant doctrines of justification": "1. Justification is defined as the forensic *declaration* that the believer is righteous, rather than the process by which he is *made* righteous, involving a change in his *status* rather than his *nature*. 2. A deliberate and systematic distinction is made between *justification* (the external act by which God declares the sinner to be righteous) and *sanctification* or *regeneration* (the internal process of renewal within man).... 3. Justifying righteousness ... is defined as the alien righteousness of Christ, external to man and imputed to him, rather than a righteousness which is inherent to him, located within him, or which in any sense may be said to belong to him."

21. Characteristically Catholic is the qualification of the Reformation "sola fide" by K. Kertelge, *"Rechtfertigung" bei Paulus: Studien zur Struktur und zum Bedeutungsgehalt des paulinischen Rechtfertigungsbegriffs* (Münster: Aschendorff, 1967). He sums up his discussion of "Faith and Justification": "In Paul faith always means obedience to the saving will of God and therefore contains an active element as a person complies with the claim of God" (225).

discussion this is the point that needs to be brought out more clearly. Justification may be the most important image for the beginning and end of the process; but the in-between stage of the process, usually distinguished as "sanctification," has to be reckoned with as well. Paul assuredly expected his converts not only to be accounted righteous but also to be transformed into better people.

- Paul uses also the language of transformation/metamorphosis for what has happened and continues to happen to Christians (Rom. 12:2; 2 Cor. 3:18).
- Christians are now being "conformed" to the image of Christ as they will in the end be conformed to his glorious body (Rom. 8:29; Phil. 3:10, 21); sanctification is a process of becoming like Christ.
- Becoming a Christian means being clothed with a new self, the replacing the old self and its practices, an inner renewing in accordance with the image of its creator, something integral to the process toward the final resurrection body transformation (2 Cor. 4:16; Col. 3:9–10).
- So, naturally, Paul expected the process of salvation to produce a tested, approved character (*dokimē*) (Rom. 5:4; 2 Cor. 2:9); he hoped to present his converts "pure" (*hagnos, eilikrinēs*), "blameless" (*amōmos, aproskopos*), "faultless" (*amemptos*), "irreproachable" (*anegklētos*), and "mature/perfect" (*teleios*) at the coming of Christ (1 Cor. 1:8; 2 Cor. 11:2; Phil 1:6, 10; Col. 1:22, 28; 1 Thess. 3:13; 5:23).[22]

It is hard to avoid the conclusion, then, that as Paul insisted on the need for faith, so he was equally insistent that his converts should demonstrate their faith by the quality of lives they lived.

- Paul expected obedience from his converts (Rom. 1:5; 6:16, 19; 15:18) and for his converts to "lead a life worthy of the Lord/ worthy of God" (Col. 1:10; 1 Thess. 2:12);

---

22. E. Petrenko, *Created in Christ Jesus for Good Works: The Integration of Soteriology and Ethics in Ephesians* (Milton Keynes, UK: Paternoster, 2011) well demonstrates that in Ephesians the transformation of the believer and of the community is integral to "salvation"; "for the writer of Ephesians salvation entails the transformation of the self and of community; these are not addenda to soteriology or its effects, so much as the practical meaning of salvation" (219).

- He looked for "the harvest or fruit of righteousness" in their lives (2 Cor. 9:9–10; Phil. 1:11)—"righteousness" used in an Old Testament sense of acts of kindness done rather than something imputed to them (Ps. 112:9).
- He expected believers to "fulfill" the law (Rom. 8:4), and to produce "good works" (2 Cor. 9:8; Col. 1:10).
- In speaking of the love that fulfills the law, Paul evidently had specific conduct in mind (Rom. 12:9–13.10; Gal. 5:13–15).[23]
- "Keeping" the requirements of the law continued to be important for Paul (Rom. 2:26–27; 1 Cor. 7:19).

In view of the above passages, it is hard to escape the conclusion that Paul not only saw righteousness as imputed, as a status attributed, but also as a quality that he fully expected to be manifested in the lives of his converts.[24] Whether we categorize it in terms of "infused righteousness" or of "sanctification" does not really matter. What is important is to recognize that this emphasis was also integral to Paul's gospel and theology. Later commentators may have found it difficult to hold the two emphases together, but clearly Paul himself did not. And rather than attempting to fit them together in some scheme spatchcocked together by minds that prize consistency more highly than honoring the full range of what Paul actually wrote and taught, we should hold together both emphases, however much the one taken out of Paul's contexts jars with the other similarly extracted from Paul's letters.

---

23. J. M. G. Barclay, *Obeying the Truth: A Study of Paul's Ethics in Galatians* (Edinburgh: T&T Clark, 1988), 94: "Although the true Abrahamic family are free from the yoke of the law, they are not free from the obligation to *work*—to turn their faith into loving behaviour."

24. Peter Stuhlmacher is most typically Lutheran in his exposition of Paul at this point; his most recent contribution is P. Stuhlmacher, *Revisiting Paul's Doctrine of Justification: A Challenge to the New Perspective* (Downers Grove, IL: InterVarsity Press, 2001). Not unimportant, then, is the critique of Stuhlmacher's earlier expositions by Mark Seifrid, "Paul's Use of Righteousness Language Against Its Hellenistic Background," in *Justification and Variegated Nomism II: The Paradoxes of Paul* (ed. D. A. Carson et al.; Tübingen: Mohr Siebeck, 2004), 39–74: "The only point where one might wish for greater clarity is in Stuhlmacher's insistence on the *inherent connection* between 'imputed' and 'effective' righteousness" (73–74). Cf. the earlier criticism of Stuhlmacher by Karl Donfried, "Justification and Last Judgment in Paul," *ZNW* 67 (1976): 90–110, reprinted in his *Paul, Thessalonica and Early Christianity* (London: T&T Clark, 2002), 253–78 (here pp. 257–60). In regard to Stuhlmacher's evident concern to be faithful to what he regards as the critical insight of the Reformation, Donfried wags a reproachful finger: "the issue is to correctly understand Paul, not the Reformation" (260).

This reminds us once more that Paul's teaching on these matters, these same twin emphases, is not dissimilar from the teaching of the Old Testament and of the Judaism of his day—back to the issue of Paul's "covenantal nomism"! Another way to pose the issue of this section is in terms of a contrast between "synergism" and "monergism." Those who want to play down Paul's emphasis on judgment according to works do so by claiming that Paul opposed the Jewish scheme of salvation because it was "synergistic," that is, depended on human cooperation with God. In contrast, so the argument goes, Paul put forward a scheme of salvation that was "monergistic," that is, solely and wholly dependent on God's doing.[25]

But now it should be clear that Paul did lay responsibility on his converts, in language that reads far more synergistically than monergistically. The classic text, Philippians 2:12–13 expresses the point succinctly: "Work out your own salvation with fear and trembling; for it is God who is at work in you, enabling you both to will and to work for his good pleasure" (NRSV); why should it prove so problematic that Paul could put both clauses in the same sentence?[26]

Before turning to the key Pauline teaching on judgment according to works, we should review one other aspect of the discussion.

Does the Fruit of the Spirit Require No Effort from the Christian?

One of the ways for those unhappy with the thought that Paul's gospel had any synergistic aspect to it is to argue that the fruit of the Spirit (Gal. 5:22–23) is the natural/spiritual outcome of having received the Spirit, for which the believer as such can claim no credit. Does that mean that the fruit of the Spirit is inevitable in every believer? Will every believer unquestionably attain, a measure at least, of love, joy, peace, patience, and so on? In contrast to the failure of the old covenant

---

25. Thus D. A. Hagner, "Paul and Judaism: Testing the New Perspective," in Stuhlmacher, *Revisiting*, 75–105: "Paul abandoned the synergism of Jewish soteriology for the monergism of total dependence upon the grace of God in Christ" (p. 92). Similarly M. A. Seifrid, *Justification by Faith: The Origin and Development of a Central Pauline Theme* (NovTSup 68; Leiden: Brill, 1992), 255: Paul "no longer viewed God as cooperating with human effort within the framework of the covenant with Israel. Now for Paul, God's act in Christ effected salvation in itself."

26. Seifrid comments appropriately on 1 Cor. 7:19: Paul's "rejection of 'works of the Law' notwithstanding, we may nicely fit Paul into 'covenantal nomism'" ("Paul's Use of Righteousness Language," 65).

to meet the demands of the law, so the argument runs, members of the new covenant are enabled or empowered to "fulfill the requirements of the law" by the Spirit (Rom. 8:4); "those who have the Spirit actually keep the law."[27] Does that mean that keeping the law is inevitable and requires no effort on the part of the believer? Those wary of attributing to Paul any degree of synergism naturally like to emphasize the second half of Philippians 2:12–13 (v. 13: "for it is God who works in you both to will and to work for his good pleasure").

In commenting on Romans 2:7–10, Peter Stuhlmacher speaks of those who have been granted "a new nature in righteousness and the spiritual ability to do what is right."[28] Roland Bergmeier comments: "The law finds true fulfilment first on the level of the Spirit.... In the mind of Paul one should speak not of a *nova obedientia*, but of an obedience now possible for the first time."[29] And Simon Gathercole speaks of "Paul's theology of the divine empowerment of Christians" ("the Spirit does offer power to fulfill the Torah under the new covenant") and thus has no qualms in concluding: "for Paul, divine action is both the source and the continuous cause of obedience for the Christian," so that "belief in final vindication on the basis of obedience" can be affirmed of Paul also.[30] Similarly, Stephen Westerholm readily agrees that those granted God's Spirit "to empower their living must express the reality of their new life in suitable behavior"; God's Spirit "enables them to serve God in a new way.... With faith that is active in love,

---

27. T. R. Schreiner, *Romans* (BECNT; Grand Rapids: Baker, 1998), 404–7; also *The Law and Its Fulfillment: A Pauline Theology of Law* (Grand Rapids: Baker, 1993): "the Spirit, not self-effort, produces obedience"; "the Spirit's work in a person produces obedience to the law (Rom. 2:26–29).... The works that are necessary for salvation ... are evidence of a salvation already given" (187–88, 203; further ch. 6); similarly *Paul, Apostle of God's Glory in Christ: A Pauline Theology* (Downers Grove, IL: InterVarsity Press, 2001), 281–82 (further ch. 12).

28. P. Stuhlmacher, *Paul's Letter to the Romans* (Louisville: Westminster John Knox, 1994), 47.

29. Bergmeier, "Das Gesetz," 75–76, citing E. Reinmuth, *Geist und Gesetz* (Theologische Arbeiten 44; Berlin: Evangelische Verlagsanstalt, 1985): "Obviously it is the function of the Spirit to bring to realization the fulfilment of the law's requirements, which became possible in the condemnation of sin" (p. 70); also O. Hofius, "Gesetz und Evangelium nach 2. Korinther 3," *Paulusstudien* (2nd ed.; WUNT 51; Tübingen: Mohr Siebeck, 1994), 75–120: "The deliverance from the Torah's judgment of death is much more at one and the same time the deliverance for that new life determined by the Spirit of God, in which, in accordance with the promise of Ezek. 36.26f., the holy will of God first of all can find and does find its fulfillment" (120).

30. Gathercole, *Where Is Boasting?* 132, 223, 264.

believers not under the law may in fact fulfill the righteousness that the law requires."[31]

But, can the first half of Philippians 2:12–13 (v. 12: "Work out your own salvation with fear and trembling") be totally absorbed into the second half (v. 13: "for it is God who works in you both to will and to work for his good pleasure")? Paul's talk of "walking by the Spirit" or "being led by the Spirit" elsewhere[32] clearly puts responsibility on the believer to so walk, to be so led. Can that responsibility be dissolved in talk of the divine enabling so to act, of which Paul also speaks? Paul certainly has no problem with emphasizing that responsibility, and in stark terms, in the very same context, as we have seen (Rom. 8:13; Gal. 6:8). Is there not a danger of subtly magicking away what for Paul was an important emphasis? To use Galatians 2:20 to remove all responsibility from the believer for any good that he or she does, since it is the indwelling Christ who does it,[33] is to eliminate the "I" as a responsible person.

The problem, however, is that Paul's ethical teaching consistently assumes that his readers were responsible people, who should be making effort—enabled by God's Spirit, of course—but nevertheless having the responsibility to walk by the Spirit, to be led by the Spirit, with the express corollary that failure to do so would have severe and possibly *damning* consequences. Does it therefore not follow for Paul that

---

31. S. Westerholm, *Perspectives Old and New on Paul: The "Lutheran" Paul and His Critics* (Grand Rapids: Eerdmans, 2004), 431–34; similarly "Paul and the Law in Romans 9–11," in *Paul and the Mosaic Law* (ed. J. D. G. Dunn; WUNT 89; Tübingen: J. C. B. Mohr, 1996; Grand Rapids: Eerdmans, 2001), 215–37: "The 'works' which Paul discounts are those of the unredeemed 'flesh'; the righteous behaviour that he requires is the 'fruit' of the Spirit borne in those who have responded to God's demonstration of righteousness with faith" (236). Similarly M. A. Seifrid, "Unrighteous by Faith: Apostolic Proclamation in Romans 1:18–3:20," in *Justification and Variegated Nomism II*,106–45: Paul "understands the gospel to work true obedience to the Law in those who believe" (124–25); "The Spirit, and the Spirit alone, effects real obedience ... the work of the Spirit is justification (initial and final) in its outworking" (private correspondence).

32. Rom. 8:4, 14; Gal. 5:16, 18, 25.

33. B. Byrne, "Living out the Righteousness of God: The Contribution of Rom 6:1–8:13 to an Understanding of Paul's Ethical Presuppositions," *CBQ* 43 (1981): 557–81: "it is through living out or, rather, allowing Christ to live out this righteousness within oneself that eternal life is gained" (p. 558); Stuhlmacher, *Romans* 120; T. Laato, *Paulus und das Judentum: Anthropologische Erwägungen* (Åbo: Åbo Akademis, 1991): "Christ does the good works of the Christians" (203); M. A. Seifrid, *Christ, our Righteousness: Paul's Theology of Justification* (Downers Grove, IL: IVP Apollos, 2000): "Christ—the new person—is present within faith, performing his works" (p. 149). D. B. Garlington, *Faith, Obedience and Perseverance* (WUNT 79; Tübingen: Mohr Siebeck, 1994), 44–71: "It is *in Christ* that one becomes a 'doer of the law'; and the Christian's loving obedience to God is nothing other than the extension to him/her of the loving righteousness of *Christ himself*" (p. 71).

how these Christians exercised that responsibility would be subject to the judgment of the final judgment? Could Paul ever have agreed that to live as a Christian requires no effort or self-discipline, no hard work, from the individual Christian? And if he expected such, would it not follow that he fully expected that such effort, such work would be among the works to be judged on the day of the Lord?

This brings us to the central issue of this book.

Judgment according to Works

Paul's teaching on the nature of final judgment is clear enough.

- Romans 2:6–11: God "will render to each in accordance with his works [from Ps. 62:12; Prov. 24:12]. To those who seek for glory and honor and immortality by perseverance in doing good, eternal life. But to those who out of selfish ambition also disobey the truth, being persuaded to unrighteousness, wrath and anger. Affliction and distress on every living person who brings about what is evil, Jew first and Gentile as well. But glory and honor and peace to everyone who brings about what is good, Jew first and Gentile as well. For there is no partiality with God."
- Romans 2:13: "It is not the hearers of the law who are righteous in God's sight, but the doers of the law who will be justified"— note that doing, not simply believing, is judged (or simply believing what is heard).
- Romans 14:10–12: "We shall all stand before the judgment seat of God.... So then each of us will give account of himself to God."
- 1 Corinthians 3:8: "Each will receive wages according to the labor of each."
- 2 Corinthians 5:10: "All of us must appear before the judgment seat of Christ, so that each may receive recompense for what has been done in the body, whether good or evil."
- Colossians 3:25: "The wrongdoer will be paid back for whatever wrong has been done, and there is no partiality."[34]

---

34. See further K. L. Yinger, *Paul, Judaism and Judgment according to Deeds* (SNTSMS 105; Cambridge: Cambridge University Press, 1999), 207–15, 277–78, who notes, inter alia, that while the "reward" in 1 Cor. 3:14–15 can be distinguished from salvation, in Col. 3.24 the reward *is* "the inheritance" (234–35).

Striking is the way Paul emphasizes the importance of this. Christians will *not* escape judgment. And the judgment will be "according to works" — that is, undeniably, surely, *their* works, not the works of Christ — works done as enabled by the Spirit, to be sure, but still *their* works. Hence, works for which they are responsible, and therefore works for which they can be judged. Paul would hardly think in terms of Christ's works being subject to judgment in the final judgment; that had already taken place in the resurrection and exaltation of Christ!

Moreover, Paul clearly intended the awareness of this unavoidable judgment to be a major factor in determining how his converts should act, especially toward others. The thought of final judgment should help prevent acts of evil, and Paul does not hesitate to hold out the prospect of reward and prize to encourage the doing of good (1 Cor. 3:14; 9:24–25; Phil. 3:14; Col. 3:24; 2 Tim. 4:8).

Notable in Romans 2:6–11 is the fact that Paul could put the issue solely in terms of doing good and doing evil. There is no mention of faith, or of the possibility that such good-doing will depend on the Spirit. Nor does Paul trouble to clarify that in his later exposition. Does Romans 8:31–39 (nothing "shall be able to separate us from the love of God in Christ Jesus our Lord") qualify 2:6–11 (God "will repay to each one according to his works") so that it no longer applies to the recipients of his letters?[35] The fact that he goes out of his way to emphasize the impartiality of God, that God has no favorites when it comes to judgment (repeated in Col. 3:25), hardly suggests that he did not really think Romans 2:6–11 still applied to those who had received the gospel.

Here again, and not least, we are confronted with an uncomfortable similarity between, on the one hand, a covenantal nomism that included emphasis on judgment on Israel's failure to obey the Torah, and, on the other hand, Paul's emphasis that Christians will not escape judgment

---

35. R. H. Bell, *No One Seeks for God: An Exegetical and Theological Study of Romans 1.18–3.20* (WUNT 106; Tübingen: Mohr Siebeck, 1998), 254–56, simply denies that the judgment envisaged in Rom. 2 applies to Christians. Contrast K. R. Snodgrass, "Justification by Grace — to the Doers: An Analysis of the Place of Romans 2 in the Theology of Paul," *NTS* 32 (1986): 72–93, who notes that "approximately three-fourths of Paul's judgment sayings refer to the judgment of Christians" (p. 93, fn.101). See further Yinger, *Paul, Judaism and Judgment*. And on Rom. 2 and 2 Cor. 5.10 see C. VanLandingham, *Judgment and Justification in Early Judaism and the Apostle Paul* (Peabody: Hendrickson, 2006), 215–32 and 199–202 respectively.

on their works. If a degree of inconsistency is evident in Judaism's "covenantal nomism,"[36] it is difficult to see how Paul can be exempted from a similar critique.[37]

This brings us right back to where we started. Rather than take one dimension of Paul's gospel/theology as a fixed given and then try to make the rest of his theology cohere with what is deemed to be most fundamental, we should rather tease out all the emphases he makes in relation to our questions. Once that is done, once we have properly respected the full range of what Paul taught on a subject, we should then try to see how the different emphases hang together and whether they cohere.

We may not find that process easy; the history of Pauline scholarship shows just how hard it is. We may find that in attempting to identify the degree of coherence Paul evidently was content with, we force them together, knocking off awkward edges to make them fit with each other; that too has been a repeated experience in the attempts to systematize Paul's theology. So perhaps we may simply have to accept, embarrassing as it may be, that we cannot discern an appropriate explanation that is both coherent and satisfying. Perhaps we need to settle for a rhetorical solution. In other words, when Paul saw that his converts needed reassurance, he made one emphasis; and when he saw that they needed to be exhorted and warned, he made another emphasis. That at least would be more faithful to Paul than trying to fit his whole teaching into a shoebox, which in the end is too small for the wholeness of his theology.

Beyond Paul

It should be clear, then, that the problem of how to relate the thought of "judgment according to works" to the gospel of "justification by faith

---

36. F. Avemarie, *Tora und Leben: Untersuchungen zur Heilsbedeutung der Tora in der frühen rabbinischen Literatur* (Tübingen: Mohr Siebeck, 1996).

37. This complaint is at the heart of critique of Paul by H. Räisänen, *Paul and the Law* (WUNT 29; Tübingen: Mohr, 1983), 186: "it would be possible to claim that Paul actually teaches salvation (or at least reward) by works! If we (reasonably enough) refrain from such a claim, it might be wise not to apply it to Paul's Jewish contemporaries either. There is a difference of emphasis ... it is not clear that the pattern itself is much different." See also Yinger, *Paul, Judaism and Judgment*, 2–4, 286–90; and VanLandingham, *Judgment and Justification*, ch. 3: e.g. "other than making Jesus Christ the tribunal, Paul has not altered Jewish belief in the Last Judgment in any significant way" (240).

and not by works" is a problem that is posed particularly by Paul and for Paul's theology and gospel. Hence discussion of Paul has been the primary and principal focus of this essay. However, on the question of "judgment according to works," Paul is by no means alone within the New Testament, including, not least, Jesus' own teaching on this subject.[38] Here we should simply note that we merely create the same problems when attempting to systematize and rationalize the full range of Jesus' teaching or to fit it all into a neatly consistent and coherent pattern with the rest of the New Testament. How, for example, if the gospel according to Paul is the normative New Testament gospel, are we to fit into it Jesus' parable of the prodigal son(s), in which there is no redemptive intermediary and no need for one? In the case of the issue here (judgment according to works), it can hardly escape notice that there is teaching in the Gospels to the effect that final judgment will be "according to works."

Jesus warns explicitly that the Son of Man "will repay to each person according to his way of conducting himself" when he comes (Matt. 16:27; see esp. 25:31–46).[39] In the words of the Johannine Jesus, at that time "those who have done good will come forth (from the grave) to the resurrection of life and those who have done evil to the resurrection of judgment" (John 5:28–29). These warnings are as pressing for the (Christian) readers of the Gospels as ever were Paul's. Matthew warns his audiences that to those who merely confess Jesus as "Lord" without obeying the Father's will, Jesus will say, "Depart from me, workers of lawlessness" (Matt. 7:21–23). Not unlike Paul (Rom. 2:13), Jesus warns that final justification will involve an assessment of what fruit each life has borne (Matt. 12:33–37). Unsurprisingly, then, imagery of reward for achievement or good deeds (works) is not lacking (e.g., 6:1–6; 10:41–42; 25:34–40). And salvation (eternal life) is

---

38. See particularly A. P. Stanley, *Did Jesus Teach Salvation by Works? The Role of Works in Salvation in the Synoptic Gospels* (ed. David W. Baker; ETSMS 4; Eugene, OR: Pickwick, 2006).

39. Recognized by Gathercole, *Where Is Boasting?* 113–19, 124–31, who also notes that Jesus in Luke 10:28 seems to make eternal life dependent on "doing" (121–24). In view of the main argument of his monograph, Gathercole is remarkably unphased by all this (the chapter is headed "Jewish Soteriology in the New Testament"), despite the possible corollary that Paul's doctrine of justification was *directed against other writers of the NT* (even Jesus?!) as much as against the soteriology of Second Temple Judaism.

spoken of as in some degree conditional on faithful endurance (e.g., Mark 13:13). [40]

When we look at the other New Testament writings, the message is no different. Hebrews warns more starkly than Paul that those who have once been enlightened and have shared the Holy Spirit, and have tasted the goodness of the word of God and the powers of the age to come, may too fall away. The ground blessed by rain, if it produces thorns and thistles, "is worthless and on the verge of being cursed; its end is to be burned" (Heb. 6:4–8). Thus for those who "go on sinning deliberately after receiving the knowledge of the truth, there no longer remains a sacrifice for sins, but a fearful expectation of judgment, and a fury of fire that will consume the adversaries" (10:26–27). "The Lord will judge his people," including "those who have trampled underfoot the Son of God, and have profaned the blood of the covenant by which they were sanctified, and have outraged the Spirit of grace" (10:29–30). "Shrinking back leads to destruction, but faith to the preservation of the soul" (10:39). Hence the writer warns his readers that there is a conditionality about their relationship to Christ — "if we hold firmly to the original commitment to the end" (3:6, 14) — and urges his readers, "Be watchful lest any fall short of the grace of God" (12:15).

James, in his warning that faith without works is dead and that justification/acquittal at the final judgment will be by works and not by faith alone (Jas. 2.12–26), is not at all so far from Paul as those have assumed who have followed Luther in trashing James, because of his qualification of justification by faith alone. [41]

One of the several points where 1 Peter can be regarded as close to Paul is his reminder that those who "invoke as Father the one who judges all people impartially according to their deeds" should consequently live their lives in reverent fear (1 Pet. 1:17). In 2 Peter 1:5–11, "entry into the eternal kingdom of our Lord and Saviour Jesus Christ" seems to be at least to some extent dependent on the recipients' self-control, endurance, godliness, mutual affection, and love.

---

40. So also Stanley, *Did Jesus Teach Salvation by Works?* 248–49.

41. See ibid., 308–11; Gathercole, *Where Is Boasting?* 116–18; P. A. Rainbow, *The Way of Salvation: The Role of Christian Obedience in Justification* (Milton Keynes, UK: Paternoster, 2005).

In 1 John 4:17 it is not faith or even abiding in God or having his Spirit that can give the recipients "boldness on the day of judgment," but love—and not just reception of God's love but loving one another (4:7–12).

Of the passages in the latter New Testament writings only one (Rev. 20:11–15) comes close to Paul's teaching in 1 Corinthians 3:10–15. In 1 Corinthians 3 judgment of Christians will test (to destruction) only the works that are built as a superstructure on the foundation of Jesus Christ. Wherever shoddy building materials have been used, "the builder will be saved, but only as through fire" (1 Cor. 3:15). However, Paul immediately adds, "if anyone destroys God's temple ['the temple which you (plural) are,' 3:17], God will destroy that person," which suggests that 3:15 is by no means the whole tale of judgment. The great white throne judgment near to the end of Revelation is one of Revelation's most fearful visions, where "the dead [are] judged according to their works, as recorded in the books … and all [are] judged according to what they had done" (Rev. 20:11–13). "Anyone whose name was not found written in the book of life was thrown into the lake of fire" (20:15). But judgment of those written in the book of life will be according to the works they have done, as recorded in the book of life. Here, too, therefore, we see another of these formulations that cannot so easily be fitted into others on the same subject.

Conclusion

How, then, can we hold together these different emphases in Paul (and Jesus and the other New Testament writers)? Can we actually reconcile "justification by faith and not by works" with "judgment according to works"? Assuredly we can maintain that any good that the believer does derives entirely from God's grace and is only wrought by the Spirit's enabling. Assuredly we can affirm that the believer never approaches the throne of grace, whether now or in the future, except as a sinner, wholly dependent on that grace. Assuredly we can say with Paul that before God there can never be ground for boasting in one's own doings but only in the glory and grace of God (Rom. 4:2; 5:11; 1 Cor. 1:29, 31; 2 Cor. 10:17; but note also Rom. 15:17; 2 Cor. 1:14; 7:4; Phil. 2:16).

But can we also deny that Paul expected his converts to become better persons because they were "in Christ" and were/should be walking in accordance with the Spirit? Can we deny that for Paul, believers do and will bear responsibility before God for their doings? Can we deny that, according to Paul, Christians too will be judged according to their works? And the same questions have to be put to the other New Testament writers.

So, do we have to say that for Paul and the other New Testament writers salvation will depend, at least to some extent, on (good) works done by the believer? It could, of course, be argued that salvation actually achieved will depend entirely on Christ and his Spirit, while also maintaining that salvation could be lost by our own efforts, or lack of effort. But is such a solution entirely satisfactory in light particularly of the Pauline teaching reviewed in this essay?

Whether we can or cannot successfully knit together the two emphases in Paul's and the others' teaching into a single coherent catechism, we surely should not fall into the trap of playing one off against the other, the naively satisfying device that blends one into the other in a way that diminishes the force of one or other, the ignoring of the one in order to give the other the emphasis that we think it deserves. Is it so serious that we cannot fit the two neatly into a single coherent proposition? Is it not more important that we should hear both and respond to both as our situations and (dis)obedience of faith require?

RESPONSE TO JAMES D. G. DUNN

ROBERT N. WILKIN

James D. G. Dunn wonders why people feel the need to reconcile Paul's teachings on assurance of eschatological salvation with those verses that seem to warn believers that they might fail to persevere and end up eternally condemned. Dunn's *apparent* conclusion is to allow both themes *equal emphasis* in Paul's work. Warning passages are aimed at the disobedient; justification passages are aimed at the faithful. It all depends on pastoral context: "Is it not more important that we should hear both [themes] and respond to both as our situations and (dis)obedience of faith require?" (p. 141).

However, his *ultimate* conclusion is different. Despite his caveat against adopting an *ordo salutis* that artificially subordinates all other aspects of salvation under one overriding norm, Dunn suggests that Paul's theology is best understood in terms of Second Temple Judaism's "covenantal nomism," where, despite an initial, merely probationary justification by faith apart from works, eschatological salvation is *ultimately* made contingent on our faithful obedience.

In other words, Dunn effectively believes that warnings trump assurance. No matter how assured we may be, that assurance is illusory. The fact is, whatever "salvation" the believer currently has is forfeitable. Hence, warnings about failing to be finally justified will be effectively more important than passages dealing with assurance of probationary justification.

Dunn comes to this conclusion because, despite stressing the importance of taking all the different "metaphors of salvation" into account, he never considers the possibility that *salvation* itself may be plural. That is, he does not consider that many of the Pauline (and other New Testament) passages traditionally interpreted as addressing the conditions for attaining or losing salvation from hell are really speaking about salvation from temporal afflictions. Is it not possible (as I have argued) that the New Testament refers to different kinds of salvation and different divine judgments, each with its own conditions, subjects, assurances, and warnings?

The Only Type of Justification That Really Matters Is Still Future

Where does the idea of a future, final justification for believers come from? Dunn thinks he finds it in Paul. Under the heading, "The Two Justifications" (pp. 122–24), Dunn finds it *striking*, to use his word, that Paul believed that "justification ... can be experienced now" (p. 124). This is striking because the only justification that matters *eternally* is still future. After citing Romans 5:1 he makes this statement:

> Yet at the same time Paul retains the more basic thought of justification, acquittal as taking place at and awaiting final judgment, using the same verb "justify" (*dikaioō*) to look forward to that final judgment (Rom. 2:13; 3:20, 30) (p. 124).

Note that for Dunn the basic concept of justification is not having a present, once-for-all standing of being declared righteous by God. No present experience of justification guarantees a future experience of final justification. Only if the believer *perseveres* will his present justification become "acquittal ... at ... final judgment."

Dunn's view is a bit like being registered for a marathon. You can pick up your runner's packet, bib number, and timing chip, and even start the race, but you can't be certain that you'll finish. You have a chance at winning the finisher's medal, but no certainty about the outcome.

In such a case, of what practical value is present justification? Its main value seems to be knowing that you're at least *in the race* to win final justification.

Unfortunately, the verses Dunn appeals to in order to establish such a final judgment for believers teach no such thing. He cites Romans 2:5; 3:3–6; and 8:31–39 as implying "that the primary reference of the law-court imagery for Paul is the final judgment." But the expression *final judgment* does not occur in those texts.

For instance, Romans 2:5 refers to legalistic Jewish unbelievers who "are storing up for [themselves] wrath in the day of wrath and revelation of the righteous judgment of God." Believers are not in view here, nor are they found in 2:6–7 (which refers, hypothetically, to those who live sinless lives).

Romans 3:6 refers to God's judgment *of the world*, but not of *believers*. Rather, it refers to the judgment of *unbelievers* during the millennium, as suggested by the only other reference in Paul's letters to *judging the world*. In 1 Corinthians 6:2 Paul says, "Do you not know that the saints will judge the world?" During the millennium believers who rule with Christ will share in His judgment of the world. [42]

Finally, Romans 8:31–39 does not mention judgment at all. Rather, it refers to the present experience of believers who are being persecuted (vv. 35–36), and Paul assures them that such persecution cannot cut them off from God's love. In verses 33–34 Paul indicates that no one can bring a charge against God's chosen ones. Why not? Evidently because those who are justified are secure. Dunn admits as much when he speaks of "the wonderful assurance held out in Romans 8:31–39" (p. 122). But given his view, how can Dunn say this? If it was possible for someone who is justified *now* to lose their justification at some *future* judgment, then clearly it *would* be possible to bring a charge against God's chosen ones. It all depends on whether or not they persevere. In such a case, Paul's assurances would not be *wonderful*; rather, they would be *cruelly deceptive*.

Is Salvation Conditional?

Dunn has an entire section entitled, "The Conditionality of Salvation" (pp. 125–28). In that section he cites a number of passages in support of his view, but none actually refers to salvation from hell. Rather, they refer to physical death or spiritual ruin in this life (which are real possibilities for believers).

Among the verses he discusses are Romans 8:13 (which actually refers to *physical* death versus *physical* life), Galatians 6:8 (discussed in my article), Romans 14:15, 20 and 1 Corinthians 8:11 (referring to spiritually demoralizing or destroying a Christian brother), 1 Corinthians 3:17 (which refers to believers who destroy the local church being temporally judged and possibly dying), and 1 Corinthians 10:9–11 (which

---

42. See, e.g., Dwight Hunt, "First Corinthians," in *The Grace New Testament Commentary*, (Denton, TX: Grace Evangelical Society, 2010), 2:728.

refers to Numbers 21 and the physical death of many Jews in the wilderness). In my essay I discussed some of the other verses he cites (e.g., Rom. 8:17; 1 Cor. 9:27; Col. 1:21–23).

Clearly, salvation *from temporal afflictions* is conditional. But *eternal salvation* is another matter entirely.

Why Only a Passing Reference to Revelation 20:11 – 15?

There is only one passage in the Bible that explicitly refers to the Great White Throne Judgment and to what goes on there: Revelation 20:11–15. (It is inferred in Matthew 7:21–23, but little is said about it there.) I would have expected that someone writing about final judgment would discuss Revelation 20:11–15 carefully. Unfortunately, Dunn only mentions it in passing at the end of the article, and his conclusion about it is puzzling: "Here, too, therefore, we see another of these formulations that cannot easily be fitted into others on the same subject" (p. 140). We are not told what Revelation 20:11–15 means, and then Dunn simply moves on to his conclusion.

A careful reading of that passage reveals a significant detail: there are two types of books. There are books (plural) of deeds, and there is the book (singular) of life. And we are told that people are cast into the lake of fire, not because of what is in the books of deeds, but *because they were not found in the book of life* (Rev. 20:15). This implies that works will not be the issue at the Great White Throne Judgment in relation to eternal condemnation. The issue, rather, will be whether one is in the book of life. See the section in my essay on Revelation 20:11–15 for more details.

Assurance and Warning?

Dunn asks an excellent question: "How, to refer to an exquisitely poignant example, are we to integrate the wonderful assurance held out in Romans 8:31–39 with the sobering warning of 2 Corinthians 5:10?" (p. 122). Unfortunately, he does not answer that question at any point in his essay, but seems comfortable accepting an impossible tension. Believers are supposedly certain of their eternal destinies, while at the same time uncertain of their acquittal at the final judgment. In other words, we are at once sure *and* unsure of whether we will be with the Lord in His kingdom. That makes no sense and is spiritually destructive.

The problem here is that 2 Corinthians 5:10 does not refer to the Great White Throne Judgment, where unbelievers will be judged (Rev. 20:11–15). Rather, it refers to the Judgment Seat of Christ, where *we* (i.e., *believers*) will be judged to determine degrees of reward in the kingdom (cf. Rom. 14:10–12; 1 Cor. 3:10–15; 9:24–27; 1 John 2:28; 4:17–19). Indeed, the verses that immediately precede 2 Corinthians 5:9–11 and are part of the same paragraph (i.e., vv. 1–8) refer to the *certainty* that we will one day soon receive glorified bodies: "We *know* that if our earthly house is destroyed, we have a building from God ... eternal in the heavens" (v. 1, italics added). Paul goes on to say that "God ... has given us the Spirit *as a guarantee*" (v. 5, italics added). Whatever Paul means in verses 9–11 cannot contradict the assurance he just spoke of in verses 1–8.[43]

Temporal Salvation Is a Process; Eschatological Salvation Is Not

As suggested above, Dunn has a one-sided concept of salvation and fails to discuss the diversity of the various types of New Testament (or Old Testament) salvation. Like the other authors in this book, he views *salvation* as routinely referring to *deliverance from eternal condemnation*. But it doesn't inevitably meant that.

On multiple occasions Dunn refers to salvation, by which he means escaping eternal condemnation, as a *process*: "It is easy, then, to forget that for Paul 'salvation' is a process" (p. 125). "A disturbing feature of Paul's theology of the salvation process is the degree of hesitation and concern he shows that it might not be completed.... The disturbing feature is that Paul regarded the possibility of apostasy, of failing to persevere, as a *real* danger for his converts" (pp. 125–26, italics his).

While I heartily agree that Paul regarded failure to persevere as a real possibility, and while I recognize that salvation *from temporal difficulties* is a process, I do not agree that Paul saw *eschatological salvation* as a process that could be reversed and end in eternal condemnation. For Paul, the moment a person believed in Christ he or she was justified by God the Father and regenerated by God the Holy Spirit, and nothing can undo either justification or regeneration (cf. Rom. 4:4–5; 8:31–39; 11:6, 29; 1 Cor. 6:19–20; 2 Cor. 5:8; Eph. 2:8–9; Phil. 1:21–24;

---

43. See ibid., 2:784–86.

3:20–21; 4:3; Col. 3:3–4). And Paul's doctrine of justification by faith alone is complemented by John's doctrine of everlasting life, which is also by faith alone (John 3:16, 36; 5:24; 6:35, 39–40, 47; 11:25–26).

The reason why Dunn thinks that eschatological salvation is a process that can be aborted by failure to persevere is because he fails to distinguish between the condition for being regenerated (i.e., faith alone) and the condition for fruitful fellowship with God and for receiving eternal rewards in the messianic kingdom (i.e., faithful works).

The bottom line is, despite Dunn's appeal to God's gracious enablement of the believer that makes perseverance possible (e.g., p. 140, "Assuredly we can maintain that any good that the believer does derives entirely from God's grace and is only wrought by the Spirit's enabling"), Dunn cannot conceive of the fact that once a person believes in the Lord Jesus, he "has everlasting life, shall not come into judgment, but has passed from death into life" (John 5:24). But that is the essence of the Lord's teaching on the new birth. If the issue is eschatological salvation, the Baptists have it right: *once saved, always saved.*

THOMAS R. SCHREINER

Agreements

James Dunn is well known for his excellent scholarship, and his exegetical skills are on display in his essay. He doesn't restrict himself to only a portion of what Paul teaches but listens to the whole of the Pauline witness. He rightly observes that Paul proclaims the justification of the ungodly and the necessity of works for final vindication.

The extent of agreement between Dunn and me is significant since we both think good works are necessary for eternal life and final justification. Still, there are differences between us or places where further clarification might prove helpful. Dunn emphasizes the tension between justification by faith and judgment according to works. Similarly, he points to the promises that God will continue the good work he started (Phil. 1:6; cf. Rom. 8:35–39). At the same time, however, there are many warnings in Paul that threaten the readers with final judgment and destruction if they don't persevere. Dunn cautions us against a facile systematizing of Paul, for dogmatic systems tend to squeeze out part of what Paul says. He says it is better to live with the tension, to resist fitting everything into a logically neat package. We must let Scripture be Scripture and admit that there may be some contradictions in Paul and the scriptural witness.

It should be said at the outset that living with tension is better than the approach that eliminates part of the scriptural witness. Dunn is on to something here. We must beware of denying the necessity of good works for final salvation by appealing to texts that teach salvation is free. Wilkin falls into this error in his essay. As Dunn helps us see, there are too many texts that require good works for final salvation. The Bible repeatedly warns that if we deny Christ and repudiate the gospel by the way we live, we will be damned. It is far better to affirm both salvation by grace and the necessity of works than it is to deny either of these teachings. We have no right to truncate the biblical witness even if we can't see how it coheres.

Dunn maintains that we find a similar soteriological pattern in Second Temple Judaism and Pauline theology, picking up Sanders's phrase "covenant nomism." I wish this matter could be discussed more fully here, but the issue is complex and can't be examined adequately here. I would suggest that the pattern of religion in Second Temple Judaism was variegated, and hence some streams of Judaism focused more on grace while others emphasized human obedience. [44] Hence, there is both continuity and discontinuity with Paul.

Disagreements

Dunn Breaks the Tension Himself

Dunn's statements regarding the tensions in Paul and other biblical writers needs to be qualified and adjusted. Indeed, Dunn himself does not adhere to the tension fully. Some texts promise that believers will never fall away, that God will keep those whom he has chosen (e.g., John 6:37–40; 10:28–30; Rom. 8:28–39; Phil. 1:6; 1 Thess. 5:24). But other texts warn believers that if they turn away from the gospel they will face eschatological destruction. They won't enter the kingdom (e.g., John 15:6; Rom. 11:19–22; Gal. 6:8; Heb. 6:4–8; 10:26–31; 2 Pet. 1:5–11).

Dunn acknowledges the tension here, but it is striking and illuminating to see that he breaks the tension as well. Dunn admits we may be unable to explain how the Scriptures cohere rationally. But he also commits himself to one side of the tension when it comes to warnings and promises, for he argues that the warnings are meaningless if believers can't fall away. Apparently, then, the promises that God will keep believers so that they will certainly be saved are qualified and modified by the warnings. The warnings, for Dunn, are used to restrict the promises, for the promise that believers will be saved in the future may not come to pass after all. Dunn doesn't fully abide by his own words about holding onto the tension, for he provides a rational solution to

---

44. See *Justification and Variegated Nomism: The Complexities of Second Temple Judaism* (ed. D. A. Carson, Peter O'Brien, and Mark A. Seifrid; Grand Rapids: Baker, 2001), vol. 1.

the tension between the promises and warnings. The promises are conditioned by the warnings, so that the warnings receive priority rather than the promises.

The Relationship between Warnings and Promises

Space is lacking to explore this matter fully, but I would like to propose another solution. [45] I agree with Dunn that believers must persevere to the end to be saved and that good works are necessary for final vindication. At the same time, the promises are not conditioned by the warnings. Instead, the warnings and promises are complementary. They are corollaries and do not stand in competition with one another. The warnings function as the means by which the promises are secured. In other words, the warnings are always effective for the elect and for those who are justified. The immediate objection is that such a view makes the warnings superfluous, for the elect always heed the warnings. But such an objection misses the mark, for it reads the warnings abstractly, as if the promises are secured apart from the warnings!

But is such a view of the warnings biblical? Two examples will have to suffice. In Acts 27 Paul receives the promise that every single person on the storm-tossed ship will live. Not a single one will die (27:22 – 26). Indeed, Paul emphasizes that there are no exceptions. The promise isn't merely that *most* will live but that *all* will live. Still, the promise does not preclude the need for warning. Paul warns immediately after receiving the promise that if the sailors are allowed to escape on the smaller boat, no one will live (27:31). Why does Paul give a warning after receiving the promise that all will live? Apparently Paul (and Luke!) didn't believe that the promise precluded the need for the warning to the sailors. Indeed, the warning was one of the means by which the promise was secured.

The promise and warning in the above text refers to physical deliverance. In Mark 13, however, the situation is quite different. Jesus warns his disciples repeatedly to be alert and to stand watch. False christs and prophets will arise, and they will attempt to lead disciples astray, and so

---

45. For a further development of what is said here, see Thomas R. Schreiner and Ardel B. Caneday, *The Race Set before Us: A Biblical Theology of Perseverance and Assurance* (Downers Grove: InterVarsity Press, 2001); Thomas R. Schreiner, *Run to Win the Prize: Perseverance in the New Testament* (Wheaton: Crossway; 2010).

they must be on guard (13:21–23, 33–37). If anyone embraces a false christ, they will not receive eternal life. Jesus warns his disciples in the strongest possible terms not to be deceived. But notice in 13:22 that Jesus says that it is not possible for the elect to be led astray! They will not embrace a false christ. Such a state of affairs is impossible for the elect, and yet he warns them not be led astray. Mark doesn't draw the conclusion that the elect don't need warnings since it is impossible for them to believe in false christs. I would suggest that he believed that the warnings were a means by which the promise is secured for the elect. The warnings and the promises are complementary, not contradictory, in the lives of those God has chosen.

But what about those who fall away? Isn't it true that some do turn away from the Lord? So doesn't that show apostasy is possible? Certainly some fall away, but notice that the New Testament, when it considers retrospectively those who fall away, says that they were never truly Christians. Consider here 1 John 2:19, "They went out from us, but they did not really belong to us. For if they had belonged to us, they would have remained with us; but their going showed that none of them belonged to us" (NIV). John clarifies that those who fell away were never truly part of the community. Perseverance is the mark of those who are genuine Christians, and true believers heed the warnings and persevere to the end.

The words of Jesus in Matthew 7:21–23 confirm what is said here. We might think that those who acted in Jesus' name by doing miracles, casting out demons, and prophesying and then turned toward evil had lost a salvation they once had. But notice what Jesus says: "I never knew you" (7:23). He doesn't say he knew them once and no longer does. Quite the contrary. Even though they appeared to belong to Jesus, they were actually never part of God's people (cf. also 1 Cor. 11:19; 2 Tim. 2:18–21).

Dunn and I agree that good works and perseverance are necessary for salvation, and that is a significant agreement, but we disagree on whether genuine believers can apostatize. I argue that the promises given to the elect will never be revoked, that those who truly belong to God will never fall away. The warnings aren't robbed of their significance, for only those who heed the warnings will persevere. But what we find in the Scriptures is that the elect always heed the warnings, and those who don't heed them reveal that they never belonged to God in the first place.

Are There Contradictions?

Dunn also makes another point in referring to the tension between the promises and the threats in Scripture. He suggests that we might have to accept that the Scriptures are actually contradictory as well. The reason we can't explain fully the tension between justification by faith and judgment according to works may be due to an unsolvable contradiction.

Dunn is nervous about dogmatic theology that levels the rough edges of Scripture. In a sense I agree. It is better to preserve tension instead of cancelling out an aspect of the biblical witness. Still, none of us can escape systematics and philosophy. To say that Scripture has contradictions betrays a philosophical and theological worldview as well. There are no neutral or objective players in the game. I think it accords better with the historic Christian tradition and the biblical witness to speak of mysteries (if we can't solve the problem rationally) instead of contradictions. Christians throughout history have acknowledged that the teaching on Jesus' humanity and deity, the doctrine of the Trinity, and the relationship between the soul and the body are mysteries that exceed our understanding. Many have posited the same when it comes to divine sovereignty and human responsibility.

I have suggested above, of course, an explanation that indicates how the warnings and the promises are not contradictory. I also suggested in my essay that works are the evidence instead of the basis of our right-standing with God. So, I am not appealing to mystery at this point. But if one rejects such solutions, it fits better with the biblical witness and the tradition of Christian theology to posit mystery instead of contradiction. The witness of Christian tradition shouldn't be dismissed lightly, for the notion that contradictions exist in the Scriptures is a product of historical-critical study (which has its own philosophical and theological standpoint), and I think it is fair to say that the Christian faith has not flourished in cultures where the historical-critical method has become mainstream.[46]

---

46. I am speaking of historical-critical study that adopts the view that contradictions actually exist in the biblical text. I am not opposed to historical-critical study that is employed with what I would call a Christian worldview.

Some Final Comments

Let me close my response by responding more briefly to some issues raised by Dunn. I would argue that righteousness is forensic rather than transformative, and yet Dunn is surely right in his main contention. When we put Paul's theology together, a wedge should not be driven between the forensic and the transformative, though the forensic is the basis of the transformative.

It also seems that Dunn misunderstands what is typically called monergism in Reformed theology. He says that Philippians 2:12–13 is synergistic rather than monergistic, presumably because it calls on believers to work out their salvation. Monergism in the Reformed tradition, however, has never denied that human beings must choose and act. Similarly, he suggests that monergists believe that since the law is fulfilled through the Spirit, no effort is required of believers. Again, he misconstrues monergism. Instead, 2:12–13 perfectly captures what monergists believe. Human beings must act and choose, but ultimately what they choose and act is attributed to God. He causes them to will and to work for his own good pleasure.

In other words, the ultimacy of God's work does not cancel out the proximate will of human beings or the authenticity and reality of human choices and decisions. God's work is not understood as cancelling out the reality of human work, nor is human responsibility dissolved, as Dunn suggests. Perhaps what Dunn writes reflects his experience of the Reformed tradition growing up, but it does not reflect the theological teaching of a John Calvin, John Owen, or J. I. Packer. A tension between divine sovereignty and human responsibility is characteristic of Reformed theology. Many Reformed thinkers, starting with Calvin, acknowledge that the relationship between divine sovereignty and human responsibility is ultimately mysterious. They do not "remove all responsibility from the believer to do good," as Dunn suggests.

Dunn refers to Romans 2:6–11 and rightly affirms judgment by works, but he also finds it significant that the Spirit is not mentioned here. But such a conclusion cuts off 2:6–11 from the rest of Romans, and even the remainder of Paul's argument in Romans 2. In 2:26–29 Paul explains that the obedience of the Gentiles stems from the work of the Spirit. The obedience described in 2:6–11 should not be sundered from the obedience produced by the Spirit in 2:26–29.

Conclusion

I have raised a few questions about Dunn's essay, but the fundamental claim in his essay is on target. Eternal life and final judgment are according to works. This theme can't be waived out of the New Testament. Grace does lead to transformation, though not perfection, in the lives of believers. Good works are necessary for salvation, though they are the necessary evidence and fruit of new life, not the basis for salvation.

RESPONSE TO JAMES D. G. DUNN

MICHAEL P. BARBER

In his famous work *On Christian Doctrine*, Augustine cautions his readers about foisting artificial explanations on obscure passages in Scripture. He writes, "It is better even to be in bondage to unknown but useful signs than, by interpreting them wrongly, to draw the neck from under the yoke of bondage only to insert it in the coils of error." [47] James Dunn makes a similar case in his essay. Faced with seemingly contradictory teachings in the letters of Paul, Dunn insists that we must avoid "the naively satisfying device that blends one into the other in a way that diminishes the force of one or other, the ignoring of the one in order to give the other the emphasis that we think it deserves" (Dunn, p. 141). I heartily concur.

I consider it a distinct honor to have the opportunity to respond to Dunn here, a scholar whose work I have long admired and from which I have learned a great deal. Although I cannot comment on every aspect of his presentation, I would like to focus on the tension he identifies in Paul's teaching regarding the role of works. To sum up Dunn's analysis, Paul's letters affirm two seemingly conflicting ideas: (1) justification is by faith apart from works (e.g., Rom 4:4–5; Eph 2:8) and (2) God will judge believers on the basis of their works (e.g., Rom 2:6–11, 13; 2 Cor 5:10–11).

While I certainly agree that we cannot reconcile every apparent discrepancy in Scripture, I humbly submit that these two aspects of Paul's teaching regarding the role of works are not necessarily hopelessly at odds. In my contribution here, I offer a Catholic explanation of Paul's message. Here I would like to explain why I believe this approach actually complements Dunn's exegesis and avoids the pitfalls he speaks about.

Following Dunn's lead, I will simply focus on Paul. I recognize that my own essay draws from various books of the New Testament and that

---

47. Augustine, *On Christian Doctrine*, 3.9.13 (NPNF1 2:560).

this might raise the objection that the approach I have proposed fails to pay due attention to the unique theological distinctiveness of each New Testament writer. I hope this reply, which concentrates on Dunn's analysis of Paul, will help alleviate such concerns.

Grace as Empowerment

In his article, Dunn turns to a text that is crucial for understanding Paul's view of good works, Philippians 2:12–13: "Therefore, my beloved, as you have always obeyed, so now, not only as in my presence but much more in my absence, *work out your own salvation with fear and trembling; for God is at work in you*" (emphasis added).

As Dunn observes, some scholars, pointing to passages such as Galatians 2:20 ("it is no longer I who live, but Christ who lives in me"), have insisted on a monergistic reading of Paul that plays down the importance of human effort. Yet, as he shows, Paul is *not* advocating a monergistic vision. Dunn writes, "To use Galatians 2:20 to remove all responsibility from the believer for any good that he or she does, since it is the indwelling Christ who does it ... is to eliminate the 'I' as a responsible person" (Dunn, p. 134). I hope my treatment of Galatians 2 in this volume will not be misconstrued as falling prey to this tendency. Dunn raises an important point here. As he notices, in Paul's teaching in Philippians 2 there are *two* agents involved, both God ("at work in you") *and* the believer ("work out your own salvation").

Moreover, as Dunn mentions, a growing number of scholars are now challenging the long-standing presupposition that divine and human agency should be seen in terms of competing categories in the Old Testament and Second Temple literature.[48] Prophetic texts hold both concepts in unison so that "God's saving agency perpetually works in the newly created moral agent" (cf. e.g., Jer. 32:39)."[49] For instance, God explains in Ezekiel, "I will put my spirit within you, and *cause you to walk in my statutes and be careful to observe my ordinances*" (Ezek. 36:27, emphasis added). Such passages reveal that Israel will learn to walk in

---

48. See, e.g., Simon Gathercole, *Where Is Boasting? Early Jewish Soteriology and Paul's Response in Romans 1–5* (Grand Rapids: Eerdmans, 2002), 263–64; Kyle B. Wells, "Grace, Obedience, and the Hermeneutics of Agency: Paul and His Jewish Contemporaries on the Transformation of the Heart" (PhD diss., Durham University, 2010).

49. Wells, "Grace," 41.

the Lord's ways, but only with his help. The presence of synergistic language in Paul is thus not surprising.

In sum, Paul does tell believers to "work out your own salvation," but not because he thinks they can earn it merely on their own power. In his mind, believers are truly capable of doing works that are salvific. Yet this is not Pelagianism. Believers only have this capacity because they have been empowered by God's grace. John M. G. Barclay therefore speaks of Paul's view of grace in terms of "empowerment"[50] and "energism."[51]

This explains Paul's emphasis on the necessity of works for salvation in Romans 2. In fact, Paul even insists that works are related to justification: "the doers of the law will be justified" (Rom 2:13). As Keener has shown, the language of Romans 2 draws on the language used later in the book to describe what Christians are enabled to do by Christ.[52]

Justification apart from Works

In Romans 4, Paul insists justification is given not as a "wage" (*misthos*) to one who has faith but as a gift. However, earlier in Romans, Paul speaks of God's "repaying" (*apodidōmi*, 2:6) each one according to their works, also using language of remuneration.[53] To resolve the apparent tension between these two passages, some have made the case that Romans 2 represents a hypothetical or rhetorical strategy that does not authentically represent Paul's theology.[54]

Not only are such readings implausible;[55] they are unnecessary. As we have seen from Philippians 2, Paul teaches that good works do in fact play a determinative role in one's salvation (Phil. 2:12; cf. also 2 Cor. 5:10; Col. 3:23–25), with the understanding that salvific works

---

50. John M. G. Barclay, "Grace and the Transformation of Agency," in *Redefining First-Century Jewish and Christian Identities* (eds. Fabian E. Udoh et al.; South Bend, IN: University of Notre Dame Press, 2008), 384 [372–89].

51. Ibid., 388 n. 38.

52. Craig S. Keener, *Romans* (Eugene, OR: Wipf and Stock, 2009), 44–45.

53. Nathan Eubank explains the economic background of this language using BDAG, in "The Wages of Righteousness: The Economy of Heaven in the Gospel According to Matthew" (PhD diss., Duke University, 2012), 74.

54. Most recently, see Douglas A. Campbell, *The Deliverance of God: An Apocalyptic Rereading of Justification in Paul* (Grand Rapids: Eerdmans, 2009).

55. See, e.g., Michael J. Gorman, "Douglas Campbell's *The Deliverance of God*: A Review by a Friendly Critic," *JSPL* 1/1 (2011): 99–107.

are only possible through the indwelling of the Spirit (Phil. 2:13). One should not therefore pit Romans 4 against Romans 2.

Likewise, at first glance, it might seem that Paul's teaching that the "doers of the law will be justified" (Rom 2:13) is irreconcilable with his insistence that one is "justified by faith apart from works of law" (3:28). However, in light of Dunn's treatment, a possible solution presents itself.

Dunn does a masterful job highlighting the way salvation is described by Paul as not simply a discrete event, but as a "process" (see the section, "Beginning and Completing," pp. 124–25). I would like to suggest that this insight allows us to make sense of Paul's teaching on the role of works.

It seems to me that when Paul explains that a person is justified by faith and not by "works of law" (e.g., Rom. 3:28; Gal. 3:10), he is speaking of the *initial* grace of justification. Indeed, his specific language of "works of law" (*erga nomou*) appears to be situated within contexts dealing with debates about the value of circumcision, which seems to have been understood as the *entry* point into the covenant (cf. Gal. 5:3; also Sir. 44:19–20). Circumcision identifies who is "in" the people of God.[56] Paul insists that things such as circumcision do not merit justification. In Romans, therefore, Paul turns to Genesis 15:6 to point out that Abraham was justified by faith *prior* to his being circumcised in Genesis 17 (Rom. 4:10). So while his opponents hold that God's blessing is only on the circumcised (3:9), Paul's point is that the inception point into the life of blessing (i.e., justification) comes by faith.

Before moving on, I must make an important point. In identifying "works of the law" with circumcision, some might complain that I have too narrowly defined its meaning. Clearly the language involves *more* than merely circumcision.[57] Yet — and this is key — the controversy over what its broader meaning entails is ultimately irrelevant to my main argument. Paul's point in Romans and Galatians is that the initial

---

56. See, e.g., James D. G. Dunn, *The Theology of Paul the Apostle* (Grand Rapids: Eerdmans, 1998), 356, 360; Thomas R. Schreiner, *The Law and Its Fulfillment* (Grand Rapids: Baker, 1993), 99.

57. Particularly helpful, at least for the meaning of the term in Galatians, is Scott W. Hahn, *Kinship by Covenant* (AYBRL; New Haven, CT: Yale University Press, 2009), 238–77. Hahn shows that the terminology has Deuteronomic significance.

grace of justification comes through faith.[58] I only highlight the link between "works of the law" and circumcision to underscore one thing: Paul's statements concerning justification by faith apart from "works of law" seem situated within contexts where there are questions about what constitutes entry into the life of blessing (= justification).

The Power at Work within Us

The initial grace of justification, then, is a gift, not dependent on works (Rom 4:4–5; 9:32; etc.). This gift enables the Christian to perform works that result from God's operative power in the believer. By virtue of their source in God, these works have surpassing value. That this represents Pauline thought is clear from Ephesians 2:8–10:

> For by grace you have been saved through faith; and this is not your own doing, it is the gift of God—not because of works, lest any man should boast. For we are his workmanship, created in Christ Jesus for good works, which God prepared beforehand, that we should walk in them.

One is *first* saved by grace alone. Yet God's grace is given to believers to empower them to do good works that far exceed what they would otherwise be capable of on the basis of human effort alone. Thus, in the following chapter, Paul gives glory "to him who by *the power at work within us* is able to do *far more abundantly than all that we ask or think*" (Eph. 3:20, emphasis added). The works the believer performs in union with Christ are therefore capable of doing far more than *all* we ask or think—they even have salvific value! That is why Paul can tell the Philippians that they must "work out their own salvation."

I think this solution to the problem of Paul's seemingly conflicting statements on the role of works fully preserves both dimensions of his teaching. Dunn is right that we must not impose readings on Paul that neatly solve apparent conflicts by muting one aspect of his message in favor of another. The Catholic view does not do that. Rather, it fully

---

58. Notably, in his commentary on Galatians, Aquinas argues that "works of the law" can thus be interpreted as referring to the whole law, "because sin is not removed nor anyone justified in the sight of God by them, but by the habit of faith vivified by charity." Thomas Aquinas, *Commentary on Saint Paul's Epistle to the Galatians* (trans. F. R. Larcher, O.P.; Albany: Magi, 1966), 80.

reflects his rich understanding of grace, namely, that it is both a free gift that brings about our salvation (Rom. 11:6; Eph. 2:8–9) and that it is empowerment to become "God's fellow workers" (1 Cor. 3:9; cf. 2 Cor. 6:1).

A CATHOLIC PERSPECTIVE: OUR WORKS ARE MERITORIOUS AT THE FINAL JUDGMENT BECAUSE OF OUR UNION WITH CHRIST BY GRACE

MICHAEL P. BARBER

The charity of Christ is the source in us of all our merits before God. Grace, by uniting us to Christ in active love, ensures the supernatural quality of our acts and consequently their merit before God and before men. *The saints have always had a lively awareness that their merits were pure grace.*
—Catechism of the Catholic Church, no. 2011[1]

The above quotation from the *Catechism of the Catholic Church* (henceforth, "the *Catechism*"), the official compendium of all of the Church's teachings,[2] beautifully summarizes the Catholic understanding of salvation and the role of works at the last judgment.[3] I

---

1. Cited from *Catechism of the Catholic Church* (2nd ed.; Vatican: Libreria Editrice Vaticana, 1997), 487 (italics added). In this article, when quoting the *Catechism*, I will usually cite paragraph numbers instead of page numbers, as is conventional.

2. At the time of its release, John Paul II affirmed that the *Catechism* faithfully and authoritatively presents the teaching of the Catholic Church: "I declare it to be a sure norm for teaching the faith and thus a valid and legitimate instrument for ecclesial communion." Apostolic Constitution, *Fidei Depositum*, 11 October 1992 (printed as a dedicatory letter in the *Catechism of the Catholic Church* [2nd ed.], 5).

3. Catholics believe that one is both judged at death ("particular judgment"; cf., e.g., Heb. 9:27)—thus allowing the believer to enter into his heavenly reward and be "with Christ" immediately (2 Cor. 5:8; Phil. 1:23; Heb. 12:23)—as well as at the end of history ("final judgment"; cf., e.g., Matt. 25:31–46; John 5:28–29). In Catholic teaching the verdict rendered at the final judgment is no different from that rendered at the particular judgment. For a fuller discussion, see *Catechism*, nos. 1021–22, 1038–41.

suspect that it may surprise some non-Catholic Christians. It obviously does not cohere with the description of Catholic soteriology many are familiar with, namely, a works-righteousness, legalistic perspective. Indeed, such a charge represents a crass mischaracterization of Catholic teaching.[4]

Of course, such distortions can be found on both sides. I know this from personal experience. As a Catholic I chose to study theology at non-Catholic institutions in part to better understand my separated brothers and sisters in Christ. I spent most of my academic career as a student learning from and with Protestants, earning a BA degree in Theology and Philosophy from Azusa Pacific University and a PhD in Theology from Fuller Theological Seminary.

I can honestly say that studying at these institutions, as a Catholic, was an overwhelmingly positive experience. I had the privilege of learning from such godly and eminent scholars as Colin Brown, John Goldingay, and Seyoon Kim. I thank God continually not only for all they taught me, but for their personal witness of faith in Jesus Christ, which had a deep impact on my own life.

I offer this essay as an irenic attempt to engage in dialogue. I hope to show here that the Catholic view of good works at the final judgment seeks to explain the entirety of the biblical witness without minimizing either passages that discuss the priority of God's grace or texts highlighting the role attributed to good works. While I do not expect all the contributors of this volume to agree with it (I expect hearty disagreement, in fact), I hope to highlight one aspect of the Catholic understanding that often gets overlooked or misrepresented — the unlimited power of God's grace. As I will show, at its root, the Catholic view of works affirms Jesus' teaching that "with God all things are possible" (Matt. 19:26),[5] including his ability to render our works meritorious.

---

4. This article seeks to expound the official teaching of the Catholic Church. Therefore I will refer to the *Catechism* and other official Church documents. One might find a theologian/writer who, identifying himself as Catholic, takes a different view than that taught by the magisterial documents of the Church itself. However, to label such divergent opinions as "Catholic" is probably not helpful since such writers' affiliation with the Catholic Church seems to play a negligible role in the formulation of their position.

5. Unless otherwise noted, all English translations of biblical texts are taken from the RSV. Any italics in biblical quotes are added.

Salvation and the Final Judgment

To properly understand the function of good works at the final judgment it is necessary to take a step back and look at the larger question of what constitutes "salvation." Though it is impossible here to offer a detailed look at the various ways the New Testament speaks of salvation,[6] what should be pointed out is that, as a growing number of scholars have noted, salvation in Christ is described as a past, present, and future reality.[7] Salvation is something that believers have already experienced. In Titus we read that Christ "*saved* us [*esōsen*]" (Titus 3:5; cf., e.g., also Rom. 8:24).[8] Yet Paul also describes salvation in terms of an ongoing process: "to us who are *being* saved [*sōzomenois*]" (1 Cor. 1:18). Similarly, we read in Acts 2:47, "the Lord added to their number day by day those who were *being* saved [*sōzomenous*]." In addition, the New Testament describes salvation as a future reality; believers "*will* be saved [*sōthēsetai*]" (John 10:9; Acts 15:11; Rom. 10:13; 1 Cor. 3:15; 1 Tim. 2:15).

We should also recognize that Scripture speaks about salvation in various words and phrases. Salvation is understood in terms of "justification," "redemption," "entering the kingdom," "eternal life," and so on. As Schreiner and Caneday have ably shown, many of these ideas are also spoken of as both past, present, and future realities.[9] Thus "justification," a concept with clear soteriological meaning in the New Testament (e.g., Rom. 5:9; 10:10; Titus 3:5 – 7), can be identified as something that has already occurred in the life of the believer (e.g., 1 Cor. 6:11) as well as taking place in the future (e.g., Matt. 12:36; Rom. 2:12 – 13).

Thus, it should be clear that, despite the way many Christians speak about it, salvation is not simply a "past event." Salvation is something that is experienced in the here and now. As Peter explains, baptism "now saves you" (1 Pet. 3:21). Paul explains, "you were washed, you

---

6. Although I do not agree with every aspect of his treatment, I must commend the extremely helpful study of this topic by Alan P. Stanley, *Did Jesus Teach Salvation by Works?: The Role of Works in Salvation in the Synoptic Gospels* (ETSMS 4; Eugene, OR: Pickwick, 2006), esp. 134–65.

7. See ibid., 134–65; idem, *Salvation Is More Complicated Than You Think: A Study On the Teachings of Jesus* (Downers Grove, IL: InterVarsity Press, 2007), 45–57; Thomas R. Schreiner and Ardel B. Caneday, *The Race Set before Us: A Biblical Theology of Perseverance and Assurance* (Downers Grove, IL: InterVarsity Press, 2001), 46–86.

8. Please note that throughout this essay, any italics in the Scripture passages have been added; they are not in the RSV.

9. Schreiner and Caneday, *The Race Set before Us*, 46–86.

were sanctified, you were justified" (1 Cor. 6:11). However salvation *also* occurs in the future. Thus some Protestant scholars describe salvation in terms of a pilgrimage (Stanley) [10] or a race to be won (Schreiner, Caneday). [11] A Catholic understanding would agree with this essential outlook, though perhaps our view would be better summed up with another image: spiritual maturation, i.e., "growing up." I will explain this in greater detail below.

For our purposes here, it is especially important to observe that language tied to salvation is linked to God's judgment and Christ's second coming.

- "I tell you, on the day of judgment men will render account for every careless word they utter; for by your words you *will be justified* [*dikaiōthēsē*], and by your words you will be condemned [*katadikasthēsē*]." (Matt. 12:36–37)
- "For it is not the hearers of the law who are righteous before God, but the doers of the law who *will be justified* [*dikaiōthēsontai*]." (Rom. 2:13)
- "And just as it is appointed for men to die once, and after that comes *judgment*, so Christ, having been offered once to bear the sins of many, *will appear a second time,* not to deal with sin but *to save* [*sōtērian*] those who are eagerly waiting for him." (Heb. 9:27–28).

To understand the role of works at the final judgment, therefore, involves understanding the nature of salvation itself.

Salvation in Christ

Although the New Testament talks about many different aspects of salvation ("justification," "sanctification," "redemption," "forgiveness," etc.), at its center New Testament soteriology is christological: salvation comes *in Christ*. [12] The question of what constitutes salvation leads us to Christ him-

---

10. Stanley, *Did Jesus Teach Salvation by Works?* 326.

11. Schreiner and Caneday, *The Race Set before Us,* 46–86.

12. See Pope Benedict XVI, *St. Paul* (San Francisco, CA: Ignatius), 25: "Christianity is not a new philosophy or a new morality. We are only Christians if we encounter Christ.... Only in this personal relationship with Christ, only in this encounter with the Risen One do we truly become Christians."

self. We are "justified," that is, we are declared/made righteous, because Christ is "our righteousness" (1 Cor. 1:30). Because we are united to him, we are righteous. He is the standard of salvation. To be saved is nothing less than to be "conformed to the image of [God's] Son" (Rom. 8:29).

The christological center of soteriology can easily be overlooked. Salvation is often understood in minimalistic terms. Many portray salvation in terms of what Christ has saved us *from*, neglecting what he has saved us *for*. Thus it is not unusual to hear popular descriptions of salvation in Christ as involving little more than "fire insurance" — that is, deliverance from the fires of hell. Yet salvation in the New Testament involves more than merely preservation from the torments of damnation. Ultimately, salvation involves communion with God in Christ.

While there has been much focus on Paul's discussion of "justification" — and rightly so — perhaps we would do well to spend time carefully reflecting on the way Paul describes his ultimate hope in Philippians: "that I may gain Christ" (Phil. 3:8). Similarly overlooked is 2 Peter's explanation of the goal of salvation: that we might "become partakers of the divine nature" (2 Pet. 1:4). Indeed, Ephesians reminds us that God's ultimate purpose is "to unite all things in [Christ], things in heaven and things on earth" (Eph. 1:10).

Salvation is nothing less than union with the triune God in Christ. As Jesus explains in the gospel of John, "If a man loves me, he will keep my word, and my Father will love him, and we will come to him and make our home with him" (John 14:23). Paul likewise explains, "I have been crucified with Christ; it is no longer I who live, but Christ who lives in me" (Gal. 2:20).

Grace and Salvation

In Catholic theology, union with the triune God in Christ is the result of God's grace. Salvation is given to us as a free gift. This is the clear testimony of Scripture: "By grace you have been saved through faith; and this is not your own doing, it is the gift of God — not because of works, lest any man should boast" (Eph. 2:8–9; cf. Rom. 11:6; 2 Tim. 1:9; Titus 3:5).

I must reiterate that Catholic teaching joyfully receives this aspect of Scripture's testimony. The quote from the *Catechism* that I started this essay with should make it clear that Catholic teaching rejects works-righteousness: "*The saints have always had a lively awareness that their merits were pure grace.*" The *Catechism* even cites Thérèse of Lisieux's view as representative of magisterial Catholic teaching: "*I do not want to lay up merits for heaven....* In the evening of this life, I shall appear before you with empty hands" (*Catechism* no. 2011).

Indeed, this section of the *Catechism* goes on to draw from the Council of Trent, which insisted on this point:

- "... in adults the beginning of that justification must proceed from the predisposing grace of God through Jesus Christ, that is, from His vocation, whereby, *without any merits on their part*, they are called." (Council of Trent, Session 6, ch. 5) [13]
- "... we are therefore said to be justified gratuitously, because *none of those things that precede justification, whether faith or works, merit the grace of justification.* For, if by grace, *it is not now by works*, otherwise, as the Apostle says, grace is no more grace" [cf. Rom 11:6]. (Council of Trent, Session 6, ch. 8) [14]

Some might make the case that the *Catechism's* teaching on the importance of grace represents a shift resulting from twentieth-century ecumenical dialogue. However, as these quotes from Trent reveal, such a view would be historically inaccurate. The Catholic teaching has always insisted that we are saved by grace. On this point Catholics and Protestants agree. To cite another passage from the *Catechism*: "Our justification comes from the grace of God. Grace is *favor*, the free and undeserved help that God gives us to respond to his call to become children of God, adoptive sons, partakers of the divine nature and of eternal life." [15]

Judgment according to Works

Catholics affirm that salvation is the result of God's free gift. Yet Catholic teaching also recognizes that there are passages in Scripture that describe good works as a criterion for salvation. In particular, over and over again, Scripture insists that God will judge each person according to his or her *works*:

---

13. Cited from H. J. Schroeder, *The Canons and Decrees of the Council of Trent* (St. Louis: Herder, 1941), 31.

14. Cited from ibid., 35.

15. *Catechism*, no. 1996.

- "For the Son of man is to come with his angels in the glory of his Father, and then he will repay every man *for what he has done*." (Matt. 16:27)
- "For he will render to every man *according to his works*." (Rom. 2:6)
- "For we must all appear before the judgment seat of Christ, so that each one may receive good or evil, *according to what he has done in the body*." (2 Cor. 5:10)
- "And if you invoke as Father him who judges each one impartially *according to his deeds*, conduct yourselves with fear throughout the time of your exile." (1 Pet. 1:17)
- "I am he who searches mind and heart, and I will give to each of you *as your works deserve*." (Rev. 2:23)
- "And the dead were judged by what was written in the books, *by what they had done*." (Rev. 20:12)
- "Behold, I am coming soon, bringing my recompense, to repay every one *for what he has done*." (Rev. 22:12)

The idea can even be traced into the Old Testament. Psalm 62 declares: "For thou dost requite a man *according to his work*" (Ps. 62:12; cf. Prov. 24:12).[16]

That works will be the *essential criterion* of judgment on the last day is clearly affirmed in Matthew 25:34–46.[17]

Then the King will say to those at his right hand, "Come, O blessed of my Father, inherit the kingdom prepared for you from the foundation of the world; for I was hungry and you gave me food, I was thirsty and you gave me drink, I was a stranger and you welcomed me, I was naked and you clothed me, I was sick and you visited me, I was in prison and you came to me."... Then he will say to those

---

16. For a full study of this passage and its influence on the New Testament texts explored below, see Kyoung-Shik Kim, *God Will Judge Each One according to Works: Judgment according to Works and Psalm 62 in Early Judaism and the New Testament* (BZNW 178; ed. James D. G. Dunn et al.; Berlin: de Gruyter, 2011).

17. Some dispensationalist writers have argued that the scene does not describe the final judgment but the judgment of nations prior to the millennium. See, e.g., Stanley D. Toussaint, *Behold the King: A Study of Matthew* (Portland, OR: Multnomah, 1980), 288–89; John F. Walvoord, *Matthew: Thy Kingdom Come* (Chicago: Moody Press, 1974), 202. Yet this clearly goes beyond the text. In fact, the imagery here patently points to the scene of the eschatological judgment. See D. A. Carson, "Matthew," *EBC* (ed. Tremper Longman III and David E. Garland; Grand Rapids: Zondervan, 2010), 585–87; David L. Turner, *Matthew* (BECNT; eds. Robert W. Yarbrough and Robert H. Stein; Grand Rapids: Baker, 2008), 604–5.

at his left hand, "Depart from me, you cursed, into the eternal fire prepared for the devil and his angels; for I was hungry and you gave me no food...." And they will go away into eternal punishment, but the righteous into eternal life.

Those welcomed into the kingdom are those who have performed works of mercy. Those who have not performed such works "go away into eternal punishment." It is the presence or absence of works that determines one's future destiny.

Interpreters have tried to find ways around this conclusion. Some have distinguished between salvation and rewards, arguing that such passages refer to benefits other than salvation itself.[18] I shall not add anything more here to what I say in my response to Robert Wilkin's essay in this volume.[19] Suffice it to say, elsewhere in Matthew the idea of "reward" is synonymous with entering the kingdom of heaven (cf. Matt. 5:46–47 with 5:20).[20] The latter idea undoubtedly points to ultimate salvation. As Dale Allison has demonstrated, Jesus' teachings in the Gospels regarding entering the "kingdom of God" and "eternal life" are best understood as expressions of Jewish hopes regarding the ultimate state of the righteous.[21] The imagery of reward therefore is best viewed as pertaining to salvation itself.

Others suggest that the deeds of the righteous are only the fruit of faith and, therefore, are not really what determine their salvation (see the essay by Tom Schreiner in this volume).[22] Others go a little further in their conclusions (see the essay by James D. G. Dunn). Nixon writes that the small acts of kindness "have not been remembered as meritorious by the righteous (presumably they are the outcome of a living

18. See, e.g., Joseph C. Dillow, *The Reign of the Servant Kings: A Study of Eternal Security and the Final Significance of Man* (Miami: Schoettle, 1992); Robert N. Wilkin, *The Road to Reward: Living Today in Light of Tomorrow* (Irving, TX: Grace Evangelical Society, 2003).

19. See also Craig L. Blomberg, "Degrees of Reward in the Kingdom of Heaven?" *JETS* 35 (1992): 159–72.

20. See the fine treatment in Stanley, *Did Jesus Teach Salvation by Works?* 273–77.

21. See Dale Allison, *Constructing Jesus: Memory, Imagination, and History* (Grand Rapids: Baker, 2010), 188–99. On the unique use of "kingdom of heaven" as an expression of the heavenly realm, see Jonathan T. Pennington, *Heaven and Earth in the Gospel of Matthew*, NovTSup 126; Leiden: Brill, 2007).

22. See e.g., John Calvin, *A Harmony of the Gospels: Matthew, Mark, and Luke* (eds. D. W. Torrance and T. F. Torrance; trans. A. W. Morrison and T. H. L. Parker; Grand Rapids: Eerdmans, 1972), 3:115–16, who makes the case that the "reward" is not merited by good deeds but is ultimately the result of God's grace.

faith and not the basis of acceptance)."[23] This reading may cohere with Protestant tradition, but it is not derived directly from the text itself.

A more sophisticated approach involves recognizing that those who are saved enter the kingdom not simply because of what they did but for whom they did it: "Truly, I say to you, as you did it to one of the least of these my brethren, you did it to me" (Matt. 25:40; cf. 25:45). The case is made that "the least of these my brethren" refers to disciples, who elsewhere in Matthew are identified as Jesus' brothers and sisters (12:46–50; 28:10).[24] Moreover, in Matthew 10, the way people treat the disciples will be a sign of their reception or rejection of the gospel (10:11–14) and ultimately seal their fate "on the day of judgment" (10:15). Thus in the scene described in Matthew 25:31–46, the works of mercy performed are ultimately an expression of how the righteous embrace the gospel.[25]

This reading is compelling. It beautifully ties together different threads of the gospel. Nonetheless, just because the works of mercy performed by the righteous are likely the result of their embrace of the gospel, to conclude that such actions are therefore *not* a criterion for salvation at the final judgment would be to go beyond the text. Such a view is untenable given one especially important consideration: if Jesus wanted to say that the actual works of mercy shown to his disciples were truly in and of themselves a criterion for entering the kingdom, it is hard to see how the passage would look much different.

With God All Things Are Possible

In fact, that performing good deeds will be a criterion of salvation is suggested elsewhere in Matthew. For example, it is the basic assumption

---

23. R. E. Nixon, "Matthew," in *The New Bible Commentary* (rev. ed.; ed. D. Guthrie and J. A. Motyer; Grand Rapids: Eerdmans, 1970), 846.

24. For a fuller discussion see, e.g., T. W. Manson, *The Sayings of Jesus* (London: SCM, 1949), 251; J. R. Michaels, "Apostolic Hardships and Righteous Gentiles: A Study of Matt. 25:31–46," *JBL* 84 (1965) 27–37; George E. Ladd, "The Parable of the Sheep and Goats in Recent Interpretation," in *New Dimensions in New Testament Study* (ed. R. Longenecker and M. Tenney; Grand Rapids: Zondervan, 1974), 191–99. This "was the most widely accepted [interpretation] until around 1800." See Ulrich Luz, *Matthew 21–28* (Hermeneia; ed. Helmut Koester, trans. James E. Crouch; Minneapolis: Fortress, 2005), 271. We might point out that this reading is not without its problems. See Klyne R. Snodgrass, *Stories with Intent: A Comprehensive Guide to the Parables of Jesus* (Grand Rapids: Eerdmans, 2008), 555–58; W. D. Davies and Dale C. Allison, *Matthew 19–28* (ICC; ed. J. A. Emerton et al.; Edinburgh: T&T Clark, 1997), 428–29.

25. Stanley, *Did Jesus Teach Salvation by Works?* 303–5.

behind the question posed to Jesus in Matthew 19: "Teacher, what good deed must I do, to have eternal life?" (Matt. 19:16; cf. Mark 10:17). Notably, Jesus does not reprove the man for his apparent "works-righteousness" attitude. Instead, after referring him to the commandments, Jesus explains, "If you would be perfect, go, sell what you possess and give to the poor, and you will have treasure in heaven; and come, follow me" (Matt. 19:21).

Again, some have tried to solve the apparent difficulty here by making the suggestion that Jesus was simply giving the standard Jewish answer to the question posed to him. In this view, Jesus' teaching is directed to Jews, not to Christians.[26] This, however, ignores the thrust of the passage. In the Great Commission, Jesus tells the disciples to teach all nations that they must observe "all that I have commanded you," without any hint of a distinction between Jews and Christians (Matt. 28:19–20).

Another explanation holds that Jesus was not talking specifically about salvation to the young man in Matthew 19, but about something extraneous to it (e.g., rewards). Yet that salvation is in view in this passage and not simply other kinds of blessings is made abundantly clear from the context. After the man declines the offer, Jesus explains it is "hard for a rich man to enter the kingdom of heaven" (19:23–24). Moreover, that Jesus is talking about salvation is clear from the disciples' response to his teaching: "Who then can be *saved* [*sōthēnai*]?" (19:25). Moreover, the story ends with Jesus talking about "inheriting *eternal life*" (19:29).[27]

Finally, it is worth noting Jesus' response to the disciples' complaint about his teaching: "With men this is impossible, but with God all things are possible" (Matt. 19:26). Here we have two critically important ideas. First, believers must do the impossible to be saved: we must be *perfect*. Jesus holds believers to this same standard in the Sermon on the Mount: "be perfect, *as your heavenly Father is perfect*" (Matt. 5:48). Note here that the perfection Jesus points to is not just human

---

26. Daniel J. Harrington, "The Rich Young Man in Matthew 19:16–22: Another Way to God For Jews?" in *The Four Gospels* (ed. F. Van Sebroeck et al.; Leuven: Leuven University Press, 1992), 1429.

27. The *Catechism* interprets this story in terms of the offer of eternal salvation in nos. 308 and 1058.

perfection but *divine* perfection ("as your heavenly Father is perfect"). This, obviously, is an unattainable goal for human beings. Second, God makes it possible for us to attain what Jesus is calling us to achieve. With him, somehow, *we can do the impossible.*

Forgive Us Our Debts

Above we alluded to passages that describe salvation in terms of a "reward." The language here is only fully comprehensible when it is understood against the backdrop of the Jewish worldview out of which Christianity emerged. As Gary Anderson has shown, in ancient Judaism sins and good deeds were closely tied to economic terminology.[28] In an important dissertation recently completed at Duke University, Nathan Eubank applies this work to the gospel of Matthew.[29]

As scholars have long recognized, the idea that sin constituted a "debt" pervades Jewish literature.[30] The most famous passage in the New Testament reflecting this understanding is found in the Lord's Prayer: "And forgive [*aphes*] us *our debts* [*ta opheilēmata hēmōn*] as we also have forgiven [*aphēkamen*] *our debtors* [*tois opheiletais hēmōn*]" (Matt. 6:12). As is universally acknowledged, sins are here described in terms of "debts." The same idea is found in other places in the New Testament, for example, the parable of the unforgiving servant, where the handling of "debt" is clearly related to the concept of sin (cf. 18:23–35).

This kind of commercial terminology permeates the New Testament. Jesus, for instance, explains that his death provides the ransom needed for salvation, i.e., the cost of redemption (Matt. 20:28//Mark 10:45). Paul describes the way every sin has its price: "the wages of sin is

---

28. See Gary Anderson, *Sin: A History* (New Haven, CT: Yale University Press, 2009); idem, "Redeem Your Sins by the Giving of Alms: Sin, Debt, and the 'Treasury of Merit' in Early Jewish and Christian Tradition," *Letter & Spirit* 3 (2007): 39–69; idem, "From Israel's Burden to Israel's Debt: Towards a Theology of Sin in Biblical and Early Second Temple Sources," in *Reworking the Bible: Apocryphal and Related Texts at Qumran* (ed. E. G. Chazon et al.; Leiden: Brill, 2005), 1–30.

29. Nathan Eubank, "The Wages of Righteousness: The Economy of Heaven in the Gospel According to Matthew" (PhD diss., Duke University, 2012). This work will be published this year by Walter de Gruyter with a new title: *Wages of Cross-Bearing and Debt of Sin: The Economy of Heaven in Matthew's Gospel* (BZNW 196; Berlin/Boston: de Gruyter, 2013).

30. See, e.g., Martin MacNamara, *Targum and Testament* (Grand Rapids: Eerdmans, 1972), 120; Matthew Black, *An Aramaic Approach to the Gospels and Acts* (Oxford: Clarendon, 1967), 140; Joachim Jeremias, *New Testament Theology* (New York: Charles Scribner's Sons, 1971), 6, fn. 15; 196.

death" (Rom. 6:23). In Colossians, Christ has saved us by canceling the debt of our indebtedness by his death on the cross (Col. 2:14).

This kind of language only makes sense in a Jewish context. As Anderson writes, "In contemporary Greek the words 'remit' [*aphiēmi*] and 'debt' [*opheilēma*] did not have the secondary meaning of 'forgive' and 'sin.' Matthew's version of the Our Father makes sense only if we assume that the wording reflects an underlying Semitic idiom."[31] Indeed, looking at ancient Jewish texts, we do in fact find sin described along these lines. In the Dead Sea Scrolls, for example, we see the covenant infidelity of Israel described along these lines: "[all] the first members of the covenant *fell into debt* [*ḥābû*]; they were given over to the sword. They had forsaken the covenant of God and chose their own will" (CD 3:10).[32]

God Will Repay Him

Given that sins were understood in terms of debts, it is not surprising to find a corollary: good deeds were viewed as a "reimbursement." One of the earliest texts suggesting this perspective is Proverbs 19:17: "He who is kind to the poor lends to the LORD, and *he will repay him for his deed*." Here it is understood that performing good deeds will lead to divine repayment.

The books of Tobit and Sirach reveal that by the first century such ideas were more fully developed. In these books the "credit" earned by good deeds is represented by the image of a heavenly treasury of sorts.

> ... if you do what is true, *your ways will prosper through your deeds.* Give alms from your possessions to all who live uprightly, and do not let your eye begrudge the gift when you make it. *Do not turn your face away from any poor man, and the face of God will not be turned away from you.* If you have many possessions, make your gift from them in proportion; if few, do not be afraid to give according to the little you have. So *you will be laying up a good treasure for yourself against the day of necessity.* For *charity delivers from death and keeps you from entering the darkness*; and *for all who practice it charity is an excellent offering in the presence of the Most High.* (Tob. 4:6–11)

---

31. Anderson, *Sin*, 32.
32. Translation taken from ibid., 34.

Help a poor man for the commandment's sake, and because of his need do not send him away empty. Lose your silver for the sake of a brother or a friend, and do not let it rust under a stone and be lost. *Lay up your treasure according to the commandments of the Most High, and it will profit you more than gold. Store up almsgiving in your treasury, and it will rescue you from all affliction*; more than a mighty shield and more than a heavy spear, it will fight on your behalf against your enemy. (Sir. 29:9–13).

Moreover, Sirach tells us that it is not only almsgiving that builds up credit in one's treasury but other good deeds as well.

Whoever honors his father atones for sins, and *whoever glorifies his mother is like one who lays up treasure*.... For kindness to a father will not be forgotten, and *against your sins it will be credited to you*; in the day of your affliction it will be remembered in your favor; as frost in fair weather, *your sins will melt away*. (Sir 3:3–4, 14–15)

By the first century, the idea that good deeds earn "credit" was clearly linked to entry into life with God after death—that is, salvation from ultimate death. The prize to be won is viewed ultimately not as earthly life but supernatural life. In Wisdom 2:22 those who have died experience a blessed afterlife described as the "wages of holiness." Similarly, *Psalms of Solomon* 9:5 explains, "The one who does righteousness treasures up life for himself with the Lord."

Not surprisingly, then, the final judgment is often described in Jewish sources with imagery reminiscent of the marketplace: scales. Such works describe how one's good and evil deeds are weighed against each other. Salvation depends on which weighs more heavily: one's good deeds or bad deeds.[33]

The Treasury of Merit and "Reward" in Jesus' Teachings

I realize, of course, that many non-Catholic Christians do not embrace Tobit and Sirach as canonical. However, it seems hard to deny that Jesus teaches a similar idea in the Gospels. As in the texts cited above, almsgiving is often identified as an act that fills a heavenly treasury. For

---

33. See *1 Enoch* 38:1–2; 41:1; 61:8; *Apoc. Zeph.* 8:5; *T. Ab.* 12 (note 12:15: "repayment" [*antapodosis*]); *t. Qiddushin* 1:13–14.

example, returning again to the story we looked at above from Matthew 19, Jesus tells the rich young man: " … sell what you possess and *give to the poor, and you will have treasure in heaven*" (Matt. 19:21). In Luke, Jesus advises: "Sell your possessions, and *give alms*; provide yourselves with purses that do not grow old, *with a treasure in the heavens that does not fail*, where no thief approaches and no moth destroys" (Luke 12:33).

Closely associated with all of this is another concept in the Gospels we have already mentioned: the understanding of salvation as a "reward." In his masterful study of economic imagery in Matthew, Eubank shows how standard English translations mask the commercial language used over and over again by Jesus. English Bibles since the King James Version generally render the Greek words *misthos* and the verb *apodidōmi* as "reward." Yet in today's usage "reward" implies that the "recompense" God gives unrelated to an employer/employee or to a creditor/debtor relationship. This is misleading. [34]

A careful look at Matthew's gospel reveals that this is *precisely* the terminology intended. Indeed, *misthos*, almost always translated as "reward," clearly carries the meaning of "wage." The present dichotomy of "wage"/"reward" is only the result of the particular way the English language has developed. At the time the KJV was translated, the English word "reward" was used synonymously with "wage," that is, the financial remuneration of a laborer. [35] In fact, in the parable of the workers in Matthew 20 it is precisely this word, *misthos*, that occurs in verse 8: the laborers are given their "wages." Let us here pause to look at this story.

The Parable of the Workers in the Vineyard (Matthew 20:1 - 16)

In the parable of the workers the owner of a vineyard hires workers at different points during a day. At the end of it, he says, "Call the laborers and pay them their *wages* [*misthos*]" (Matt. 20:8). Those who had worked from the beginning of the day become angry when the owner gives those who started working at the eleventh hour the same wage they received. The owner defends himself, saying, "Am I not allowed

---

34. Eubank, "Wages of Righteousness," 74.

35. See ibid., 76. Eubank mentions that the Oxford English Dictionary cites Adam Smith's eighteenth-century work, *Wealth of Nations*: "A little school, where children may be taught for a reward so moderate, that even a common labourer may afford it" (II. v. i. 370).

to do what I choose with what belongs to me? Or do you begrudge my generosity?" (20:15). Much could be said here about this parable, but let us highlight two things. First, the parable is clearly about "the kingdom of heaven" (20:1). Given the usage of the concept in Matthew, it seems difficult to deny that here we have a teaching that relates to salvation.

Second, given the first point, the parable teaches that salvation is given as a "wage." Some have tried to obscure this fact by focusing on the owner's unexpected decision to give those who were hired at the end of the day the same wage as those who had started in the morning. Highlighting this, France claims the story reveals, "It is all by grace."[36] Stanley follows the same line of thought, "We are at the grace and mercy of a generous landowner to come and call us to his vineyard."[37] I agree that salvation is, as the *Catechism* affirms, "pure grace" (no. 2011 cited above), but is the aim of this story to minimize the role of works—or is it something else? As Eubank states, "The point of the parable can hardly be that 'everything depends upon grace' since the early workers received exactly what they worked for, though Matthew 20:11–15 certainly warns those who have done more work against begrudging God's generosity with those who have done less."[38] Indeed, all were paid for doing *some* work; none were paid for *not* working at all. If the story were meant to teach that salvation is given only as a gift with no relation to works, one would expect the vineyard owner to walk into town handing out money to everyone he met, without any negotiations or further expectations.

In fact, Eubank points out that the story is best read in light of what immediately precedes it: the story of the rich young man, who, unlike the disciples, refuses to leave all his possessions and follow Jesus (Matt. 19:16–30).[39] The story, then, likely functions as an extended answer to the disciples' question: "Who then can be saved?" (19:25). While this man has kept the commandments, Jesus suggests that technically the man has not done enough to be perfect. The apostles, who have left everything, have done much more. Nonetheless, by placing the parable

36. R. T. France, *The Gospel of Matthew* (NICNT; Grand Rapids: Eerdmans, 2007), 752.
37. Stanley, *Salvation Is More Complicated Than You Think*, 83.
38. Eubank, "Wages of Righteousness," 108.
39. Ibid., 101–12.

of the workers immediately after this story, Matthew provides us with hope for the man: God is a merciful judge.

Indeed, this idea has its parallels in Jewish literature describing divine judgment. [40] In sum, Jesus teaches salvation is not simply the result of a cold calculation of credits and debits. Wages are paid out in connection with labor, but not in strict proportion to labor. The parable thus teaches the necessity of works alongside the generosity of God in paying out more than was earned.

A similar idea is found in the parable of the talents in Matthew 25:14–30. There, once again, we find divine judgment described in terms of financial imagery. This time we hear about a master who returns from a trip to collect money he has entrusted to his servants. Notably, the different servants who invested wisely each end up with a different amount (the first has eleven talents and the second only four). In fact, in Luke's version, this prompts a protest from the servants (cf. Luke 19:25). Suffice it to say, the parable does not support the idea that in the end all receive the same recompense. In addition, it is noteworthy that God rewards his servants with abundance. As Eubank remarks, Matthew insists that "heavenly wages go beyond what workers earn by strict dessert, but it is equally clear that this generosity is a generous wage for work done rather than an unmerited gift." [41]

Salvation as a Wage

It is this kind of economic imagery that is obviously in play in Matthew 16:27: "For the Son of man is to come with his angels in the glory of his Father, and then he will repay [*apodidōmi*] every man for what he has done." It is likewise no wonder that Jesus describes the final judgment in terms of the "settling of accounts" (cf. 18:23). Moreover, the sheer volume of passages describing salvation as a wage/reward (*misthos*) in Matthew is alone overwhelming. To name but a few:

---

40. See e.g., *2 Baruch* 24:1–2. Likewise, see *T. Ab.* 14:1–8 [A], where souls whose good and evil actions are equally weighted enter into paradise due to the intercession of Abraham and Michael. The emphasis clearly falls on God's "boundless" mercy (14:9). For further analysis of such passages, see Chris VanLandingham, *Judgment and Justification in Early Judaism and the Apostle Paul* (Peabody, MA: Hendrickson, 2006), 66–174; Simon J. Gathercole, *Where is Boasting: Early Jewish Soteriology and Paul's Response in Romans 1–5* (Grand Rapids: Eerdmans, 2002); Kent Yinger, *Paul, Judaism, and Judgment according to Deeds* (SNTSMS 105; ed. Richard Bauckham; Cambridge: Cambridge University Press, 1999).

41. Eubank, "Wages of Righteousness," 115.

- "But I say to you, Love your enemies and pray for those who persecute you, *so that you may be sons of your Father who is in heaven* ... For if you love those who love you, what *reward* [*misthos*] have you? Do not even the tax collectors do the same?" (Matt. 5:44–46)
- "Beware of practicing your piety before men in order to be seen by them; for then *you will have no reward* [*misthos*] from your Father who is in heaven. Thus, when you give alms, sound no trumpet before you, as the hypocrites do in the synagogues and in the streets, that they may be praised by men. Truly, I say to you, *they have received their reward* [*misthos*]. But when you give alms, do not let your left hand know what your right hand is doing, so that your alms may be in secret; and *your Father who sees in secret will reward* [*apodidōmi*] *you*."(Matt. 6:1–4)
- "And when you pray, you must not be like the hypocrites; for they love to stand and pray in the synagogues and at the street corners, that they may be seen by men. Truly, I say to you, *they have received their reward* [*misthos*]. But when you pray, go into your room and shut the door and pray to your Father who is in secret; and *your Father who sees in secret will reward* [*apodidōmi*] *you*." (Matt. 6:5–6; cf. 10:41–42)

Put simply, to argue that Scripture teaches that salvation is the result of "faith" alone and that works *themselves* are not rewarded with salvation flies in the face of Jesus' teaching. One can only come to this conclusion through a tortured reading that obscures these texts' plain sense by imposing on them preconceived theological ideas.

James and Justification

So far we have failed to discuss the text that perhaps most clearly links salvation with works: James 2. Here, of course, we find the only place in Scripture where "justification" and the phrase "faith alone" appear together: "You see that a man is justified by works and not by faith alone" (Jas. 2:24). While some have argued that James's view is simply that works only justify an individual before other humans—that is, from the standpoint of an outside observer [42]—this fails to account for

---

42. See John MacArthur, *James* (The MacArthur New Testament Commentary; Chicago: Moody Press, 1998), 137–39.

what is explicitly stated. James, via what are obviously rhetorical questions, insists that works in fact justified Abraham and Rahab. "Was not Abraham our father justified by works, when he offered his son Isaac upon the altar?... And in the same way was not also Rahab the harlot justified by works when she received the messengers and sent them out another way?" (2:21, 25). Nowhere does James imply their justification by works involved merely outward appearances. Nor does he suggest that it is really the faith that accompanies the good works that actually justifies. Rather, works do justify the believer. [43]

By Faith through Grace

So are we saved by grace alone or by something else? Protestants would affirm that we are saved by grace alone. Of course, what this really means for most Protestant Christians is that we are saved by grace through faith alone.

For many Protestants, the act of faith is not itself a "work." This preserves the concept of grace; salvation is accomplished without any works. Yet even Protestants must affirm that to receive salvation one must still *do* something—one must believe. The insistence that salvation is the result of grace does not entail a rejection of the need for a human response. Strictly speaking, someone could argue that because salvation is said to be the result of divine gratuity, this means that a person needs to do *nothing at all* to be saved.

A more nuanced understanding, of course, would recognize that here we are insisting on a false dichotomy between grace and the believer's response to it. Scripture teaches that the human response *itself* is the result of grace. Paul declares: "No one can say 'Jesus is Lord' except by the Holy Spirit" (1 Cor. 12:3). Similarly, Jesus responds to Peter's confession of faith by insisting: "Flesh and blood has not revealed this to you, but my Father who is in heaven" (Matt. 16:17). Along the same

---

43. Many commentators harmonize Paul and James by pointing out that the former speaks of *initial* justification, the latter *final* justification. Such scholars acknowledge that while initial justification takes place by faith, final justification involves works. See, e.g., Patrick J. Hartin, *James* (SP 14; ed. Daniel J. Harrington; Collegeville, MN: Liturgical, 2003), 165–67. Hartin (p. 167) cites Augustine: "Therefore the opinions of the two apostles, Paul and James, are not opposed to each other when the one says that man is justified by faith without works, and the other says that faith without works is useless; because the former (Paul) speaks about works that precede faith, while the latter (James) speaks about those that follow faith; as even Paul shows in many places" (*De diversis quaestionibus LXXXIII Liber Unus* 76).

lines, in the gospel of John Jesus teaches: "This is *the work of God*, that you *believe* in him whom he has sent" (John 6:29). Thus, with our separated brothers and sisters, Catholics affirm that we are saved by grace through faith and that this faith is the result of *God's* work within the believer: To quote the *Catechism:* "*Faith is a gift of God, a supernatural virtue infused by him.*"[44]

Nonetheless, though faith is understood as the result of God's action, it is still an act performed by the believer. It is not as if believers are coerced into faith. Rather, God's grace moves them to freely assent; they are truly the ones who believe, though with divine assistance.

Work Out Your Salvation

Above we discussed the danger of establishing a false dichotomy between grace and faith. Catholics would insist that we must also be careful about doing the same with regard to good works. Here we can point once more to Paul who told the Philippians, "*Work out your own salvation* with fear and trembling; *for God is at work in you*, both to will and to work for his good pleasure" (Phil. 2:12–13). If faith is the result of God's action within us, the same is true of works.

It is important to recall that salvation involves more than just deliverance from sin. Salvation involves being fully incorporated into Christ, so that, with Paul, the believer can truly say, "it is no longer I who live, but Christ who lives within me" (Gal. 2:20). Paul therefore can tell the Philippians to "work out your own salvation" because ultimately the good works they do are truly the product of God working within them. This means no one can boast of his or her own salvation (Eph. 2:8–9); it is only through grace that one can do such good works.

Nevertheless, we are also saved for accomplishing good works (Eph. 2:10). No one can claim to do meritorious good works on his or her own power. As Jesus says, "apart from me you can do nothing" (John 15:5)—that is, nothing that avails for salvation. Yet because of union with Christ, Paul can speak of "the power at work within us" that "is able to do far more abundantly than all that we ask or think" (Eph. 3:20).

---

44. *Catechism*, no. 153. See also Thomas Aquinas, *Summa Theologiae*, I-II, q. 109, art. 6 and 9.

Traditional Protestant theology would agree that Christ's power within us is capable of doing far more than we could ever ask or think, with, apparently, one exception: it is not capable of empowering the believer to perform meritorious works. In the Catholic view, however, all things are possible with God, *including the performance of meritorious works.* From a Catholic point of view, works themselves can be considered through the lens of Jesus' statement, "With men this is impossible, but with God all things are possible" (Matt. 19:26). As we saw in our analysis of Matthew 19 above, this was exactly the point underscored by the context of this verse—human beings must do something to be saved, but what they must do is impossible. Nonetheless, Jesus affirms that God will enable believers to do the impossible, namely, works by which believers can have eternal life.

Put another way, salvation is first by God's grace and not by works. One receives Christ not because one has performed any good works. However, once one has become united to Christ, one is capable of doing what was previously impossible. In Catholic teaching, works performed by those in union with Christ have meritorious value.[45] They cannot *not* have meritorious value. Why? Because they are the result of Christ's work. The believer says, "It is no longer I who live, but Christ who lives within me" (Gal. 2:20).

The good works of the believer *are* the good works accomplished by Christ in him or her. To insist that the believer's works lack meritorious value is to claim that *Christ's* work lacks meritorious value. To say that believers can perform meritorious works is therefore not to detract from Christ's redemptive work; rather, it is the denial that believers can do meritorious works through Christ that detracts from his power and glory. If the Catholic view is wrong, it is ultimately so because it gives God too much credit. If the Catholic understanding is mistaken, it is because we believe God is able to do more in believers by grace than Protestants believe.

Of course, I do not think the Catholic view has erred in attributing too much to the grace of Christ. In fact, Paul explains that salvation

---

45. See Council of Trent, Session IV, chap. 16: "For since Christ Jesus Himself... continually infuses strength into those justified, which strength always precedes, accompanies and follows their good works, and without which they could not in any manner be pleasing and meritorious before God, we must believe that nothing further be wanting to those justified to prevent them from being considered to have, by those very works which have been done in God, fully satisfied the divine law."

involves nothing less than being "conformed to the image of [God's] Son" (Rom. 8:29). Christ fully shares his sonship with us so that we are truly "sons in the Son." Catholics take Jesus at his word when he says, *"All that the Father has is mine*; therefore I said that *he will take what is mine and declare it to you"* (John 16:15). Thus, since Christ has the capacity to merit, he merits for believers the capacity to merit with him. In other words, if salvation is truly Christocentric—if it involves being conformed to the image of Christ—it necessarily involves our ability to merit in him. Good works are not simply the *fruit* of salvation; they are part and parcel of it. Without them we are not fully "like Christ."

Suffering for the Sake of the Body

Thus Paul explains, "Now I rejoice in my sufferings for your sake, and *in my flesh I complete what is lacking in Christ's afflictions for the sake of his body, that is, the church"* (Col. 1:24). This is an astonishing passage. As Thomas Aquinas explains, it could be misinterpreted as teaching "that the passion of Christ was not sufficient for our redemption, and that the sufferings of the saints were added to complete it." Yet, citing 1 John 2:2, Thomas firmly rejects such a reading: "But this is heretical, because the blood of Christ is sufficient to redeem many worlds." How do we interpret this then? Thomas states:

> Rather, we should understand that Christ and the Church are one mystical person, whose head is Christ, and whose body is all the just, for every just person is a member of this head: "individually members" (1 Cor. 12:27).... We could say that Paul was completing the sufferings that were lacking in his own flesh. For what was lacking was that, just as Christ had suffered in his own body, so he should also suffer in Paul, his member, and in similar ways in others.[46]

Paul's suffering completes what is lacking in Christ's afflictions only in the sense that Christ's redemptive work now must be lived out in his mystical body.

Moreover, we should point out the ecclesial nature of all of this. Salvation is not simply communion with Christ but also communion with

---

46. Cited from Thomas Aquinas, *Commentary on Colossians* (trans. F. R. Larcher; Naples; Sapientia, 2006).

all believers. Thus, "if one member suffers, all suffer together; if one member is honored, all rejoice together" (1 Cor. 12:26). Paul's suffering redounds to the benefit of the entire mystical body—he makes up what is lacking not only for himself but, through his union with Christ, what is lacking in the body itself. [47]

Salvation As Maturing in Sonship

So how can we affirm *both* that salvation is by God's grace and not by works *and* that salvation involves Christ imparting to believers the capacity to merit? Isn't this contradictory? Not if salvation is more than a moment in time. One must keep in mind that salvation involves a process, including past, present, and future dimensions.

The initial moment of saving grace is, of course, identified with baptism in Catholic teaching. As Peter explains, it is "baptism" that "now saves you" (1 Pet. 3:21). [48] This is rebirth, "the washing of regeneration" (Titus 3:5). As Paul says, "you were washed, you were sanctified, you were justified" (1 Cor. 6:11). We are united with Christ and therefore saved (cf. Rom. 6:3–4; Gal. 3:27; Col. 2:12). By baptism, we are made members of the body of Christ (cf. 1 Cor. 12:13).

It should be emphasized that in Catholic theology baptism is not understood as a work accomplished by human beings, but rather as the work of God. For Catholics, the fact that one *receives* baptism and does not administer baptism to oneself illustrates in a visible way that no one can save themselves by their own actions performed independently of God or the believing community of the Church. [49] For Catholics, infant baptism highlights in an especially profound way the gratuitousness of salvation: "Since the earliest times, Baptism has been administered to children, for *it is a grace and a gift of God that does not presuppose any human merit*" (*Catechism*, no. 1282; italics added). [50]

---

47. See also Jean-Nöel Aletti, *Saint Paul: Épître aux Colossiens* (Paris: Gabalda, 1993), 134–37.

48. That Paul identifies baptism with justification has been persuasively argued in the recent work of Protestant scholar Michael Gorman, *Inhabiting the Cruciform God: Kenosis, Justification, and Theosis in Paul's Narrative Soteriology* (Grand Rapids: Eerdmans, 2009), 73–79.

49. This point is made in Joseph Cardinal Ratzinger, *Church, Ecumenism and Politics: New Endeavors in Ecclesiology* (San Francisco, CA: Ignatius, 2008), 19.

50. Space precludes a defense of infant baptism here. For a fuller defense of the practice see Bryan Holstrom, *Infant Baptism and the Silence of the New Testament* (Greenville, SC: Ambassador, 2008); Gregg Strawbridge, *The Case for Covenantal Infant Baptism* (Phillipsburg, NJ:

For Catholics, baptism is truly a saving event. The baptized is united with Christ. One is "reborn" and made a "son" in the Son. One is saved by God's grace and not by works. Yet salvation is more than just a discreet moment in time. It involves being conformed to the image of Christ. To put it simply, the sons must "grow up." They are justified by grace alone, but for the purpose of performing good works (cf. Eph. 2:8–10). Saved initially by grace, through uniting himself with Christ, a person is further saved by faith, and, moreover, "justified by works and not by faith alone" (Jas. 2:24).

Conclusion

The Catholic understanding of works at the final judgment preserves the entirety of the biblical witness regarding salvation. Salvation is a moment *and* a process of maturing in sonship. Initially we are saved by grace and not by anything we do. However, God's grace in the believer allows him or her to do the impossible: perform works meritorious of salvation. And it is by these works that the believer is truly saved — he or she is fully conformed to the image of the Son of God. All that the Son has been given by the Father he shares with those united to him by grace (John 16:15) — including his capacity to merit.

Strikingly, even John Calvin allowed for the idea that good works could be understood as a means of salvation:

> ... the efficient cause of our salvation is placed in the love of God the Father; the material cause in the obedience of the Son; the instrumental cause in the illumination of the Spirit, that is, in faith; and the final cause in the praise of the divine goodness. In this, however, there is nothing to prevent the Lord from embracing works as inferior causes. But how so? In this way: Those whom in mercy he has destined for the inheritance of eternal life, he, in his ordinary administration, introduces to the possession of it by means of good works.... *For this reason, he sometimes makes eternal life a consequent of works*; not because it is to be ascribed to them, but because those whom he has elected he justifies, that he may at length glorify

P&R Publishing, 2003); Joachim Jeremias, *Infant Baptism in the First Four Centuries* (trans. D. Cairns; Eugene, OR: Wipf & Stock, 2004 [1960]); Meredith G. Kline, *By Oath Consigned: A Reinterpretation of the Covenant Signs of Circumcision and Baptism* (Grand Rapids: Eerdmans, 1968).

(Rom. 8:30); he makes the prior grace to be a kind of cause, because it is a kind of step to that which follows.[51]

Given the plethora of passages describing the role of good works in salvation, it is not surprising that Calvin would make such a statement.[52]

Nonetheless, it would certainly be wrong to conclude that Calvin agreed with the Catholic Church. Indeed, many will point out that the Church's teaching, while perhaps tolerable, remains in practice dangerous since it is too easily misunderstood. Many Catholics, some might observe, appear to neglect the teaching of grace. To this claim I would simply point out that no view of salvation is immune from being misinterpreted and misunderstood.

In closing, Catholic doctrine affirms the importance of works without hedging on the priority and unlimited power of grace. Grace is so effective it is *even* able to render weak and sinful humans capable of performing meritorious works. Protestants may disagree with the Catholic understanding, but let it *not* be said that this is because Catholics have a low estimation of grace. To say the Catholic view is incorrect is to say Catholics attribute *too much* to grace!

According to Catholic teaching, then, salvation is, ultimately, "pure grace." At the final judgment, good works play a role in our salvation, but only because they are the result of God's work within us. The Catholic view is expressed well by Augustine. Speaking of the final judgment, he writes, "*Then God will crown not so much thy merits, as his own gifts.*"[53] Or to put it in the words cited from the *Catechism* above: "*The charity of Christ is the source in us of all our merits before God. The saints have always had a lively awareness that their merits were pure grace*" (*Catechism*, no. 2011).

"Now to him who by the power at work within us is able to do far more abundantly than all that we ask or think, to him be glory in the church and in Christ Jesus to all generations, for ever and ever. Amen" (Eph. 3:20–21).

---

51. John Calvin, *Institutes of the Christian Religion* (trans. H. Beveridge; Grand Rapids: Eerdmans, 1975), 3.14.21.

52. For further discussion, see Joseph Wawrykow, "John Calvin and Condign Merit," *Archiv für Reformationsgeschichte* 83 (1992): 73–90.

53. *Sermon 120* 10. Cited from St. Augustine, *Sermons on Selected Lessons of the New Testament* (Oxford: James Parker, 1845), 2:879.

ROBERT N. WILKIN

Michael Barber has done a fine job explaining some of the nuances of Catholic soteriology. His thesis is summarized by his opening (and closing) quote from the *Catechism of the Catholic Church* (abbrev. *Catechism*):

> *The charity of Christ is the source in us of all our merits* before God. Grace, by uniting us to Christ in active love, ensures the supernatural quality of our acts and consequently their merit before God and before men. *The saints have always had a lively awareness that their merits were pure grace.* (pp. 161, 184, italics his)

Evidently, Barber believes the invocation of *pure grace* at the end of the statement rescues the Catholic position from accusations of teaching salvation by works. He writes:

> I suspect that it [the statement cited ending in *pure grace*] may surprise some non-Catholic Christians. It obviously does not cohere with the description of Catholic soteriology many are familiar with, namely, a works-righteousness, legalistic perspective. Indeed, such a charge represents a crass mischaracterization of Catholic teaching. (p. 162)

I fail to see why the statement cited *obviously* denies works-righteousness and a legalistic perspective. After all, it has long been understood that for Catholics grace was something (perhaps an infused quality) given to believers to empower them to do the works necessary to be finally saved. Apart from such empowerment, the works would be impossible. But even *with* the empowerment, works are not automatic. Believers must work hard their entire lives if they wish to stay saved and finally merit final salvation.

The official Catholic position is more nuanced than a simple determination of whether one's good works in some sense outweigh one's bad works. (Barber does not say *how* God will evaluate our flawed works to determine our destiny.) Nevertheless, I would suggest that, in spite of his denials, Barber's position *is* clearly one of works-righteousness.

After all, what reason would Barber give to explain why some people will be damned? Presumably he would *not* say the reason was the insufficiency of God's grace. The fault cannot lie there because God's grace can do the impossible. Rather, Barber would say the problem was with the persons themselves, namely, that their works were culpably insufficient. Perhaps they didn't cooperate with God's grace enough or didn't take advantage of the means of grace available to them.

Whatever the case, if someone dies outside of "God's grace and friendship" (*Catechism* 1030); if he dies having sinned gravely against God, his neighbor, and himself and has not met the needs of the "poor and the little ones" (*Catechism* 1033); if he has willfully turned away from God and has persisted in his sin "until the end" (*Catechism* 1037), that person will be damned because of what he did and because of what he failed to do. In other words, for all Barber's talk of grace, at the end of the day he would say that salvation finally depends upon *our own efforts*. Those efforts may not technically be meritorious or effective apart from God's grace, but they are necessary—and without them no one can be saved. That is the essence of legalism and salvation by works.

Eternal salvation attained by God-empowered works is a far cry from what we find in the New Testament. It clearly teaches that everlasting life is given to sinners as a gift when they simply believe in Jesus for that gift. This is what Jesus taught (e.g., John 3:16; 5:24; 6:28–29, 35, 37; 11:25–27) and what His apostles taught (e.g., Acts 15:7–11; 16:30–31; Eph. 2:8–9; Titus 3:5; Jas. 1:18; 1 John 5:9–13). The quality of our fellowship with God in this life and the eternal rewards and position of authority we will have in the life to come do depend on living a life of faithful obedience to Christ. But the conditions for eternal salvation and eternal rewards are entirely different.

The Most Important Evidence Is Not Discussed

I cannot emphasize enough the importance of studying John on the topic of eternal salvation and judgment. Other than an out-of-context quotation of John 6:29 (p. 179), Barber does not discuss the Lord's teaching on regeneration in the Fourth Gospel.[54] Since John's gospel is the only evangelistic book in the Bible (John 20:30–31), Barber's failure to deal with that gospel is startling.

In John 5:24 the Lord said that believers "shall not come into judgment." Is that reference not an essential one to discuss in a book dealing with final judgment? That verse needs explanation, as do all of the verses that condition everlasting life on faith in Christ, not on works.

Moreover, John 6:29, a verse Barber cites to *support* his position, actually teaches *against* it, if considered in context. In the preceding verse, Jesus' audience asks, "What shall we do, that we may work the works of God?" Notice the plural "works." Like Barber, the crowd assumes that eternal destiny depends on one's works. It is significant, I think, that in his answer, Jesus speaks not of *works* (plural) but of a single *work*. And what is that one work we must do? "This is the work of God, that you believe in Him whom He sent." Jesus is drawing a contrast here. Believing in Him is the only "act" that one can do to obtain everlasting life. Of course, faith is a passive action. We are presented with Jesus' message of everlasting life, and we either believe Him or not. Hence, everlasting life is not of works (John 6:28; Eph 2:9), but it is of faith.

Barber Teaches Works-Righteousness by Conformity to Christ

Barber states, "Paul explains that salvation involves nothing less than being 'conformed to the image of [God's] Son' (Rom. 8:29)" (p. 165). A few pages later he says, "Salvation is more than just a discreet moment in time. It involves being conformed to the image of Christ.... Salvation is a moment [*sic*] *and* a process of maturing in sonship.... It is by these works that the believer is truly saved—he or she is *fully conformed* to the image of the Son of God" (p. 183, emphasis added).

There is *some* truth in what Barber says. God does guarantee that all who are born again by faith in Christ will be conformed to His image, *when He returns* (cf. Rom. 8:29; Phil. 3:21; 1 John 3:2). When we are raised and glorified, then and only then will we be conformed to His image. Until that time, whatever Christlikeness we now experience still

---

54. Barber does quote John 14:23 and 16:15 as well, on pp. 165, 181, and 183, but those verses say nothing about regeneration.

falls short of His glory (Rom. 3:23; Phil. 3:12; 1 John 1:8, 10). We are still in fallen bodies that sin, suffer, and die and that lack the fullness of everlasting life. But despite our expectation of one day being fully Christlike, there is no process whereby we somehow merit eschatological salvation.

It is unnerving how Barber makes conformity to Christ's image a condition for our eschatological salvation, as if it could be achieved by our own (God-empowered) works. How is it that any living human being can be said to be *fully conformed* to the image of Christ *in this life*? Only the Lord Jesus is sinless. If one must, over time, be conformed to Christ's sinless image *in this life* in order to escape eternal condemnation, then no one will escape.

Given that understanding of eschatological salvation, no person could have assurance of eternal destiny. They will never *know* prior to death if they will spend eternity with the Lord. Indeed, under such teaching they should be sure *that they will be eternally condemned*. The situation is hopeless. But assurance of everlasting life is something that every believer does know as long as he or she continues to believe God's testimony (John 5:24; 1 John 5:13).

The Concept of Salvation Receives Inadequate Explanation

Barber (like Dunn and Schreiner) uncritically cites verses using the words *save* and *salvation* as though they automatically refer to regeneration or to spending eternity in Christ's kingdom. I commend Barber for at least considering "the larger question of what constitutes 'salvation'" (p. 163). But his answer does not show the range of uses of *sōzō* and *sōtēria* in the New Testament. Not all references to these terms speak about salvation from hell. Most actually refer to salvation from some temporal trouble or affliction. For example, he cites 1 Timothy 2:15 (without any discussion), where Paul says, "she will be saved in childbearing," as an example of future salvation from eternal condemnation (p. 163). Yet the context does not support that interpretation. The context refers to women not being able to teach in the meeting of the local church (1 Tim. 2:12–14). How will a woman *be saved* from such a potentially frustrating situation? "She [singular] will be delivered [or saved] through childbirth if they [plural, that is, her children] continue in faith, love, and holiness, with self-control" (1 Tim. 2:15).

In the same way Barber cites (but without any discussion) Romans 10:13 as teaching future salvation from eternal condemnation. Yet that verse clearly refers to deliverance from *temporal wrath* in this life, as verse 14 says: "Therefore how shall they call on Him in whom they have not believed?" Believing must precede calling, just as hearing must precede believing in the next question of verse 14. Thus the ones being *saved* in Romans 10:13 are believers, not unbelievers. They have already been united to Christ, so that is not Paul's concern. Verse 13 is a quote of Joel 2:32, which refers to *the temporal deliverance* of Jewish believers in the tribulation when they will cry out to Messiah. Romans 10:13–14 is not concerned with salvation from the lake of fire. It is concerned with deliverance from God's wrath in the here and now (cf. Rom. 1:18–32; 13:4–5).

Likewise, while Barber discusses Philippians 2:12 and the expression "work out your own salvation" (p. 179), he fails to consider the context. In three pages he fails to discuss the use of *sōtēria* in Philippians or even anything in the context. The words "your own salvation" are in contrast to an earlier statement in the letter: "For I know that this will turn out for salvation [*eis sōtērian*] for me through your prayer and the supply of the Spirit of Jesus Christ" (Phil. 1:19). What was *Paul's salvation* ("salvation for me")? It was not salvation from hell or union with Christ. That salvation was already accomplished by faith in Christ, apart from works. Rather, Paul knew that their prayers and the power of the Holy Spirit would result in his *successfully enduring the persecution he was undergoing* during his Roman imprisonment.

In other words, "your own salvation" is compared to Paul's salvation and refers to the believers in Philippi *successfully enduring their persecution* at the hands of unbelievers. The reason why Paul refers to "fear and trembling" is because he is reminded of the Judgment Seat of Christ, where, though eternally secure, believers will nevertheless be held accountable for their works and will be rewarded accordingly, hopefully experiencing confidence before the Lord and not shame (cf. Luke 19:16–26; 1 Cor. 9:24–27; 2 Cor. 5:9–11; 1 John 2:28). Philippians 2:12, like many of the other verses Barber cites in defense of his position, has nothing to do with salvation from eternal condemnation.

Conclusion

In summary, *pure grace* is not being empowered by God to save ourselves by perseverance in faithful works. Rather, pure grace is being given the free gift of everlasting life and eternal security, without ever again having to fear coming under God's eternal judgment, simply by believing in Jesus' promise (John 3:16; 5:24).

RESPONSE TO MICHAEL P. BARBER

THOMAS R. SCHREINER

Agreements

Michael Barber helps us avoid some common misunderstandings of Catholic theology, and at the same time we see points of contact established between Protestant and Catholic theology. For instance, Barber reminds us that Catholic theology teaches that the good works of believers are due to God's grace. Catholic theology should not be confused with Pelagianism. In popular circles Protestants too often wrongly believe that Catholic theology is entirely bereft of grace. We also find common ground in the already/not yet dimensions of salvation. Whether we speak of justification, redemption, the kingdom, or eternal life, there is an already but not yet dimension to God's saving work in our lives. Furthermore, Barber's essay is Christ-centered. He affirms that Christ is our righteousness and emphasizes that the goal of our salvation is communion with God in Christ.

Disagreements

Works as a Criterion

Barber apparently thinks he differs from me in maintaining that "good works" are "a criterion for salvation" (p. 166), saying works are "the *essential criterion* of judgment on the last day" (p. 167).[55] Barber says I don't believe works are a criterion since I say they are a fruit of faith. We have to be careful that we don't talk past one another at this point, for I am happy to say works are a criterion of salvation at the final judgment if what we mean is defined carefully. I would argue that they are an essential criterion in terms of evidence or fruit, but it is incorrect to say, against Barber, that they provide merit or are a basis of our salvation in

---

55. I think it is overstated to say works are "the essential criterion."

any way. In other words, when I use the word "evidence" or "fruit" in relation to works, I am not saying that works are unnecessary. They are an essential fruit or evidence. If the works aren't present, the person will be damned! That's a criterion!

The Problem with Merit Exegetically

What I object to, however, is the notion that the works are meritorious. In other words, Barber's claim that works bring merit at the final judgment doesn't square with the biblical evidence. Barber attempts to show that merit fits with a right understanding of Scripture since the Scriptures speak of wages, repayment, and reward in texts that speak of a final recompense. It is certainly the case that repayment imagery is used in some texts that refer to the final reward given to believers (cf. Rom. 2:6–10). Barber also points to the parable of the workers in the vineyard where the laborers are given wages, and the wages relate to salvation (Matt. 20:1–16). He sees a similar connection where the final reward is explicated in terms of recompense in the parable of the talents (25:14–30).

In other words, Barber rightly shows that the language of recompense and reward is used in the Scriptures, and occasionally financial imagery is appealed to ("wages"). The question, however, is whether the language and imagery denotes *merit*. Certainly believers are rewarded or paid, but what do the biblical authors mean by such expressions? To say that the final judgment is described in terms of reward or wages doesn't necessarily lead to the conclusion that the reward is merited. Such a notion can't be read out of the parable of the laborers in the vineyard, for granting some the wages of eternal life for one hour of work is not merit but grace! Citing parables to defend a theology of merit is precarious in any case, unless such a teaching is clearly one of the main points of the story. We must beware of pressing details of the story in parables.

The fundamental problem with Barber's essay surfaces with the word and connotation of the term *merit*, which hails from the Latin word *meritum*. Why is it that works don't merit a final reward? Well, God demands perfection (Matt. 5:48), and works would only merit a reward if they were done perfectly. But even as Christians we all sin in many ways (Jas. 3:2). The continuing presence of sin in believers is evident, for Jesus taught us to pray regularly for the forgiveness of sins (Matt. 6:12). Clearly, Jesus taught this prayer to his disciples because they needed to pray for forgiveness until death. Perfection is never ours in this life (Phil. 3:12–16). Indeed, the injunction to ask for forgiveness of our sins (cf. 1 John 1:9 as well) was one of the fundamental arguments Augustine used in his polemic against Pelagius, showing that believers always stand in need of grace.

I don't see how works can be meritorious when the standard is perfection and when it is evident that Christians don't meet the standard. Barber says after believers are united with Christ they can do the impossible so that works "have meritorious value" (p. 180). But how can that be so if believers continue to sin after their conversion? Barber's solution affirms that works are meritorious because of God's miraculous grace, even though they are not strictly meritorious. At that point, the word merit seems to be deprived of its typical meaning. What does it really mean for works that are not strictly meritorious to be counted as meritorious? More fundamentally, where does the Bible articulate such a notion? I don't see how saying that God makes the impossible possible really solves the problem, for how does God make what is not meritorious to be meritorious?

Barber derives the notion that God miraculously makes works meritorious from the story of the rich ruler (Matt. 19:16–30). I would suggest that the following terms describe the same reality in the account: "eternal life" (19:16), "perfect" (19:21), "treasure in heaven" (19:21), entering the kingdom of heaven (19:23), and being saved (19:25). The impossible thing God does is to transform someone's heart so that he or she becomes a disciple of Jesus instead of clinging to riches. I don't see any evidence here that the impossible thing God does is make our works meritorious. The rich ruler allegedly kept all the commands of the Decalogue, but it counted for nothing if he didn't become a disciple of Jesus. Jesus makes it clear that the issue at stake is salvation (19:25). The story doesn't teach that our inadequate works can somehow be counted as merit. It teaches that salvation is a miraculous work of God.

The Problem with Merit Theologically

It is possible that the disagreement between Barber and myself is ultimately semantic. For Protestants and Catholics both believe works are necessary for eternal life.[56] Catholics affirm that God crowns our

---

[56]. I realize some Protestants would disagree with me here. Given the nature of the response, I am not qualifying every statement.

merits, so that in his grace he counts our works as merits even though they fall short of God's perfect standard.[57] Is that really so different from saying that God rewards us with eternal life, even though our works after conversion are imperfect?

At one level, we could say that Protestants and Catholics aren't far apart, for both believe rewards stem from God's grace. We have seen that there is certainly common ground between Catholics and Protestants, for we both affirm the grace of God. Still, the devil is in the details. Or perhaps it is better to say that the meaning of words like merit and reward have to be placed in a larger theological context. In Catholic theology, merit is part of a system in which the sacraments play a crucial role in salvation so that justification receives a definition quite different from what we typically find in Protestant theology. For instance, Catholic theology teaches that justification is a process that continues throughout one's life,[58] whereas Protestants typically contend that justification is forensic and not transformative.

One's understanding of merit, then, is tied closely to one's understanding of justification. In the Catholic system justification is a process and works play a role in the renewal of the person. There is not time or space to defend the view that justification is forensic, but it is obvious that one's notion of final reward or what Barber calls merit will be interpreted in radically different ways if one disagrees on the nature of justification.

Protestants emphasize that salvation is a gift of God, so that God justifies the ungodly (Rom. 4:2–5). As a corollary believers can be assured of final salvation because justification depends on faith and is not based on works (John 20:30–31; 1 John 5:12–13). Catholic theology, however, rejects the notion that anyone can be certain of final salvation apart from special revelation and teaches that those who are justified can lose their justification and finally be damned. Reformed Christians believe that those who are now justified (for whom God's end time verdict has been declared in advance) will certainly be saved on the last day (Rom. 5:9). Set against this backdrop the Catholic

---

57. *Catechism of the Catholic Church* (New York: Doubleday, 2003), no. 2006–2011 (pp. 541–42). For the catechism I am supplying first the paragraph number and then the page number of my edition.

58. *Catechism of the Catholic Church*, no. 1989, 1995 (pp. 536–37).

understanding of merit and reward looks remarkably different from the Reformed understanding.

The disparity between Catholics and Protestants, of course, has a long history, reaching back to the Reformation, for the magisterial Reformers (Luther, Zwingli, and Calvin) believed in the effective grace of God in election. Such a view, of course, goes back to Augustine and also has roots in Aquinas. We think here of the famous debate between Luther and Erasmus on the bondage and freedom of the will.

The disjunction between Catholic and Reformed theology is reflected in their understanding of human freedom. Catholic theology today clearly endorses a libertarian view of human freedom, a view defended by Erasmus over against Luther.[59] Indeed, many of the early fathers espoused the same view, and such a view also has its defenders in Protestant theology, particularly in the Arminian wing of Protestantism. Catholic theology disputes the notion that grace is effective. In other words, grace ultimately depends on free will.[60] Merit is a result of grace, but the grace given can be resisted, and so those who obtain merit do so ultimately because of their free will.[61] "Moved by the Holy Spirit and by charity, *we can then merit* for ourselves and for others the graces needed for sanctification, for the increase of grace and charity, and for the attainment of eternal life."[62]

I would argue that one of the major issues that caused a rupture of the church at the time of the Reformation was the theology of grace. In other words, Catholic theology was semi-Pelagian, while the theology of the magisterial Reformers was Augustinian. Time and space are lacking to discuss this matter in the depth it deserves, but we must recognize that simply saying that both Protestants and Catholics believe in grace is too simplistic. Luther wrote *The Bondage of the Will* because his view of justification was tied to his view of election and the effective

---

59. The Council of Trent (Session 6, Chapter 1) affirms the continuing power of free will, by which they mean what is called libertarian freedom philosophically. Canon 17 rejects the Reformers' understanding of predestination. Cf. also *Catechism of the Catholic Church*, no., 1993 (p. 537), where the freedom of the human will is given ultimacy.

60. Many Protestants today would also agree with such a judgment, though in Arminian theology the freedom of the will to choose is typically ascribed to prevenient grace.

61. "The fatherly action of God is first on his initiative, and then follows man's free acting through his collaboration, so that the merit of good works is to be attributed in the first place to the grace of God, then to the faithful" (*Catechism of the Catholic Church*, no. 2008 (p. 541).

62. *Catechism of the Catholic Church*, n. 2010 (p. 542). Italics theirs.

grace of God. Romans 11:5–6 is of crucial importance here. Salvation is all of grace, for God chooses effectively whom will be saved. Yes, Catholics believe in the grace of God, but ultimately grace can be resisted by the human will. Catholics teach the grace of justification can be lost.[63] The Reformers categorically rejected such an understanding of grace.

Readers might think I have wandered far from the essay Barber has written! My point is that the Catholic notion of merit takes on quite a different hue when human choice is ultimate in salvation, when justification is construed as a process, and when the salvation given at conversion can be lost. The term *merit* in the Catholic system assigns a contribution to salvation, which according to my reading of the Scriptures can't be harmonized with the scriptural witness as a whole. In other words, we can only understand the significance of merit when it is placed into the context of Catholic doctrine as a whole over against Protestant doctrine.

Conclusion

Barber and I agree that good works are necessary for salvation, but at the end of the day we have a dramatically different understanding of what is meant by this formulation. As a Catholic he sees them as a human contribution to salvation, so that they play a crucial role in justification. As a Protestant, I would argue that justification is by grace alone and through faith alone and in Christ alone. True faith always produces love (Gal. 5:6). Good works are a fruit of faith and constitute necessary evidence of the genuineness of faith, but they are not the basis of salvation or justification. For forgiveness and justification are only ours through the crucified and risen Savior, Jesus Christ.

---

63. Council of Trent, Session 6, Chapter 15; *Catechism of the Catholic Church* (no. 162, p. 50) says about faith: "Faith is an entirely free gift that God makes to man. We can lose this priceless gift."

JAMES D. G. DUNN

Areas of Agreement

Grace Is Fundamental

I found myself warming to Michael Barber's "Catholic perspective." It is ecumenical: it effectively chops down the "dividing wall" between Roman Catholicism and Protestantism, which has prevented mutual respect and bred suspicion as to the gospel of both and the faithfulness of each to biblical teaching. Grace is as fundamental to both systems, even, arguably (as Barber provocatively suggests), more fundamental to Catholic teaching. [64]

Jesus Is Close to Jewish Soteriology

It is biblical: the Protestant dismissal of the Old Testament's and early Judaism's soteriology, too often dismissed as "works righteousness" and "synergistic," is shown clearly to be at best misleading since it is so much of a piece with Jesus' own teaching on reward. My own argument that the New Testament writers teach a form of "covenantal nomism," not very different from the teaching of Old Testament and early Judaism, is reinforced.

Perhaps most important, Barber has no inhibitions in trying to show how the legal analogy of justification and judgment and the schema of incorporation in/into Christ can be held together in fruitful integration. [65] Even if we might quibble over use of terms like

---

64. "The Catholic teaching has always insisted that we are saved by grace. On this point Catholics and Protestants agree" (p. 166). "If the Catholic understanding is mistaken, it is because we believe God is able to do more in believers by grace than Protestants believe" (p. 180).

65. "We are 'justified,' that is, we are declared/made righteous, because Christ is 'our righteousness' (1 Cor. 1:30)" (p. 165). "Salvation involves more than just deliverance from sin. Salvation involves being fully incorporated into Christ" (p. 179).

"merit," [66] Jesus' readiness to use the concept of "reward" should surely go a long way to calm any excessive Protestant sensitivities on that score.

Specific Comments on Jesus' Teachings

The central issue for this volume is posed by Paul's teaching on justification by faith. Michael Barber focuses chiefly on the Gospels, and I have no complaint about that, though it may miss what has been the heart of the battle. But it is, of course, of fundamental importance that Jesus' teaching be fully taken into view. Some presentations, indeed, seem to imply that the (true) gospel only begins from and after Jesus' crucifixion and resurrection; that is, Jesus' own teaching is not (yet Christian) gospel, and the "Jewishness" of his teaching can be passed over without any qualms. But it would be folly to reassert "the historical Jesus"/"Christ of faith" dichotomy on this point, as though Jesus' own teaching could be regarded as defective because it was not yet completed by his passion.

And when we do take seriously Jesus' teaching, preserved, after all, in the form of "the Gospels," it is exceedingly hard to avoid the emphases that Barber has brought out. I too have been impressed by Eubank's thesis, particularly his treatment of the parable of the workers in the vineyard (Matt. 20:1–16). Important elements of the parable have been too often overlooked, or they are submerged in the attempt to interpret the parable as an expression of pure grace. To be sure, the workers who work only for the last hour (no reasons given as to why their labor had not been engaged earlier in the day) are treated generously—graciously, we may of course say. But those who have worked all day are paid the wage agreed when they were engaged, the wage they had earned. Nothing in the parable denies their right to that wage. And if the parable is indeed a parable of the kingdom, that is of kingdom values, and of relations between the king and his subjects, then the failure to bring out a stronger note of "sheer unmerited grace" (payment entirely unrelated to work done for all workers) must be significant.

---

66. "Since Christ has the capacity to merit, he merits for believers the capacity to merit with him. In other words, if salvation is truly Christocentric—if it involves being conformed to the image of Christ—it necessarily involves our ability to merit in him. Good works are not simply the fruit of salvation; they are part and parcel of it. Without them we are not fully 'like Christ'" (p. 181).

Reading Eubank's thesis reminded me that Jesus' saying, "I came to call not the righteous but sinners" (Mark 2:17), should not be taken as a rejection of "the righteous," as though "righteous" was a condemnatory term. An implication that can be more readily drawn is that it was sinners who needed to hear the call of grace; the righteous had no such need—they were "righteous"! Similarly, when Jesus rounded off another parable by affirming to complainants that "the tax collectors and the prostitutes are going into the kingdom of God ahead of you" (Matt. 21:31), he evidently was not denying that the complainants had a place in the kingdom. He was certainly breaking down the boundaries by which the religious thought that sinners were debarred from grace; he was not erecting new barriers to shut out the religious.

The same point comes through in the parable of the prodigal son (Luke 15:11–32). I had always been a little nonplussed by the father's response to the elder son's complaint: "Son, you are always with me, and all that is mine is yours" (15:31). Did Jesus include that simply for dramatic effect, part of the drama's scenery? Should we assume that the quite popular variant title for the story, the "Parable of the Prodigal Sons," has a better grasp of Jesus' intention? Or should we rather see the father's response as an affirmation of the elder son and of the closeness of his continuing relation to the father? Of course, the father is distressed at the elder son's legitimate disparagement of the younger son, but did that affect the elder son's standing with the father? And if the parable images the righteous Pharisees' disparagement of "sinners," then does it not make the same point as just drawn from Mark 2:17? If the righteous are condemned for their dismissal of sinners as offensive to God, then many Christians who strongly disapprove of the beliefs or practices of others as debarring them from salvation should be relieved that while grace reaches out to the sinner, it does not exclude the righteous.

Areas of Concern

Only a few notes of disquiet came to mind as I read Barber's essay— apart from his assigning me a place only "a little further" from those who "suggest that the deeds of the righteous are only the fruit of faith and, therefore, are not really what determine their salvation" (p. 168), which I read with something of a surprise.

Blending Passages from Different Authors Should Be Avoided

One was the tendency to blend together passages from the Synoptic Gospels, from John's gospel, from Paul and James and Revelation. Although in this case most of the blending is justified, the danger has to be guarded against of contriving a "New Testament teaching" on some subject that takes too little account of the distinctive emphases of each individual author or indeed sometimes of each individual document. It has been precisely the tendency to draw out one particular emphasis or metaphor or line of argument from Paul, or from the New Testament, to treat it as the dominant model or mould, and to squeeze the rest into it, knocking off or ignoring their corners and edges that do not so easily fit in, which has been the bane of so many reconstructions of Paul's theology.

Faith Is Not the Same As Faithfulness

On another point of critique, Barber's treatment of James and justification (pp. 177–78) needs to acknowledge that James 2:14–26 does seem to be in reaction to Paul's teaching on the subject: the parallel between 2:14–26 and the sequence of Romans 3:27–4:22 is too close to be accidental. That includes the recognition that James was also echoing an interpretation of Genesis 15:6 that was current in the Judaism of the time, as evidenced by 1 Maccabees 2:52, an interpretation Paul was challenging in Romans 4:1–12. Paul was in effect protesting against the understanding of "faith" as "faithfulness." Of course, Barber is right that for Paul too, true faith expresses itself in faithfulness—"faith working through love" (Gal. 5:6). But Paul's point is lost if faith is simply collapsed into faithfulness. Faith for Paul was no more and no less than trust—as he argued in his exposition of Genesis 15:6: "Abraham believed God" means no more and no less that Abraham trusted God's word of promise, when everything else told him it couldn't happen (Rom. 4:18–21).

Faith Is Not a Human Act

This observation also makes me a little nervous when Barber insists that faith "is still an act performed by the believer" (p. 179). To believe (aorist), along with the commitment of faith, is certainly an act. But in contrasting Abraham's faith with his subsequent action, his being circumcised or (as implied) his readiness to offer up Isaac, Paul was making the point that unless faith is distinguished from human doing, human action, it is misunderstood as the basis for relationship between God and the believer. The "grace through faith" summary of Paul's soteriology means that for Paul, saving faith is in its essence the reception of saving grace. To be sure, the fact that faith expresses itself in obedience ("the obedience of faith") means that Paul's argument in Romans 4:1–12 was vulnerable to the response that Abraham's faith had expressed itself in his performance of circumcision, and that without that response it would not have been true faith; it was dead (Jas. 2:17–18, 24, 26). But Paul thought it important, nonetheless, to press the point that faith in itself is nothing more than trusting God.

Baptism Does Not Occur without Faith

This also makes me a little nervous about Barber's comments on baptism. By failing to mention faith in relation to baptism, he feeds Protestant suspicion by allowing in a hint that baptism works with an *ex opere operato* efficacy (p. 182). But faith is so integral to conversion-initiation in the New Testament texts that to leave it out runs the risk, once again, of distorting the fundamental character of faith as the basis on the human side of the divine/human relationship; and that it is faith that is and marks the start of the Christian life. Certainly infant baptism "highlights in an especially profound way the gratuitousness of salvation" (p. 182), but the importance of incorporating the expression of faith into the infant baptismal ceremony has rarely been forgotten. It is rather significant, is it not, that Barber quotes 1 Peter 3:21, "baptism … now saves you," but leaves the quotation at that point and fails to complete it: "baptism … now saves you … as an appeal to God for [or 'from'] a good conscience."

In an ecumenical dialogue there is something of central importance here: that the common ground on which all Christians can unite is faith in Christ, or faith in God through Christ; and any addition to that faith, "works of the law," but also traditional rituals, creedal statements, and the like, effectively undermine the gospel. This was one of the most important lessons that Paul taught us (Gal. 2:16), and we lose sight of it at our peril.

Summary

In sum, Michael Barber shows that a fruitful dialogue between what were old entrenched positions (more entrenched on the Protestant side, to be honest) is now a realistic prospect and should be all the more fruitful through our shared understanding of biblical teaching. But in cutting away the misunderstandings and misinterpretations and in demonstrating that some contrasts have been overdrawn and exaggerated, we must not forget the distinctives and the emphases that Jesus and Paul in particular found it necessary to insist on.

THE PUZZLE OF SALVATION BY ███████
GRACE AND JUDGMENT BY WORKS

ALAN P. STANLEY

What did you expect when you began reading this book? Perhaps you already had a view on the role of works at the final judgment and wanted to see if anybody else held your view. Maybe you had no view and thought you had better become informed. Or perhaps you didn't even realize that there was a variety of views on this issue. Whatever the case, it's easy to approach a book like this expecting it to answer all your questions. That would certainly be nice. Mind you, given that the whole point of the book is to present four views, we shouldn't be surprised if we find ourselves coming away with even more questions. But if the book has served its purpose well, I hope our questions will now be more focused and directed with more clarity. At the very least we should now be able to see where the major battles are to be fought.

As we look back on what has been written, we might think of the role of works at the final judgment like a jigsaw puzzle box filled with pieces. The only difference is that there is no picture on the front of the box to show how all the pieces are to come together. However, by and large, the four contributors have all been given the same box with the same number of pieces—the Bible, particularly the New Testament—to work with. Not surprisingly each one has put together the pieces differently.

Interestingly though, the approach in putting the pieces together has been relatively similar. That is, it has been impossible for each contributor to examine the role of works at the final judgment without first looking at the role of works prior to the final judgment. In other words, the pieces to this puzzle are not limited to those passages that speak of judgment in the life hereafter. For the Christian, and indeed for every human being, what happens then is intractably related to the lives we are living now. Invariably this has meant that each contributor has written at some length on the relationship between works, grace, faith, and salvation.

What, then, is the exact role of works at the final judgment? How have Robert Wilkin, Tom Schreiner, James Dunn, and Michael Barber put the pieces of the puzzle together? What do their four pictures end up like?

Robert Wilkin: *Black And White* – Believers Won't Be At The Final Judgment

We might describe Wilkin's final picture as black and white—that is, there are no apparent grey areas. *Black:* the New Testament teaches over and over again that once a person believes in Jesus Christ, he or she is saved (has eternal life) once and for all. *White:* since the final judgment determines where people will spend eternity and since, for the Christian, this question has already been answered when they believed, there is no need for believers even to be at the final judgment.

But there are all those "pieces in the box" that speak of believers being judged by works. Where do these pieces fit? Believers will be judged by their works, but not at the final judgment (the Great White Throne judgment); rather, they will be judged at the judgment seat of Christ. Only Christians will appear at this judgment, and therefore what is at stake is not eternal salvation but eternal rewards. Hence, those Christians who have faithfully persevered in good works will be rewarded while those who have been unfaithful will not be rewarded—though they will still be saved. For example, the servant who sat on his money remains a "servant" in spite of his unfaithfulness (Luke 19:11–27). What he forfeits is not his place in the kingdom but his *role* in the kingdom—he does not get to reign over any cities.

A key point here is that in Wilkin's approach to sorting out this puzzle, entering the kingdom or to gaining eternal life is not the same as *inheriting* the kingdom or eternal life. Everyone who believes in Jesus Christ enters the kingdom and has eternal life, but only those who persevere actually inherit them. Hence, when Paul promises that those who sow to the flesh will reap corruption and those who sow to the Spirit will reap eternal life (Gal. 6:8), he is not contrasting those who will not be saved and those who will. Rather, he is contrasting those who will not reap the experience and benefits of reigning with Christ. Both groups *have* eternal life, but only those who do not grow weary in doing good (6:9) will "reap" eternal life.

In Wilkin's final picture, then, the colors of the various pieces do not run into one another. There are essentially only two colors. Eternal life/salvation is a free gift whereas rewards are given or withheld on the basis of perseverance/works. If we keep these pieces of the puzzle in mind, we will avoid putting together a distorted picture. So quite simply, any Bible passage that is overtly at odds with salvation by grace through faith (e.g., Gal. 6:7–9; Col. 1:21–23) must be speaking of something other than a believer's eternal salvation. "We do not harbor hidden fears that we will appear at the final judgment only to find we were never saved. Rather, we believe Jesus' promise that the one who believes in Him 'has everlasting life … [and] shall not come into judgment …' (John 5:24). We rejoice in this security. Let us not go through life fearful of the final judgment. Believers will not be judged there" (p. 50).

Tom Schreiner: *A Coherent Blend* – At the Final Judgment Works Demonstrate Who Are Saved

Schreiner agrees with Wilkin when looking at half of the pieces to the puzzle: "Salvation is not secured by works but by faith" (p. 77); "human beings cannot be justified or saved on the basis of their works.... Justification must be apart from works" (p. 78). But as Schreiner moves on to look at some of the other pieces, he sees a different picture emerging. "Paul disavows justification by works in some texts, but then in other verses he teaches that we are justified by works" (p. 78). Hence Paul could say, "[God] will grant 'eternal life to those who seek glory and honor and incorruptibility by patiently enduring in a good work' ([Rom.] 2:7)" (p. 78). While in Wilkin's picture these two pieces can never fit together, Schreiner sees a coherent blend. The pieces fit quite naturally *because* the new covenant promised that a time would come when God's Spirit would enable his people to obey him. Hence, for those who believe in Jesus Christ "obedience … stems from the new covenant work of the Holy Spirit," and this Spirit-wrought obedience results in eternal life (p. 81). Thus, for Paul at least, "works play a role in the final judgment. They are necessary for final salvation" (p. 81).

So, according to Schreiner, what role do works play at the final judgment? First of all, they are not meritorious. Works do not merit salvation at the final judgment. But nevertheless "works are necessary for eternal life" (p. 83), but only inasmuch as they are "necessary evidence and fruit of a right relation with God. They demonstrate, although imperfectly, that one is truly trusting in Jesus Christ" (p. 97). Works, then, are necessary for eternal life only because faith *alone* in Jesus Christ is necessary for eternal life.

So there is some tension here as Schreiner puts this puzzle together, but nothing that should cause a distorted picture. The following needs to be kept in mind: "The verdict of the final day is announced in advance for those who trust in Jesus" (p. 91). Hence, "the justification that is ours when we believe guarantees final glorification so that believers are assured that they are right with God when they believe" (p. 91). But even though "salvation and justification are through faith alone ... such faith is living and vital and always produces works" (p. 98). Hence, those works will be put forward as evidence at the final judgment.

James Dunn: *We Simply Don't Have All The Pieces* – Salvation at the Final Judgment Will Depend, to Some Extent, on Works

James Dunn's putting together of this puzzle is not so neat. In fact, there may even be some gaps; but not for any other reason except that we haven't been supplied with all the pieces. Dunn himself is reluctant to invent or force pieces where there is no coherent fit. The end result may not be as pretty, but it is, according to Dunn, faithful to the Scriptures.

Dunn's distinct point is that the writers of the New Testament were not writing a systematic theology. Paul's teachings, for example, on faith and works are borne out by the different contexts, problems, and circumstances to which he responded. Paul did not write his letters as a disengaged theologian trying to cover all points. He did write, however, as a concerned missionary/pastor seeking to address real life issues, which, as it turns out, does not provide all the answers we would like on this subject.

Dunn, then, rather than squeeze and impose pieces together just to satisfy our desire for a complete, consistent picture, prefers simply to allow the pieces to lie where they fall and let the gaps remain. The resulting picture is that salvation is a "now but not yet" reality, a process in which "Christians most typically are 'those who are (in process of) being saved'" (p. 125). But this raises the question: Do those who have begun this process complete it? Philippians 1:6 would seem to answer, yes: "I am confident of this, that the one who began a good work in/ among you will complete it by the day of Christ Jesus." But Galatians 3:3 leaves room for doubt: "Are you so foolish? Having begun with the Spirit, are you now made complete with the flesh?" Thus, "a disturbing feature of Paul's theology of the salvation process is the degree of hesitation and concern he shows that it might not be completed.... The disturbing feature is that Paul regarded the possibility of apostasy, of failing to persevere, as a *real* danger for his converts" (p. 126), a possibility that the apostle believed to which even he was susceptible (see, e.g., 1 Cor. 9.27).

Hence, Dunn concludes, "part of Paul's pastoral theology was his all-too-real concern that faith could once again be compromised and cease to be simple trust, that commitment could be relaxed and resolve critically weakened. The result would be an estrangement from Christ ... and the loss of the prospect of resurrection life" (p. 127). Thus, Paul's gospel might indeed promise salvation to those who believe, but that salvation was also "conditional, at least in some degree, on his converts' 'obedience of faith'" (p. 128). And if obedience (or sanctification, if we prefer that term) is a condition for salvation, it follows that the fulfillment or nonfulfillment of the condition awaits the final judgment. If we were to ask Dunn what salvation at the final judgment ultimately depends on, our works or the work of Christ—thinking back to the debate between Wright and Piper—Dunn would answer: Why should we choose?

This may not be the neat and tidy picture we'd like, but it is, as Dunn evaluates the puzzle, faithful to the pieces we have. The closest that Dunn comes to nailing something down is to say that Paul emphasizes one piece of the puzzle in certain contexts and another piece in other contexts. When reassurance is needed, the work and grace of Christ receives emphasis, but when believers need pulling into line, works and judgment get airtime.

Michael Barber: *A More Sophisticated Approach* – At the Final Judgment Works Will Merit Salvation

Barber attempts "to show here that the Catholic view of good works at the final judgment seeks to explain the entirety of the biblical witness without minimizing either passages that discuss the priority of God's grace or texts highlighting the role attributed to good works" (p. 162). How can these two pieces of the puzzle coexist? The answer is that salvation is by God's grace and yet *also* by works. Both sets of passages present these two truths. Works will be the criterion by which believers will be judged at the final judgment (see, e.g., Matt. 25:31–46). Quite simply, "It is the presence or absence of works that determines one's future destiny" (p. 168).

Now as to how the pieces of this puzzle fit together, the answer is a little more complex. Barber, in his words, takes "a more sophisticated approach" (p. 169). Both Jewish tradition and the Bible itself view sins as debts and good works as repayment. Good works, then, merit salvation or eternal life. Hence we find Jesus telling people to give to the poor in order to gain heavenly treasure (e.g., Matt. 19:21; Luke 12:33). Many will think that the picture emerging here is that Christians simply need to make sure they perform more good works than bad in order to gain eternal life. Barber warns against such an understanding for it fails to take into account the other piece of the puzzle — grace!

Good works, and even faith, are humanly impossible apart from God's grace. People cannot sell all they have and give to the poor. People cannot do good works. However, God's "grace is so effective it is even able to render weak and sinful humans capable of performing meritorious works" (p. 184). Hence, once a believer is united to Christ, they have the capacity to do what they could not previously do. That which was once impossible is now possible. Believers now, by God's grace, have the capacity to carry out works that merit salvation.

But we must remember that in Barber's putting together of the pieces, salvation is a process: past, present, and future. So to say that works merit salvation is not to say that works get one *converted*. It is to say, rather, that it is only through *these works* — works performed by the power of grace once a believer is converted — that one is truly and finally saved. Hence, just as works play an indispensable role in our salvation, so too they play an indispensable role at the final judgment, but this is only because they are the result of God's powerful, working grace within the believer.

As we look at Barber's final picture, this obviously requires a careful and thoughtful reading, especially by those who are more familiar with the Protestant understanding of salvation. The works of a believer have meritorious value but only because they are the result of Christ's work.

"To insist that the believer's works lack meritorious value is to claim that Christ's work lacks meritorious value" (p. 180). So in Barber's arranging of the pieces, all the glory goes to God. If there is any weakness, any error here, it is, according to Barber, that the Catholic version gives God too much credit and attributes to Christ too much grace.

Focusing the Discussion
The Priority of Grace

Remarkably—since this book presents four different views on the role of works at the final judgment—all four contributors agree on the priority of grace or faith. All affirm, for instance, Ephesians 2:8–9: "For it is by grace you have been saved, through faith—and this is not from yourselves, it is the gift of God—not by works, so that no one can boast."

Wilkin: "Clearly the one who simply believes in Jesus has eternal life. The New Testament is united on this point" (p. 27); "eternal life comes to the believer as a gift" (p. 31); "salvation is a free gift that comes through faith in Jesus Christ" (p. 32); "the sole condition of having eternal life … is faith in Christ" (p. 47); "the only requirement is faith" (p. 48).

Schreiner: "Justification, then, is a gift given and received" (p. 75); "salvation is not secured by works but by faith" (p. 77); "[salvation] is granted by God as a gift, as a witness to his astonishing love" (p. 77); "salvation and justification are through faith alone" (p. 98).

Dunn: "Assuredly we can affirm that the believer never approaches the throne of grace, whether now or in the future, except as a sinner, wholly dependent on that grace. Assuredly we can say with Paul that before God there can never be ground for boasting in one's own doings but only in the glory and grace of God" (p. 140).

Barber: "Salvation is given to us as a free gift. This is the clear testimony of Scripture" (p. 165); "the Catholic teaching has always insisted that we are saved by grace" (p. 166); "salvation is first by God's grace and not by works" (p.180); "according to Catholic teaching, then, salvation is, ultimately, 'pure grace'" (p. 184).

Disagreements

This agreement, of course, in many ways is rather broad. For instance, in spite of Barber's insistence that salvation is ultimately pure grace,

Wilkin thinks that his "position is clearly one of works-righteousness" (p. 186). So which is it, pure grace or works-righteousness? Clearly, Wilkin and Barber differ as to what exactly pure grace means. We need, therefore, to pay attention to how writers use their terms. The discerning reader will pay particular attention to context—which is true whether we are reading scholars or the Bible.

What this means, however, is that as readers we all have our work cut out for us. One thing I hope this book has done is to show that we cannot so easily dismiss the views of others without thoughtful engagement. It is all too easy for readers to pick up a book like this and with the information they already have accumulated in their time as believers, simply latch on to one view and rather dismissively—and perhaps disrespectfully—brush the others to the side. But each of these four scholars deserves respectful attention. Who knows? You might be persuaded. I personally have found that before critiquing someone's point of view, it is always helpful to try and put myself in their shoes, to try and see the text with their eyes, and to seek to really understand where they are coming from. Otherwise, I'm tempted to write them off before giving them a hearing. The four contributors here have given us good models, I think, in how to go about responding to one another thoughtfully.

In thinking about the main areas of disagreement between the four, it might be helpful if we think about what we ourselves are now left with. Are there still pieces of the puzzle that need to be sorted through? If you're wondering how to sort through these pieces yourself, let me suggest three crucial questions that have regularly surfaced in this book and can't be avoided.

Three Crucial Questions

What is the nature of saving grace and faith? This question particularly sets apart the first view (Wilkin) from the three that follow. Wilkin defines faith as mere assent to the truths of the gospel. Wilkin himself acknowledges that this is indeed a key point of contention when he says, "Many would agree that there is a necessary connection between believing in Jesus and obeying His commandments. I would not" (p. 39). Schreiner also acknowledges this as a key point of contention: "while Wilkin and I agree that faith alone saves, we disagree on the nature of faith and on its relationship with works" (Schreiner's response to Wilkin, p. 51).

The issue is whether faith in Jesus Christ and the grace received inevitably leads to obedience. In other words, is there a real and direct connection between faith and works, so that the latter cannot properly occur without the former; or is faith isolated from obedience? Can someone resist sexual immorality, for instance, without believing in Jesus? Both Schreiner and Barber stress that "faith alone" does not mean that faith is alone. For Schreiner, someone who believes in Jesus also trusts in Jesus and so will respond, albeit imperfectly, trustingly to his commands. For Barber, as for Schreiner, grace is effective, a power that actually transforms those who believe in Jesus Christ. For Wilkin, though, to say that salvation is by grace through faith is to say that salvation is and can only be limited to a point in time, that is, conversion, and therefore obedience is a separate issue. This leads us to our second question:

What is the nature of salvation? This question also sets apart Wilkin from the others, though Schreiner sits somewhere in between Wilkin and Dunn/Barber. The issue is whether salvation is limited to a point in time (Wilkin), a process where the outcome may perhaps be jeopardized (Dunn, Barber), or a process that has begun but its completion is nevertheless guaranteed (Schreiner). The point to wrestle with is whether there is a legitimate tension between being saved now and not yet being saved. Is salvation present once for all from the time of conversion?

Both Wilkin and Schreiner would say yes, salvation is irrevocable. However, that's where the agreement stops. Wilkin would argue that if salvation cannot be revoked, logically this means that a failure to persevere does not jeopardize one's place in eternity; it will, however, jeopardize one's role and experience in eternity. Schreiner, by contrast, would argue that since perseverance/works are necessary for salvation and eternal life, a failure to persevere or the absence of works casts doubt on whether a genuine conversion actually occurred. Dunn likewise says, "the verdict of justification can be pronounced now, already, to those who accept his gospel and believe in Jesus Christ" (p. 122), though he is not at all willing to say that justification is irrevocable (e.g., "Does Wilkin really think that when people first believe, they believe forever, so that it can be said finally and for every case that 'eternal life is decided [that is, finally and irrevocably decided] at conversion,'" Dunn's response to Wilkin, p. 61)?

Practically speaking this is probably a more important issue to settle than explaining the relationship between works and salvation at the final judgment. If salvation is not in some sense complete at conversion, then all believers will appear at the final judgment (Schreiner, Dunn, Barber). If, however, salvation is complete at conversion and there is no need for perseverance or works, then there is no need for any believer to be at the final judgment (Wilkin). This leads us naturally to the third and final question:

What is the nature of the biblical teaching on salvation? By this I am referring to something that has cropped up frequently in this book, and of course in many ways is really the essence of the debate: Should we give more weight to one set of texts (grace) over another set (works)? Should one set be subordinate? Does one trump the other, making that one more important? Remember that all four writers affirm the priority of grace, but for Wilkin this means that salvation by grace means that it cannot in any way be by works. This is not the case, however, for the other three. Schreiner, Dunn, and Barber all state plainly that Spirit/grace-produced works are indeed a prerequisite for (final) salvation. Each has a distinct ways of explaining the role works play (Schreiner: evidence; Dunn: certainly necessary; Barber: instrumental/meritorious), but they all agree that works do come into play for the Christian at the final judgment.

What Does the Bible Say?

The principal of the Bible college where I work, when students bring up this or that scholar or this or that creed or tradition to support an argument, will simply reply, "What does the Bible say?" Ultimately that is the question we must all wrestle with. Of course, the four contributors here all claim that they are indeed asking that question — and yet still we have different answers. But that's fine, because they have all asked and continue to ask that question. The challenge is now for us to ask the same question, "What does the Bible say?"

The answer we come to may differ from our tradition or denomination, or even what we would like. But the issue is whether we have diligently and faithfully looked into the text. It matters little whether

Luther, Calvin, Wesley, or the Pope disagree with it. What matters ultimately is whether we have faithfully handled the biblical text. For those of us who have a particular calling to teaching and preaching that text, this is especially apt. However, we would all do well to pay attention to the apostle Paul, and since our topic has been judgment, it seems apt to finish with his words from 1 Corinthians 4:2–5:

> Now it is required that those who have been given a trust must prove faithful. I care very little if I am judged by you or by any human court; indeed, I do not even judge myself. My conscience is clear, but that does not make me innocent. It is the Lord who judges me. Therefore judge nothing before the appointed time; wait until the Lord comes. He will bring to light what is hidden in darkness and will expose the motives of the heart. At that time each will receive their praise from God.

SCRIPTURE INDEX

SUBJECT INDEX